BREAK ME

BREAK ME

BREAK ME

The Wolf Hotel #2

K.A. TUCKER

Copyright © 2016 by Kathleen Tucker

All rights are reserved. No part of this book may be reproduced or transmitted in any form or by any means without written permission of the author. For more information visit katuckerbooks.com

This book is a work of fiction. The names, characters, places, and incidents are products of the writer's imagination or have been used fictitiously and are not to be construed as real. Any resemblance to persons, living or dead, actual events, locales or organizations is entirely coincidental.

ISBN 978-1-990105-37-1 (paperback)

Editing by Hot Tree Editing

Cover design by Shanoff Designs

Published by K.A. Tucker Books Ltd.

one

"Crap, crap, crap..." I pace around the dining table, my arms hugging my stomach in attempt to quell the nauseating churn as I dwell on the contents of those e-mails.

The confidential ones that Henry told me under no circumstances to read.

Now I know why.

Henry's a... what, a rapist? Is that what that lawyer, Dyson, meant when he said Kiera is pressing criminal charges for forced sexual intercourse? What on earth did Henry do to his last assistant? His *married* assistant.

Whatever it was, it was enough to try and buy her off with a couple hundred thousand dollars and a gag order. That's what Henry and his dad were talking about, that day I overheard them talking on the phone. Kiera is the "unfortunate situation" that Henry was sure was resolved, which means Henry's father knows all about this.

Is it true? Is it possible that this beautiful, complicated man who made sure I didn't end up at the bottom of the bay that first night, who didn't so much as kiss me back when I drunkenly threw myself at him the first night, is the type of man to force himself on a woman?

I don't know Henry at all. I can *think* I know him. I can pine over those intimate moments—about him carrying my inebriated butt home, about him in the woods that day, with his protective arm around me to calm me about the grizzly, about the worried look on his face when I was sick on the boat—and I can convince myself that he would never force himself on a woman. I can picture his handsome face and perfect masculine form, and tell myself that he'd *never have* to force himself on anyone because no woman would ever *not* willingly give herself to him.

But I don't really know him. I've known him for a hot minute. I'd be an idiot to convince myself otherwise. I'd be the silly farm girl everyone believes me to be.

I groan. My exciting summer of escape, my chance to shed the pain that Jed caused and the control my mother holds over me, this intoxicating cloud that has consumed me since the moment I met Henry, it's all over. Everything has changed with the accidental stroke of a key.

Why did I have to read that e-mail? Why couldn't I have remained ignorant?

Then again, if what that lawyer says is true, I'll be hearing about it soon enough anyway. Around the same time that everyone else does. And then they'll all be looking at me, his new assistant. Wondering, questioning. Has the billionaire heir to Wolf Hotels forced himself on his latest assistant, too? Am I one of those "similar indiscretions" that Henry and his lawyer will want to discuss? How many are there?

What if everyone figures out that we've slept together?

What if they call me to testify at Henry's trial? I'll be under oath. I'll have to admit that we've slept together but that it wasn't rape, that it was consensual—*very* consensual—and then the media will hear about it and report it. It'll be all over the newspapers, and Mama and everyone in Greenbank will be talking about how I willingly had a sexual relationship with Henry Wolf, the rapist, and Reverend Enderbey will preach at Sunday service about how I was tempted by the devil.

"Crap, crap, crap!" I can barely breathe, my chest is so tight with panic.

I just don't get it! Henry is aggressive and mercurial and he can be an outright ass in public, but he's never actually done anything to harm me, or that I didn't want, or enjoy. So what exactly happened between him and this Kiera? Does he have a thing for sleeping with his assistants? Did she say no and did he not accept it?

A squeal escapes me as the shrill ring of my work phone cuts into the silence of Penthouse Cabin One, temporarily paralyzing me.

There's only one person who could be calling me on that line.

I let it ring once... twice... three times, and if I don't get it soon, he's going to know I read those e-mails that I wasn't supposed to read. Should I even care? Do I have a right to be 100 percent appalled with him and not feel guilty? Hell, yes, I do!

Unless there's been some big misunderstanding. Unless that tiny voice in the back of my head that tells me this can't be true is right.

Either way, I'm not going to find out by avoiding his calls.

"Get it together, Abbi," I mutter as I round the table and head for the desk where my phone sits. Where he had me naked and spread out only yesterday morning. God, it was only yesterday! I've only been working for him for a week! For all the time we've spent together, it feels like an eternity ago. It's like the moment Henry touched me, I fell through this strange rabbit hole into an alternate reality, where time and intelligence don't matter.

All that has mattered is hot inappropriate sex with my boss.

But now I've been kicked out of that rabbit hole, and into a swirl of confusion, panic, and overwhelming disappointment.

"Hello? Hi. Hey." I purse my lips together to stop myself from babbling, as I tend to do when I get nervous.

"I need you in the lobby right now." Henry's deep melodic voice fills my ear, only now it's the abrupt version I get whenever we're in public, not the husky one he reserves for sending shivers through my body.

I know what I'm supposed to say. *Yes, Mr. Wolf, I'll be right there.* I'm supposed to grab my things and run to him. But when I open my mouth, I'm hit with the overwhelming urge to demand the truth. I let this man inside me, after all. I gave him something personal and private and cherished. I gave him *me*. I have a right to know if my life is about to be thrown into a mixer and set to high speed because of something horrible that he did.

"Abbi!"

I jump at the bark in my ear. "Yes?"

"Did you hear me?"

This isn't a conversation for the phone. "I'll see you in a few minutes."

"No, I won't be there. I need you to greet the reporter from *Luxury Travel* magazine."

I frown. "Roshana Mafi?" The exotic beauty who is receiving flowers with a personally written card from

Henry? I thought he was meeting all the key media contacts himself.

"Yeah. Sure," he mutters dismissively. I can hear his dress shoes click against the floor. He's likely in one of the lower-level staff areas. Wherever he is, it's quiet and he's walking quickly.

"What time will she be there?"

"How the fuck would I know?" he snaps, but then heaves a sigh. "Ask Belinda. I have some important calls I need to make."

Not any I scheduled because his calendar is clear for greeting key guests. I'm guessing one of those calls is to his attorney. Henry's stressed, that much is obvious.

"Should I have Belinda greet her instead?"

"No. There was an incident between them years ago. She hates Belinda."

I roll my eyes. I'm not going to ask for details. "Okay. Is there anything specific you want me to tell her?"

"That I'll see her later. Actually, send Michael to her for an in-room massage. She'll like that and it'll keep her occupied."

"Okay." I hold my breath, waiting to hear the line go dead so I know I can hang up.

There's a long pause. "What took you so long to answer?" Suspicion laces his tone.

"Peeing. I mean, restroom," I blurt out, because it's the first thing that comes to mind. I cringe, waiting for him to call me a liar, to confront me.

"Make sure she gets settled in." The line goes dead.

"Who did he say he's meeting with?" Belinda's black patent heel taps impatiently on the marble.

"He has a few important calls to make."

"More important than *this*? Show me his calendar." Glossy crimson claws stretch for my iPad, but I hug it tight to my chest, earning her sigh of frustration. "Well, doesn't he have you trained well already."

I say nothing and stare out at the dark blue waters and, beyond that, an endless sea of evergreens reaching all the way to the mountain range, still capped with white in mid-May. Alaska is still as breathtakingly beautiful as the first time I took it in.

Only, the magic of Wolf Cove has been sullied.

"Does this have to do with his father coming in? Because I swear, every time William Wolf is within a mile radius, Henry starts acting all reckless."

"Maybe. I don't know. He didn't say." That e-mail from the lawyer makes me think that telling Henry's father about the pending charges and the lawsuit is not going to be easy. I wonder how his father is going to react. It sounds like he holds Wolf Hotels' reputation on a pedestal.

The ferry rounding the corner distracts Belinda from pressing me for more information about Henry's whereabouts. "Okay, ten minutes and counting. Here's her room key." She thrusts the card toward me. "She's staying in Penthouse Cabin Two."

"Beside Henr—I mean, Mr. Wolf?" Henry was adamant that he is *always* Mr. Wolf outside the privacy of his cabin walls.

"Yes. As requested by Mr. Wolf, himself. Call Housekeeping and ask them to deliver her welcome package in exactly five minutes; we don't want the ice bucket melting. And have her liaison ready. She needs to be fully entertained until Mr. Wolf frees himself from whatever it is that he's doing."

"Already taken care of. Michael will be coming shortly."

"Massage?"

I nod. "Mr. Wolf's request."

She gives a small nod of satisfaction, adjusting her heavy black-rimmed glasses and smoothing her movie-star blonde waves. "Roshana Mafi needs to be impressed. We need nothing short of an exemplary review from her. Can you handle all of this?"

"Yes."

"Really? Because your breasts are practically hanging out."

My eyes drop to my gaping shirt in a panic, where the top button has slipped out of the slightly too-large buttonhole again. It's a replacement blouse, after Henry tore the buttons off my other one. "This button won't hold," I mutter, fumbling with it as my cheeks heat.

"The cleaners should have a safety pin for you to use until we can get you another shirt. Button your blazer. That might help." At least Belinda doesn't sound mad about it. As the hotel manager, she's next in charge below Henry. She also wears low-cut tops that intentionally flaunt her breasts, so this is a pot and kettle moment if there ever was one.

I fasten the single oversized button at my waist. I don't know how much that really helps though. It's more for fashion than function.

"Okay. Do you remember everything I told you?" She's never hidden the fact that she thinks I'm dimwitted.

I make sure my head is turned away when I roll my eyes. "Yes. I'll be fine." In truth, I'm so preoccupied with the e-mail bomb I opened this morning, I've barely listened to a word Belinda has said. But I'm not too worried, because if what Henry's attorney wrote is true, then no exemplary review will save Henry or Wolf Hotels from the coming shit storm.

"Oh, and one more thing... Roshana's a viper. Don't take anything she says personally."

I heave a sigh. *Great. Can't wait.*

two

Roshana Mafi's curvy body sways as she climbs the front stairs with purpose, the bellhop trailing along the ramp alongside her with her flamboyant zebra-print suitcase. She's even more exotic than the picture in Belinda's prepared file suggested. In that studio picture, she was posed, sitting prim and proper in a cobalt-blue suit, her shiny raven hair combed smooth, the white background only amplifying the rich bronzed tone of her skin.

Her hair is still shiny and smooth and her daring snow-white suit is still prim now, but with the wilderness as a backdrop and her large near-black eyes glossy with the crisp, fresh sea air, there's a sexy wild quality to counter the polish.

I fist my hands to keep from wringing them together. I shouldn't be nervous to meet her. I shouldn't care at all. But, as far as Roshana Mafi and *Luxury Travel* magazine are concerned, I represent a part of Wolf Cove, and regardless of Henry and his brewing legal troubles, I don't want to reflect poorly on this place. It's a beautiful hotel and destination, and too many employees paid a lot of money to get themselves to Homer for a job. I've only been here for a few short weeks and I don't want to think about leaving anytime soon.

But I'm guessing that once everyone finds out that I've been sleeping with my boss, I'm going to be on a plane back to Greenbank, Pennsylvania and my overbearing mama and that lying bastard, Jed.

I push that reality away for now and step forward, forcing a wide smile. "Miss Mafi?"

Her eyes roll over me, assessing the fitted plum skirt and white silk blouse that makes up my liaison uniform, before settling on my face. "That's right."

"Welcome to Wolf Cove. My name is Abbi and I'll be escorting you to your—"

"Where is Henry?" Her voice carries one of those cool, naturally condescending tones that instantly puts me on edge.

"He was called away on an urgent matter but he asked me to tell you that he would connect with you as soon as he is able. He sends his apologies."

She sniffs with displeasure but says nothing.

Is she unhappy because the owner wasn't here to roll out the red carpet for her? Or is it because *Henry* wasn't here to meet her? I noticed her use of his first name, but I was under the impression that Henry has never met her before. No doubt she's done her research, as he has done his. Has the handsome billionaire caught this magazine writer's eye?

Maybe she showed up at Wolf Cove with plans to do more than just write an article.

Did Henry write that private note with plans to do more than just provide her with quotable lines?

Is that why she's staying in the penthouse cabin directly beside his?

"You can lead me to my suite any time now."

"Right." I push aside the conflicting burn of jealousy and force a wide smile, adjusting the blazer that Belinda handed to me this morning—a more professional look when receiving guests. "Please follow me."

∼

"Is this your first trip to Alaska?"

Roshana makes a sound that resembles a yes, though I can't be sure. She barely said a word as I led her down the covered path and into her cabin. Truth be told, I'd rather listen to the wheels on the cart as the bellhop trails us than strike up conversation with this woman.

"Well, I'm sure you're going to love it. Wolf Cove is magical."

Her gaze flitters about the main room, taking in the vaulted ceilings and designer detail with lightning speed, her expression hard. It's identical to Henry's, decorated with a pleasing contract of creams, whites, and metal against wood, and nothing that anyone in their right mind could complain about.

"In the bedroom, please." She waves indigo-blue-lacquered nails toward the bellhop, though he was already moving in that direction.

I head for the main desk phone, the closest one. "The Penthouse Cabin comes with your very own personal service staff. All you need to do is hit the button marked liaison"—I press the prominent button on the phone and not three seconds later, the servants' door creaks open—"and Andy will make himself available to you."

"Hello, Miss Mafi. It's a pleasure to be of service for your stay." Andy, a tall and fit attractive blond guy with an

Australian accent, flashes his brilliant dimpled smile. I was standing in the lobby next to him a half hour ago when Belinda told him to use that smile on his guest, no matter what time of day or night—and day or night is exactly when he'll be holed up in those tiny servants' quarters awaiting Roshana's call, should she require it.

Roshana's icy exterior softens for just a moment, just like Belinda quietly predicted it would at the sight of her personal servant.

"Michael will be arriving in about ten minutes to provide you with a full-body massage, compliments of Mr. Wolf. He's Mr. Wolf's personal masseuse."

All I get is a slight nod in response.

"If there's nothing else, I'll leave Andy to give you a tour of your suite and walk through the itinerary prepared for you. It's full of all the sightseeing and pampering that Wolf Cove has to offer." Because I'd really like to get back to the quiet confines of Cabin One, where I can pace around the dining table and fret over our criminal boss in peace.

When Roshana says nothing, I take that as my cue to leave.

I'm halfway to the door when I hear her call out, "Tell your employer that I'm disappointed I wasn't more of a priority for him." She delivers that in an airy voice, but I know that it's meant to be a warning. It's supposed to send me running to Henry in a panic, for fear of an unflattering write-up in this magazine of hers.

But I for one know he had way bigger issues than a mediocre review. "Certainly. Until then, please accept his welcome note and his apologies." I gesture to the arrangement of Siberian Phlox and Lupine wildflowers sitting on the dining table, wishing I could have snuck in here earlier to read the message he wrote to her.

I dart out the door before she can pass along any more threats, and rush toward Cabin One, my swipe card clutched tightly in my fist. I enter through the servants' quarters as usual, because regardless of how freely I move through the suite once I'm inside, I need to keep up appearances for anyone outside.

"For fuck sakes! I will not let her destroy my life. Just do what needs to be done, God dammit!"

three

My hand flies out to stop the door from shutting noisily, and then I tiptoe closer to the staff entrance into the main cabin, my blood pounding in my ears. As usual, the door is ajar to allow me easy, welcome access into Henry's space. Only now I suspect that if Henry knew I was here, he wouldn't be speaking so openly.

What sends a shiver down my spine though is the part about "doing what needs to be done." What exactly "needs to be done" to the woman accusing him of rape and about to ruin his life?

Suddenly it doesn't seem like such a smart move to be eavesdropping. Yet I can't help myself, wrapping my arms around my chest in a comforting hug as I listen to the man I was head over heels for only twenty-four hours ago rant and rave to someone over the phone.

This is a different side of Henry. Even when he's pissed off, he has always maintained an air of cool arrogance and calm. Of control. He's no longer controlled here. I think he's scared, and for good reason.

"I don't give a fuck! You're my lawyer and I'm in Alaska, trying to run a new hotel that has cost me millions of my own money. I have a media event this weekend, I can't deal with this right now! I'm not asking *you* to do it. Hire your guy to do it."

Oh my God. Do what? Hire his guy? I cover my mouth to keep from gasping out loud.

"Of course my father's telling you to settle. He doesn't want this to go to court. Can you imagine the news?" There's a long pause as Henry listens to someone on the phone, and then he erupts. "God dammit!" I jump at the sound of a loud crash against the hardwood. Something shattering. A lamp, possibly? "They don't need a DNA test to prove that's my semen. I can tell you right now that it is.... Fuck, I can't remember? Three weeks ago? Four? She must have kept them.... Why is she doing this to me? I mean, come on. I gave her three months of paid leave, we set her up with a ludicrous severance package. I wrote her a glowing letter of recommendation. She said she was going to sign. *You* said she was set to sign. So tell me, what changed? No, this is on her, not me. It didn't have to go this way... No... No! Fuck, no! I don't care if your firm represents Wolf Corporate. You are my lawyer and you are going to do what I ask." Each word coming out of his mouth sounds more ominous, more conspiring. I shouldn't be hearing any of this.

"Listen to me very carefully, Dyson. I don't care if I have the money to pay her off. I will *not* be threatened and extorted on some bullshit accusation. She's just pissed because she wanted a white picket fence and three kids, and that's nothing I can give her.... Well, she *is* obviously *that* hurt, if she's held on to month-old panties and accused me of rape.... Are you fucking kidding me? I've *never* forced a woman, Dyson. She wanted it as much as I did. She fucking *begged* me for it."

So, he's claiming that what Kiera says is a lie. Is that true? Or should I expect denial to the bitter end from him? *She begged me for it.* Isn't that the classic rapists' answer?

Or is it the truth? Henry's a powerful man with lots of money. A gorgeous, powerful man who, within days, already has me ensnared in an intoxicating web where I'll do anything he asks of me.

And women can be vindictive creatures. Back in Greenbank, Billie Jo Clayburn caught her husband, Matt, in bed with another woman one night. The next day, after he left for work, she drained their bank accounts, sold their car, his golf clubs, his family heirlooms, his suits—basically, everything he valued—to a Pittsburgh pawn shop and hopped on the first plane to Europe, all before he clocked out for the day. For the rest of the summer, she posted pictures on Facebook of herself in the laps of various men, thanking Matt for working so hard to give her the trip of a lifetime, and wishing him and his boss's wife a happy life.

Needless to say, Matt was left jobless and penniless, and couldn't do much about it because he was the cheating bastard in the first place.

Hearing Henry deny the awful allegations brings a tidal wave of relief for me, because I so desperately want to believe he wouldn't do such a thing. But it's quickly flattened by a bursting ache of reality and hurt.

He was screwing his last assistant, too.

And I just handed over my virginity to him. So freely.

My stomach roils with the stark reality that, while he may have quickly invaded my every thought and wish, I'm nothing more than a plaything for him. A convenient and quick sexual fix.

Something rattles and Henry curses under his breath—it sounds like he kicked a chair leg or something. I sense him pacing. "Of course the detective is going to investigate. She handed him my semen on her clothes and some bullshit lie from her husband about bruising. I'm guessing they'll be calling for my DNA sample by the end of the weekend. I can be uncooperative but that'll make me look guilty, and they'll eventually get it anyway. Either way, they'll match it and arrest me. *That can't happen*, Dyson! Yes! Of course I'm freaking out! If the media catches wind, it won't matter that it's all bullshit... Who, Kiera? No, she has no clue..."

Kiera has no clue about what?

Henry heaves an exasperated sigh at whatever his lawyer said. I wish this were over speakerphone. "I'm guessing that dickless husband of hers is behind all this, anyway. Found out he can't please his wife anymore and he doesn't like it."

Clearly he doesn't value marriage vows. Strike two, as if potential female predator wasn't a big enough strike one.

"Yeah, do it. I'll have security let you in."

I'm holding my breath, waiting as Henry listens to the person speak on the other side, the cabin dead silent.

That's when my personal phone starts ringing. The one sitting inside my purse.

I stifle the urge to hiss with panic as I fumble for it, the strap of my purse slipping off my shoulder in the process. It hits the floor with a soft thud. I dive for it, cursing under my breath as I root through the pocket with frantic hands, finding it and flipping the silence button on the side. Hoping the noise will go unnoticed.

I'm still on my knees with my head bowed when the door creaks open wider and Henry's polished black shoes appear in front of me.

"I've gotta go. Call me when you're in my office and I'll give you the code to the safe," Henry demands, his voice unnaturally calm as compared to a moment ago, though no less hostile.

I take my time collecting the few items that spilled from my purse while I decide what to do. What should I say? Do I play dumb? Do I say I just got here? Do I pretend I don't know a thing, and smile and wait expectantly for him to kiss me?

Tell me to strip?

Fuck me on his desk? In his bed?

Even as appalled as I am with him right now, I'd be lying if I said the thought of having him touch me doesn't spark heat between my thighs. He's turned me into some sort of sex deviant. But I can't just sit here on my knees as if I'm waiting for him to unzip his fly. I finally dare look up, in time to see his hand stretch out in front of him, palm out.

It could be considered a gentlemanly offer, and yet from Henry Wolf I hear the command.

Sliding my fingers over his calloused palm—he must have earned those splitting wood—I ease to my feet. I take a deep, calming breath before I let my gaze climb his firm, hard body, his charcoal designer suit as perfect and out of place in the wilds of Alaska as on any other day, before meeting his eyes. The cold, steely blue in them instantly creates knots in my stomach.

"You have a *bad,* bad habit of eavesdropping, Abigail," he whispers.

He knows I hate being called Abigail, but now's not the time to remind him of that. I clear my throat to avoid sounding weak and fearful. "I didn't want to interrupt."

"Liar." His lip twitches with amusement, but it falls off so quickly. "What exactly did you hear?"

Here's the moment of truth. Lie and smile, or confront him with what I know. Which is it?

I've never been good at confrontation. In fact, I'm downright terrible at it. I take after my father in that. It's why my mama is able to so effectively bully us both into living the Bernadette Mitchell way. It's why I didn't punch Jed in his lying, cheating face when he told me to wait for him while he sowed his wild oats. It's why I've been so good at denying reality since I met Henry.

I don't want to deny reality again. Yet, I have to be smart, because it's clear Henry doesn't take too well to anything that feels like a threat.

Henry's eyes dip down to my white blouse, and I know that the button has slipped through the hole once again. As it is, the shirt doesn't do a good job of hiding my ample cleavage—apparently one of his favorite things about me.

I let go of his hand and fold my arms over my chest in a weak attempt to deny him any pleasure from my body as I fix the button. But when his eyes meet mine and I see the heat in them, I know it will take more than that.

"I heard something about a woman who was 'begging you for it.' And her husband."

That seems to douse whatever lurid thoughts Henry may be having. He sighs and turns, heading back into the main cabin. I trail without thought, desperate to hear how he's going to answer this. What he's going to say. I already know the truth, or at least part of it.

I frown when I see him head for the crystal decanter. "It's barely noon."

"It's five o'clock somewhere," he mutters, pouring himself a glass of the amber liquid.

"You sure you want to be doing that, with all the media coming in? And your father? What are they going to say?"

"The smell of scotch on my breath is the least of my problems right now." I watch his Adam's apple bob with a gulp, my mouth parting involuntarily at the memory of running my tongue along the sharp jut. It's far from the only part of him that I've enjoyed running my tongue over.

Silence hangs around us as Henry turns his back to me and stares out the window for a long moment, taking in the priceless view of the waters and tree-lined shores that make up Wolf Cove, a secluded inlet off Kachemak Bay that Henry's family has owned for generations, the place where Henry decided to open his luxurious Wolf Cove Hotel.

"My last assistant has just filed a civil suit against Wolf Hotels for wrongful dismissal, along with a police report that I forced myself on her. She has a pair of panties with my semen on it, and her husband is claiming she came home after meeting with me with bruises on her arms from where I restrained her when I assaulted her. They've opened a police investigation and will likely arrest me. Kiera's asking for ten million to settle out of court for the civil suit, and my father will force me to pay it out of my coffers to minimize Wolf Hotels' involvement with my mess. If I'm charged with anything that looks like sexual assault, then there is no way my father can hand over controlling share of Wolf Hotels to me. In both cases, the board of directors will demand my resignation as acting CEO immediately."

It's basically everything I just overheard, and yet somehow it feels more real, hearing him tell me firsthand. I simply stand there with my mouth hanging open in shock.

"And did you?"

"Did I what?" His head whips around and I feel the full effect of that glare in the pit of my stomach. "Did I *force* myself on her? No. *Of course* not."

I swallow against the discomfort of that weight. "But you slept with her." My voice sounds so small and weak. Hurt.

Realization fills his face. "I tell you that I'm about to lose everything I've been working for because someone is *falsely* accusing me of rape, and you're upset that that I even fucked her in the first place?" He shakes his head, bitter amusement twisting his features. "The answer is yes, I fucked my last assistant. But it wasn't forced; she was very willing. Does hearing that make you feel better?"

No. Not at all. "I just thought...." My voice trails off as the ache in my chest swells. "I don't know what I thought."

He runs his hands through his mane of hair the color of roasted chestnuts, sending it into sexy disarray. I can actually see the tension cording the muscles in his neck and shoulders. He's worried, and rightfully so. At best, he's going to lose Wolf Hotels and have his life dragged through the mud. At worst, he could go to jail.

"I'm so sorry she's doing this to you. If there was some way to help you, I would. Please know that."

He opens his mouth but pauses, his eyes trailing over my body. His dress shoes click against the hardwood floor as he approaches slowly, setting his drink on the side table on his way past, the glass hitting the surface with a loud clunk. "You thought—" his voice has softened somewhat by the time he stops right in front of me, his index finger sliding beneath my chin to tilt my head back to meet his gaze, also softened "—that I've never slept with an assistant before. That you were an exception."

I want to deny it, but I falter. *Yes.* That's exactly what I thought. Why did I think that? Did he ever say anything to make me think this was different for him? Or did I simply *want* to think that this whirlwind thing between us was uncontrollable and kismet and special? That *I* was special.

He levels me with that intense stare, waiting for me to answer.

"I thought this wasn't something you normally do," I finally admit.

"And what if I said *this*"—his free hand waves back and forth between us—"*is* different? That, from the moment I met you out on that dock, all belligerent and adorable, I knew you were different. Would you believe me?"

Would I? I already know I'd *want* to believe it. Wouldn't any normal woman, when she meets a man who consumes her thoughts? Whether we want to admit it or not, don't we all secretly pine over the hope that the man will fall head over heels for us, grow weak with lack of control, not be able to stop thinking about us?

Or is that just the naïve romantic fools like me?

I play back all the things Henry has said to me. What was it exactly he said this thing between us is? I'm getting over an idiot ex and fucking my boss for the next four months. Henry's running a hotel and fucking his assistant for the next four months. *That's all it is.* I can't forget that part. He said that, too. He never committed to more.

And yet, despite his words, I have somehow convinced myself that there is a deeper connection between us.

I may be spineless sometimes, and naïve most of the time, but I won't knowingly let myself be downright stupid. "No. I wouldn't believe you if you told me that."

"Right. And you shouldn't." He nods, more to himself than me. "So I'm not going to bother standing here and trying to convince you otherwise. But do you *really* believe I would force myself on a woman? Have I ever forced myself on you?"

My gaze searches his chiseled freshly shaved jaw as flashes pass through my mind—Henry, naked; Henry, undressing me; Henry, thrusting into my waiting body—and I can't keep my breathing from growing ragged. "No. Never." He's been forward, and dominating, and he has taunted me, but he has never forced himself on me. I've always wanted it. *Always.*

But did Kiera? She was married. Did she say no to him, even once? "Could you have been mistaken by what she wanted? Maybe you misunderstood her?"

His jaw turns hard. "No, Abbi. I didn't misunderstand anything. Not when she propositioned me time and time again, not when she told me she—" He cuts himself off, closing his eyes. "Not when we both decided it was best she find another job because I couldn't give her what she wanted." The mask he keeps firmly in place over his features slips, showing the vulnerability, the anger, the disgust—and a touch of fear—beneath. "I never touched her in any way she didn't want. You need to believe me when I say that."

Why? Why do I *need* to believe him?

Besides the fact that I already *do*.

He searches my eyes and must see that answer because his face softens and his shoulders sink with a heavy exhale. Reaching up to gently graze my cheek with the back of his knuckles, he whispers, "I didn't know how to tell you. I *wanted* to. I just found out last night, and I've been trying to get a handle on it all before I unnecessarily worry or scare you."

"And should I? Be scared?"

His hands settle onto my hips with a tight grip. He leans forward and burrows his face in the crook of my neck, his warm breath tickling my skin in that delicious way. "*I am*," he finally admits in a whisper. "I never expected her to do this to me."

Even as jealousy pricks my heart for whatever intimacy

he's shared with his past assistant, that he's here with me now, allowing me to see such a vulnerable side to him in the face of personal ruin, makes me want to shelter him. Protect him.

I revel in the feel of his sinewy muscles beneath my fingers as I slide my hands up his arms to his shoulders, to the back of his neck, cupping it in a comforting gesture. "They'll investigate and find out that she's lying, and everything will be okay."

I'm not sure I believe that, but he needs to hear it right now.

I'm also not sure that I won't get burned in this fire, if I'm somehow dragged into this mess. But, so what if everyone back home finds out I slept with my boss? There are far worse things that I could be doing. Plus, it's a summer job that'll be long over by then. I'll be fine. I need to stop being so selfish. I may not deserve the fallout of Henry's previous indiscretion, but Henry definitely doesn't deserve what she's doing to him.

There's still the matter of a husband, though. "You knew she was married."

"She told me they were separating."

"But they weren't actually separated."

He sighs and pulls away from me, wandering over to pick up his glass and take another sip. "I've never claimed to be a saint, Abbi. You know that. We were working together for months before I laid a hand on her. Twelve-hour days, weekends. We started getting close. She said she was miserable in her marriage, and she was attracted to me. So, I finally gave her what she wanted." He polishes off the glass. "Just like I gave you what you wanted, when you wanted to get over your ex. Remember? The idiot who asked you to wait for him while he fucks his new girlfriend?" Even from a good five feet away, I can feel his eyes touch me like fingertips drawn over my body, dipping first to my mouth, then to the top button of my blouse, no doubt a shift away from popping open again. "Or have you already forgotten? Maybe I did my job too well."

"He broke up with me. And he wasn't my husband."

Henry reaches up to loosen his tie and then closes the space between us smoothly, his size dominating me. I take an instinctive step back, only to find my back hitting the wall. "Do you *really* care about who I fucked in the past, and whether they were married, Abbi? The past is the past. We've all made mistakes." With one more step, his hands find purchase on the wall on either side of me, effectively caging me in.

God, how has it turned so hot in here, suddenly? How does he do that? I'm supposed to be disgusted by him right now—and part of me is—but all I can do is inhale that intoxicating cologne and absorb the heat radiating from that firm, powerful body, and remind myself about how good those hands and that mouth have made me feel, time and time again.

"Yes. I do care." It's my feeble attempt to take the moral high road, and I don't believe myself. Henry's arched brow tells me he doesn't either.

Probably because I'm quite literally panting right now.

"I don't know. I don't know what to think about any of this," I finally admit.

With a flick of his fingers, the button on my blazer pops open. With another flick, the top button of my blouse pops next, followed by the one below it, exposing the simple cotton bra I have beneath. Not exactly sexy, but I didn't come to Alaska with anything that could be classified as "sexy," and besides, there aren't a ton of sexy options for my D-cup breasts that don't cost a small fortune.

"You need to get out there. All those journalists and...." My words fade with a gasp as he pushes my blazer off my shoulders. His hands quickly work the rest of my shirt until the buttons are unfastened, my shirt is sliding from my shoulders, and my bra straps hang loose at the crooks of my elbows, exposing my swollen breasts to the cool air and Henry's searing gaze.

I know exactly where this is heading. As controlled as Henry can be, he also likes to finish what he starts.

Sure enough, he hikes my skirt up and hooks his hands around the backs of my thighs. With little effort he has me hoisted and pinned to the wall with his body, his impressive erection pressing between my legs, his mouth dipping down to take my nipple in.

A moan escapes my lips as my head falls back against the wall. I enjoy the feel of his wet tongue against my flesh and the threat of his teeth as he teases lightly. I free my arms of my bra straps so I can weave my fingers through his hair, fisting his mane tight as I shamelessly writhe against the pressure between my legs.

With one last hard—almost painful—suck, he lets my breast fall from his mouth and comes up to meet my lips. Trapping me against the wall with his pelvis, he reaches up to cup my face with both hands, and then plants the softest kiss on my lips. "I had no interest in starting up anything after that mess with Kiera. I was going to focus on Wolf Cove and taking over Wolf Hotels officially, and then find myself someone appropriate. But I met you and that all went to shit. This all happened so fast, and I wasn't expecting it at all."

I stare into his beautiful blue eyes, unshielded by their

usual mask, and I revel in his whispered words, in the promise they hold. Is it really possible? Could this powerful, overwhelming man feel something for me? I mean, I know he's attracted to me. That in itself is still a shock to me, but the proof is pressed against me right now, and he's proved it many times over.

But... what is he saying? That this could this actually be the start of something *more*?

A warm flood of emotion washes over me.

I close my eyes, reveling in the feel of his hot breath skating over my neck again.

"You should know by now that I love making a woman scream, but not from pain. And I love making a woman shake, but not from fear." His teeth graze my earlobe. "And you know what gets me hard? A woman who's dripping wet for me. Who can't keep her legs together when I'm around. Who can't hide the fact that she's turned on and begging to be touched." He drops one hand down to force it between us. I gasp as the pad of his thumb slides over me, gently brushing my swollen clit through my nylons and my soaked panties.

I dive forward to kiss him but he pulls back a touch, his lips hovering over mine, skating teasingly over them with each whisper spoken.

"I know I have no right to ask this, but please, stick with me through this. Don't make me lose you—this—because of her."

"Of course." I can't imagine going anywhere that means not having this man's lips on mine.

"Do you remember what I said I need when I'm stressed?"

I nod, blood rushing to my groin in anticipation.

He pulls back just far enough to show me his eyes, to let

me see the flurry of intense passion, anger, and wild desperation in them. "I've never been more stressed in my life. And I *need* you, right now. Please."

I want to make him feel better. I want to give him exactly what he wants.

four

I barely get the "Yes" out before his mouth is on mine, crushing me in a frantic kiss that steals my breath and my heartbeats. I revel in it, fisting his wavy hair as his tongue dances with mine in a desperate way that I haven't experienced with him before. After the roller coaster of emotions I've experienced since waking up on his rug last night, I'm likely just as desperate.

I barely notice us moving, and then suddenly we're in front of the dining table and he's releasing my legs and yanking my nylons and panties down.

"Don't rip them," I warn. "They're my last pair."

"Fuck. I don't have the patience for these damn things."

"I'll do it." I reach for them but he growls, "No!" and seizes my wrists, pinning them behind my back, confining me. I tug playfully against the restraint, giggling. He pauses, a curious look on his face.

"What?"

In answer, he slides the loosened tie from around his neck. Winding the silky material around my wrists, he secures my hands behind my back.

"What are you doing?"

"Trust me." His mouth is on mine again, his teeth nipping at my bottom lip. "Turn around."

I do, without a thought, letting his fingertips coax me until I'm bending over the table, my cheek resting against the smooth wood, staring at my reflection in the giant wall mirror across from us. It's positioned perfectly to reflect the entire tawdry scene.

"You like seeing yourself like this?" Henry asks. I watch him peel my nylons and panties down to my knees and push my skirt up to settle around my waist, exposing me to the cool air and to him. He reaches forward and runs a finger along my slit. A hiss escapes his lips. "Dammit, Abbi."

I smile at my reflection. "I know." I'm soaking wet for him, and growing all the more so by the second, watching this all unfold.

He fumbles with his belt buckle and unfastens it. His zipper follows quickly. He pushes his dress pants and boxers down to reveal his powerful thighs, freeing his impressive erection. "I wish we could just stay here all day. I would show you so many things," he mutters, stroking himself slowly, his eyes on my most private area, even as mine are locked on his reflection.

"What do you want to show me?" I'm already tied up and bent over the dining table. I'd say today's lesson is quite robust.

His hands hook the front of my hips and he adjusts my body slightly, angling my ass upward and pushing my thighs as far apart as my nylons bunched at my knees allow, until I can feel my lips spreading apart and the head of his hard cock nudging at the entrance. He hasn't put on a condom and I haven't asked him to. After feeling him come in me yesterday and last night, I don't ever want to wear a condom with him again.

I woke up this morning after a day of incredible sex, sore. Now, I clench my muscles with anticipation.

But Henry's hips still, and he lets his tip rest against me, teasing me. "Are you sure you want this?"

"Yes, of course," I pant, my eagerness almost too much.

"I'm not forcing you, am I? I don't want to be *mistaken* here."

I hear the hint of sour humor in his tone and, given my current vulnerable position, it's annoying. I push back in answer, thrusting my hips. His cock slides through my slit, coating it with me.

He groans, fumbling with the buttons of his dress shirt, getting them undone and the shirt off in record time, leaving him in only a white v-neck undershirt. His hard cock juts out just behind me, already lined up.

The anticipation is making me ache. I test the binding around my wrists. It's loose enough that my arms feel relaxed, but I won't be getting free.

"Are you watching?" He plants a hand on either cheek, grabbing a firm hold of my flesh, opening me up, his thumb skating along my crack, pushing against the tight hole.

I clench reactively. "Yes."

"Good." He sinks into me with one slow but forceful push, filling me so completely, making me cry out from the pleasurable pain. Again, he freezes. "Does this hurt? Are you sure you want this? I thought you did but I could be mista—"

"Stop it." He's making fun of me and my body is pulsing with need.

"You want me to stop?" He begins sliding out.

I fight against the binding on my wrists, desperate to reach back and grab his hard cock. "*Please.*"

"Please, what? Tell me what you want, Abbi? I need to hear it so I'm sure I'm not mistaken." There's a touch of anger in his voice, but I don't think it's directed at me.

"I want you inside me. I want to still feel you inside me tonight when I go to—" My words cut off with a cry as he thrusts into me.

And again, and again, his fingers squeezing my hips so tight that I'm not sure I won't be bruised. I'm enthralled with the sight of Henry, his powerful legs straining as he drives into me from behind, his fingers digging into my flesh.

"You like watching, don't you?"

My agreement comes out in a moan. I thought I'd be embarrassed, witnessing something like this, but it only turns me on. Good God. A few days with Henry and I've already shed all my inhibitions. I'm doing things I couldn't even imagine. Things I didn't even know were "things."

I can't move much and so I don't try, content to let Henry do the work as I watch him pumping in and out of me at a deliciously hard, fast pace, making my entire body rock and my breasts rub against the cold wood.

"I need to feel you." His hands loose their grip of my hips to reach over his head and grab hold of his undershirt. He yanks it off and tosses it to the floor, revealing that perfect upper body of rippled muscle. Rough, calloused hands slide over my curves to fit beneath me, one settling on my clit, seizing the bundle of nerves between his thumb and finger; the other to cup the front my neck, securing me gently as his body folds over mine, until his chest meets my back, all while he continues mercilessly driving into me.

Somewhere overhead I think I hear a helicopter but I'm

unable to focus on anything but how incredible this feels, that tingling buildup at the base of my spine beginning.

"This *is* different," he whispers, pressing his lips against the back of my neck.

My heart blips. "What?"

For a long moment, he doesn't speak, and I begin to think I only wished I heard him. And then.... "You. Me. This. It *is* different, Abbi. I can't explain how or why, but I need you to believe that."

"I do," I moan, blood beginning to flood between my legs, swelling my flesh, my core begging for relief.

I do because I need to. Because Henry is quickly becoming *everything* to me.

"You're mine."

"I'm yours."

"I want this to work between us."

"Yes!" I manage to get out through pants.

"You're about to come," he grits out, his cock swelling more inside me with each thrust, telling me he's not far behind me. His fingers, now slick, work against my clit with a sense of urgency, hard and fast circles that make me want to spread my legs wide for him.

The rush hits me and my muscles begin to contract. In answer, he angles his hips to thrust harder into me, the sensation so overwhelming I'm unable to hold back my cries of ecstasy as a mind-paralyzing, explosive orgasm rips through my body, leaves me a quivering mess.

"Fuck!" Henry presses his mouth against the back of my neck to muffle his cries. I can feel his cock pulsing inside me, spilling his semen into me, leaving me slick and sore and so utterly satisfied.

Silence surrounds us as we lie on the table, limp, him draped on top of me, his heartbeat pounding against my back. I stare at his handsome profile as he catches his breath.

Finally he turns to meet my gaze in the mirror with hooded eyes. "Every time we do this, I just want it more."

I smile at him. "Me, too."

"I think I should just keep you here and fuck you for the next three months."

"How is that any different than what's happening right now?" I smile.

"I'd have to fire you."

Oh. "I don't think I like the sound of being fired."

"You'd get over it."

"And what would everyone say?"

"That you must know how to suck a mean cock."

"Oh my God. No." I giggle.

"I love your laugh." He closes his eyes and heaves a sigh.

"I know. We have to go."

"We have to go." Laying a kiss on the back of my shoulder, he pulls himself up and quickly unties my wrists, examining the creases in the silk material with a frown. "Well, this one's ruined."

I peel myself off the table but have to lean against the table for support momentarily, my legs wobbly.

Henry smooths my skirt down over my hips, then reaches up to fill his hands with my breasts, running the pads of his thumbs over my nipples. "You good?"

"I think so."

I'm treated to one deep kiss, my head falling back as Henry plunders my mouth with his tongue. "Thank you. For believing me, and sticking by me." He breaks free abruptly and, tugging his pants up, he heads for his bedroom. "I have to be out there when my father lands or he'll tear me a new one. He's going to tear me a new one anyway."

The Mr. William Wolf, tearing Henry a new one. I can't imagine that, considering how daunting Henry himself can be. But I shouldn't be too concerned about that. Now that I'm no longer ensnared in Henry's overpowering haze, I remember the real issues at hand.

And the fact that I'll be meeting very important people shortly, with Henry's cum running down my thigh.

There's nothing graceful about this. I fish my blouse and bra from the floor and walk awkwardly to the small powder room to clean up, my nylons and panties still down at my knees.

We reappear in the living room at the same time, Henry looking perfectly put together again, aside from the tie around his neck, which he's in the process of retying. The first time he's ever done that himself in my presence.

"So, your dad knows all about this already?"

"Yes. I had the pleasure of making that call to him early this morning. I didn't have much choice. I couldn't have him hearing about the lawsuit through our attorneys. It's always fun to explain to your father that the police have evidence with your semen all over it." He stops in front of me, holding the silky material out. "This is navy blue, right? It works?"

"Yes. You've guessed correctly this time." I smile, reaching up to finish tying it for my poor color-blind boss. My smile slips off quickly, though. "And what about what she's claiming you did to her? Does your dad believe you?"

His gaze drifts to the window and water beyond, the tension radiating from him again. "I think he does. I *hope* he does. But it doesn't really matter. I still fucked up."

"Because you broke corporate rules and slept with your assistant."

"And William Wolf is all about rules and leading by example."

"Why does he care that much about who you sleep with?"

"Because it reflects poorly on the company. Because I'm in a position of power and it's wrong. Because it'll muddy my focus on the company, and risk the livelihood of the thousands of people's lives who depend on me." A sardonic smirk curls Henry's lips. "He's probably afraid that I'll start cancelling important meetings so I can stick my face in my assistant's pussy."

I roll my eyes. "You would *never* do that."

Henry smiles, but there's no mirth. "He warned me not to hire someone I was attracted to. In a high-stress job like this, when you spend so much time together.... He's had to fire more than one VP because of it." He bows his head. "Clearly, I didn't listen to him. And I sure as hell didn't learn my lesson."

"So, what happened, exactly? Your assistant wanted a relationship and you didn't want to give it to her?"

"I've never been cut out for normal relationships." He sighs. "That's always where things seem to fall apart with them."

"*With them?*" I feel my eyebrows popping with shock. How many other assistants have there been?

He waves a dismissive hand at me. "Women, in general. Kiera was the first assistant I got involved with."

I don't know if that's a comfort to me or not.

Either way, my gut tells me he's telling me the truth. Or maybe it's my heart, because I want to believe him. And, while finding out that he slept with his last assistant still stings, it's a sting that will fade quickly. After what Jed did to me, this is really nothing. We can get through this. To what end, I'm not sure.

But Henry said he wants this to work out. He wants *us* to work out.

"So? Now what?"

"Now I get to listen to my father berate me for several hours, and then kiss people's asses for the next forty-eight hours so they'll give Wolf Cove glowing write-ups." Cool, abrupt Henry is back.

"And what about the lawsuit, and the charges?"

He reaches out to flatten my disheveled hair. "Dyson's going to arrange a meeting with her to try and persuade her not to go through with this."

"And by 'persuade' you mean *talk* to her, right?" I haven't forgotten the conversation I walked in on.

Henry gets my meaning right away. "Fuck, of course, Abbi! What do you think I am, a thug?" He shakes his head. "If she wants to play hardball, she's going to have to deal with what I'm willing to pitch, and it won't be pretty, but I didn't start this. She needs to realize the repercussions of her lies. All the personal dirt that's going to be revealed in court about our relationship."

"You're hoping she'll recant." I lean into his chest to feel his warmth. "I hope so, too."

"Listen... I need you to do something for me."

I frown, because I can tell this is serious by the stern look on his face. "Of course, anything."

"If we sort out this mess with Kiera, I'm in the clear. But, if my dad then finds out that I turned around and got involved with you, it's over. I'm done."

"He'll give the company to Scott?" The monkey who weighs gold, according to Henry.

Henry heaves a sigh. "He threatens it, but honestly I can't see him giving Wolf Hotels to Scott. If the police press charges, I'll have to step down immediately, leaving the CEO spot vacant. My guess is that he'll appoint someone from the outside and force us to offer an IPO. He'll take Wolf Hotels public. My brother and I'll be able to cash in our 10 percent each and walk away if we want, but the business will be protected. Our family will no longer own it. My grandfather was completely against that."

I shake my head.

"What? Why are you shaking your head at me?"

"Nothing. It's just.... You know, you probably shouldn't have slept with me."

He chuckles, bowing his head. "You know, you're right. And if I'd known what Kiera was going to pull, I probably would have tied my dick in a knot to keep myself from using it. But I honestly thought she'd sign the severance package, we'd go our separate ways, and what I did with my dick while in Alaska wouldn't be such a hot topic."

"What you do with your dick is a very hot topic, for *everyone* around here." I hear the comments every day as we pass both staff and guests. Feel the eyes. Henry is an enigma and everyone seems to want a part of him.

And I seem to be getting a bigger part of him now. An emotional part. Henry's opening up to me, showing me an imperfect, vulnerable, self-deprecating side to him that I would never have believed existed.

It makes my heart swell. Even with the topic at hand.

And yet, something about this doesn't add up. "If you're charged, why can't your dad just take over again until you can clear your name? Didn't he run it for years?" He seems quite involved, still.

Henry's gaze drops to the floor, a somber mask settling over his features. "Because my father has pancreatic cancer and it's terminal."

"I'm... so sorry." I wasn't expecting that.

He nods. "They've given him three more years at most. He wants to spend them relaxing on an island somewhere, knowing that he made the right decisions about our family legacy. That's why I've been acting CEO for the last eighteen months."

"That's just.... I'm so sorry. I can't even imagine my dad dying."

"You two are close?"

I smile. "Yeah." He's a man of few words, and he hates the phone so much that I'll be lucky to talk to him once while I'm here, but he was the one who spent hours in the fields, teaching me how to catch a baseball. He was the one who hugged me while I cried and told me that Jed doesn't deserve me, even as Mama chirped in the background, minimizing Jed's "mistake." Even thinking about saying good-bye to him forever makes my throat close up and my eyes water.

A sympathetic smile touches Henry's lips as he peers down at me. "I'm guessing your dad and my dad are very different. Still... it'll be a shock when he's gone. But giving me controlling share of Wolf Hotels is the right decision, and I know he wants to do it."

"Well, I don't plan on telling your father what we've been doing, so...."

"I'm not worried about you telling him. I'm worried about him finding out." Henry's chiseled jaw tenses. "I don't know what's going to happen in the next few weeks, but I'm guessing there are going to be lawyers asking questions, and if the media gets hold of the story, they'll be asking questions. There may be a detective calling. Staff.... They'll all be asking you. I'm going to be under a microscope, which means you're going to be under a microscope. If there's anything at all you might have said about me already, to anyone...."

"I haven't told a soul."

"Are you positive?"

I frown, racking my brain for anything I may have said about Henry that could be misconstrued. "Oh my God."

Henry's eyes flash. "What?"

"That text to Jed, the one when we were in the boat. You know, about you staring at my breasts?"

"Shit. Right. That was my fault." He pauses. "Okay. Text him back and tell him you were just kidding, trying to make him jealous. Tell him I'm a dick but I don't pay any attention to your boobs or any other part of you."

"Okay." I groan, remembering the e-mail to Lucy. "I also told my friend over e-mail that I thought you were really hot."

He smirks. "Don't worry about that one. There are plenty of those floating around about me. Doesn't mean I slept with all those women."

I roll my eyes. "What do I say if someone flat out asks me if we've... *you know*." Good grief. The man just had me tied up and bent me over a table and I still can't use the actual words?

Henry doesn't seem to notice. "Then you honor the confidentiality contract that you signed on your first day working for me."

"But that's not...." I frown. Does sex with Henry fall under that contract?

"Listen to me very carefully, Abbi. No one can know about us. You tell anyone who asks—*anyone,* including my father—that you are my assistant and I'm your boss, and we have a professional relationship. You know nothing about my previous assistant or anything that may or may not have transpired."

"You expect me to outright lie to *your father*?"

He smirks. "Why not? You lied to your own mother."

"This is different."

He heaves a sigh and, while he's being patient with me, I think his patience is running out. "Do you want everyone on this resort and your family and friends at home to know how much you love fucking your boss?"

He knows the answer to that as well as I do. "But what if the police ask me?"

"Let's hope it doesn't get that far." He sounds much more calm about the whole situation than he was twenty minutes ago.

But I'm not. "But what if it *does* get that far?" I press.

"Then you tell them that you're my assistant and you have signed a confidentiality agreement that keeps you from discussing me at any length. I can hire a lawyer to protect your rights. And if they ask whether I've ever forced myself on you, you say no because that's the truth. Anything beyond that is none of anyone's fucking business as far as I'm concerned. My relationship with you has no bearing on what happened between Kiera and me."

"I'm a terrible liar, Henry."

"Yeah, I've noticed," he mutters wryly, adjusting the front of my blouse and holding out my blazer for me. "Come on. We need to go."

I barely have time to grab my iPad. With one hand at my back, he gently herds me toward the door as my mind still churns with all the fears and worries that were suppressed for those brief stolen moments of intimacy, all the more potent now that I know the truth and my heart has nothing but affection for this man once again.

Henry's touch disappears the second we step outside. He enacts the unspoken two-feet-at-all-times distance rule between us, that's intended to steer people clear of any suspicions of inappropriate behavior between boss and assistant. It's so much harder when I'm so desperate to reach out and touch him, to hold on to the private connection we shared for a little while longer.

I sigh.

"What now?"

"Nothing. Just preparing for the asshole version of you again," I mutter, steeling myself.

He chuckles, but I'm not laughing.

Will two feet be enough? If Kiera's claims get out in the media, and people start looking at us under a microscope, it'll be impossible for me to hide the way Henry stirs my blood and makes me hot, how I'm hyperaware of where he is in the room at all times, how I'm constantly checking my phone to see if he has messaged, how I can't keep the stupid grin off my face when I think about him unzipping his pants in front of me, of how hard he gets for me.

They'll know right away.

"I can hear you thinking," he grumbles under his breath as we make our way along the covered path.

"I can't help it. I'm overwhelmed. This all has me frazzled."

"I can't have you frazzled right now. I need you levelheaded."

"Levelheaded. Right." If I were levelheaded, I probably wouldn't have let my boss under my skirt. I surely wouldn't be fantasizing about life with Henry after Wolf Cove. Will I visit Henry in New York? Will he visit me in Chicago for my last year of college? I won't be a Wolf Hotel employee by then, so we can make out in the middle of the street and no one can say a word.

Maybe I should let him fire me so I can just stay in his

cabin, ordering room service and having sex with him for the rest of the summer. Sure, it might get kind of boring, and I wouldn't be earning any money, and I'd be the talk of the entire hotel, but....

Suddenly, I notice that Henry's not beside me anymore. I stop and turn to find him just standing there, watching me, a strange look on his face.

"What the fuck am I thinking, bringing you with me to meet my father?" He glances at his watch. "I need you to make yourself scarce. Parading you around will only irritate him right now."

"Okay?" I'm not going to take offense to that. Honestly, it's a relief. If Henry's nervous to see him, then I shouldn't be there.

His jaw clenches. "And do me a favor; stay the hell away from Scott. He's a fucking weasel, but he's slick and perceptive, and he's probably sharpening his knife to plunge it into my back. He's been waiting for something like this to happen since my dad appointed me CEO and not him, and he'll want to make sure he has plenty of ammo. He'll lie and manipulate and interrogate you until he gets the answer he wants."

I feel my face blanch. "Interrogate?"

Henry drops his voice to a low murmur. "Hell, he won't even need to interrogate you. One look at those big golden eyes and those plump lips and those fucking beautiful big tits, and he'll know there's no way I was able to resist you."

His words pull a soft gasp from my lips. "Okay. I'll keep away from him."

"I should have hired a male assistant. Or an elderly woman." He sighs, his gaze skating over my body. "You know, one day, when this is all over and I officially control the company, I'm going to strip you down and fuck you right here."

Blood rushes to my head with the abrupt change in subject, and his flash pan change in demeanor. Private Henry is back, but we're not in private. "*Here*?" I look around. It's a secluded path, screened from bugs, shielded from the elements above, surrounded by dense bush and only used by the three Penthouse Cabins' guests and the staff catering to those guests. I rarely ever pass anyone on my way to and from Henry's place. It's quite peaceful and private. Still, just beyond those trees, maybe a hundred feet away and definitely within earshot, is a resort full of people.

What Henry's talking about is basically exhibitionism. Is he serious?

One glance at the hard look on his face tells me he is.

My body, which can still feel him inside me, responds immediately. But this isn't good. The lines between Private Henry and Public Mr. Wolf are beginning to blur for him. "I think you need to focus on your various serious problems at hand," I warn him in a slow, careful voice.

His jaw clenches. "Believe me, those problems are still *very* much in the forefront of my mind. I'm just setting something to look forward to once they're all resolved. You know, goals."

"Goals." I drop my gaze to the front of his pants, to the bulge forming. Goals for his dick, apparently. Which is exactly what got him into his current problems. I do believe that Henry is a smart and shrewd businessman. He's just not thinking clearly right now, and he has a lot to lose by not thinking clearly. He *does* need me to be levelheaded because he can't seem to be. "Okay, how about we focus on more responsible goals for now."

He closes the distance, breaking the two-foot rule.

"What are you doing?" I hiss, glancing around.

"Trying to hold on to what we had back there for a little longer." He jerks his head toward the cabin. "Trying to avoid reality."

So, he felt the deep connection too. My heart swells. "I didn't think Henry Wolf avoided anything."

"That's because you haven't met my father yet."

This must be what Belinda was talking about when she said Henry gets reckless with his father's imminent approach. Only, I think it's been amplified by the Kiera mess. The combination seems to have really thrown Henry for an emotional loop.

And I have the overwhelming urge to hide him from the world until he can get a grip on himself because this version of Henry should not be talking to *anyone*. "Why don't I grab the truck and an ax, and we can drive out to that spot to cut some wood."

His brow arches with playful curiosity. "Right now?"

"Right this instant. Just say the word."

He frowns. "You'd actually go back there?"

"Yes."

"Even with the grizzly bear lurking around?"

A shiver runs down my back at the thought of those beady eyes and sharp claws. "Even with the grizzly bear lurking around."

"He could be more aggressive this time around."

"Then we'll get eaten. That's a really good way of avoiding reality."

Henry's head tips back and he belts out a deep, hearty laugh that makes me smile wide. I wish he laughed more. With a deep groan, he continues walking along the path. "Thank you. I needed that."

I fall into step with him again. "So, do you want me to just go back to my cabin?"

"No. He'll know I'm hiding you. Fucking suspicious old man," he mutters.

"Sounds like a *smart* suspicious old man," I correct. "So, where do you want me?"

When I glance up to see the smirk on his face, I immediately hear the potential innuendo in my question. "Stop it!"

"Okay. Okay. You're right. You need to start behaving, Abbi. This is getting to be too much."

I roll my eyes. "I'm suddenly feeling very ill. I should go rest for the day."

"Or, you know what? Better yet, get one of the Outdoor crew guys to drive you over to the old cabin."

I frown. "Your grandparents' place?" The one we were at just yesterday?

"Yeah. Some of the media wants to see the original Wolf family cabin that inspired all this, so Paige sent a team over this morning to clean and stage it for tomorrow. Make it look less abandoned. I want you to head over there to keep an eye on things."

"Until when?"

"Until you hear from me. Stay until the last of them leave. If they're done early and you have to come back, you can take the rest of the day off. I'll be holed up with my father until late tonight, anyway."

"And tomorrow, for breakfast and the entire morning," I remind him. I'm the one who slotted that into Henry's calendar.

"Fuck. I can't wait until he's back on his helicopter and gone," he mutters as we round a bend in the covered path.

Two stone-faced men are strolling down the path toward us.

I hear a quiet hiss of "shit," under Henry's breath. He speeds up to meet them head-on, leaving me in the background.

"I hope you've been more cordial to your guests than you have your own family." The older man, who bears a remarkable resemblance to Henry only with silver hair, calls out, his strides toward us measured and purposeful, his suit falling gracefully with each step. It's Mr. William Wolf. I recognize his voice from the phone call, and he sounds no less annoyed now.

"You're early." Henry reaches out to clasp hands with his father before shifting his attention to the younger man standing next to him. "And you're not supposed to be here yet."

This has to be Henry's brother, Scott. Aka the weasel. Aka the interrogator. Aside from the same chestnut-brown hair, they bear no resemblance to each other. Scott is attractive in his own right, but it's more of an average boy-next-door appeal, his jawline less pronounced, his eyes more sloped, and his nose daintier.

Scott smiles easily up at him, as if the noticeable height difference—*at least* six inches, I'd peg Scott at five foot eight—doesn't bother him in the least. "I wasn't going to, but with the nightmare our company is facing thanks to you, I thought it would be wise."

"Right." Henry's tone drips with irritation. "Belinda has you both set up in the main lodge. We need the cabins for media this weekend."

"Is that where you're staying?" The scornful smirk on Scott's face tells me he already knows the answer and is just trying to stir the pot.

Henry simply glares at him.

God, the tension radiating around these three men is enough to choke a horse.

Henry turns slightly toward me. "That'll be all, Abbi."

Up until now, I've felt like an invisible bystander. Thankfully. But now two fresh sets of eyes have landed on me and are sliding over my body, scrutinizing every curve.

"Yes, Mr. Wolf." I dart around them, happy to get far away.

From behind me, I hear his father ask, "Who is that?"

"Her name is Abbi Mitchell," Henry answers calmly.

There's a pause and then, "You're kidding me. Right? Is this a joke?"

I'm around the bend and, thankfully, out of earshot of Henry's answer.

five

The maintenance truck chugs along the service road, splashing through the ruts. Rain swept through the area in the early hours, leaving puddles that likely won't dry out for days, thanks to the cool spring temps.

In the back of the truck are two mattresses stacked side by side, still in their packaging. It's heading toward the gates, so I have to assume it's going to the cabin. There's really nowhere else for anyone to go.

A stir of nerves flutters in my stomach as I take in the two male figures sitting inside. I can't see their faces but I can feel their eyes on me all the way from here as I wait for them. I've always been nervous under the scrutiny of males. Or anyone, really. I'm not one for attention.

Hugging my body against the spring chill, I distract myself while I wait by focusing on the decorative fence and hedge that hides the "work" part of the property from the magical guest side. It's like the Wizard of Oz here, with all service areas well hidden from guests' view by curtains of one kind or another.

The truck comes to a squeaky stop in front of me.

"Well, if it isn't the Wolf's right hand," Connor drawls, his brawny arm resting against the open window, grinning at me from behind aviator glasses. He's wearing the Wolf Cove t-shirt and seems unbothered by the cool air. I shouldn't be surprised given when I met him—the first night I was here—he was flaunting that body of his through the staff village in nothing but a towel, fresh from the shower room.

A guy sits beside him who I've never met, but I've noticed with Connor plenty. He has haunting green eyes and buzzed dark hair, and seems to gain as much notice from the female staff as Connor does when he swaggers through the dining hall. I'm pretty sure the two of them are roommates. They're definitely attached at the hip.

"You waiting for us, boss?"

I burst out in a giggle, unexpectedly. "*Boss?*"

He shrugs and lifts his sunglasses. Pretty blue eyes the color of cornflowers dip down my cleavage. Thank God for this blazer, at least. "Like I said, you're Wolf's right hand. That gives you a lot of power around here."

I can't help but sense he's implying something sexual with that hand reference. Seeing as I know exactly where mine have been lately, I guess he wouldn't be wrong. "Is there any chance you could give me a ride over to the Wolf cabin?"

He opens the door and slides out, his poorly laced construction boots hitting the dirt with a thud. "Perfect timing. Hop in."

∽

"I didn't know you could get here by road."

"Road" may not be the right word for this, I accept, as I struggle to stay in my seat, sandwiched between these two guys, my arms folded across my chest to help alleviate the jolt of pain every time we hit a rough patch. I'm used to driving farm trucks over bumpy lanes, but this is a claustrophobic one-lane path through dense bush, with tree branches scratching against the truck's paint most of the way.

"They cleared it three years ago when they started building the hotel. It's meant for maintenance, which is why it's not in the best shape. Best to come through here on an ATV, to be honest. It's too narrow for more than one car and it's a real bitch when you get halfway down and meet another truck."

"That happened this morning. That's why we're using these now." The other guy, Ronan, holds up the maintenance crew walkie-talkie that he radioed in to before we turned down the entrance, telling everyone on the frequency that we were heading in.

"I guess people aren't meant to drive to this cabin." I never noticed the entrance the day Henry and I went out to cut wood, but I'm not surprised. The trees form an effective canopy to hide the newly built road. Plus, I was entirely distracted by Henry.

"No, all these places around here are water entry only," Connor agrees.

They're supposed to come up in their boats, look up and marvel at the rustic cabin Henry's grandfather, the great and powerful gold mine and luxury hotel chain owner, built himself sixty years ago. Just like we did, yesterday.

We hit an especially bad pothole and I wince, the pain jarring to my chest. "How much longer?"

"Another minute or two."

"Can you try to avoid the bumps? It can't be good for the mattresses."

"I'm trying my best, hun." I feel Connor's sideways glance on me, on my chest, and my cheeks flush. It feels like high school track and field all over again, with the girls running laps and the boys watching from the bleachers. I made the mistake of asking Jed once why they liked to hang out there and he explained the appeal of large-breasted girls and bouncing.

I'm beginning to think Connor's hitting these bumps intentionally.

"So, how's life under the big man?"

Stressful.

Amazing.

Disastrous.

Enlightening.

Frustrating.

What's the right answer? All of the above?

I offer a weak smile to no one in particular. "It's fine."

"Is he really the asshole everyone is saying he is?" Ronan asks, reaching up with a muscular tattooed arm to grip the handle above his door. He has a deep, raspy voice, the kind you'd expect to hear when a guy first wakes up.

"Is that what they're saying?"

"After canning Rachel like he did? She spent over a grand of her own money on a ticket to get here and he fires her for doing her job, which is appeasing the guests. So, hell yeah. Dick move by a spineless dickhead."

Rachel. One of my five roommates, who was literally walked off the property and sent home on the ferry for giving away free high-end alcohol and sleeping with a guest.

Henry once told me to not defend him, to agree with the

verbal swings at him. Otherwise people might start suspecting what was going on between us. I don't know if that's such a good idea now, given this mess with Kiera. He doesn't need an army of angry employees calling for his head if this thing blows up.

"He's not the worst. He's strict, but he's fair." I shrug. "He's been decent enough to me, I guess. When I don't screw up." I want off the topic of Henry. "What about you guys? How's the Outdoor crew?"

"Great group. They have us working hard but we have a lot of fun, too," Connor says, his hand scratching over the day-old blond stubble on his chin. There's an entire page on male grooming requirements in the employee handbook that specifies men must be either clean-shaven or keep a neatly trimmed beard. There are also rules about covering up tattoos but Ronan's not too concerned about that. I'm guessing the rules don't apply to these guys.

"You know, I was actually hired to be in the Outdoor crew." Seems crazy just thinking about it now.

"No shit." I turn to smile at Connor, in time to see his eyes flittering over my body, sizing me up. "So, what happened?"

Henry happened. "Nothing really. This other job came up and it seemed like a good opportunity. But I still miss being outdoors." Truthfully, if Henry and I weren't doing what we're doing, I'm afraid I'd be miserable.

"You should take a sabbatical."

I laugh. "A sabbatical?"

"Yeah, a paid leave for study."

"I know what one is. I just don't see how you figure I should get one."

"From your current job. Just for a week."

"I can't just ask for a week off to 'study' in another department." I use fingers to air quote Connor's ridiculous notion of studying the Outdoor crew.

"Sure you can. You're above the law around these parts. You can do whatever you want."

I snort. "Yeah, right."

"Come on. Come and work with us. It'll be fun." Connor grins. "There are some great opportunities with us, too. You'd learn lots."

On my other side, Ronan muffles his laughter with his hand, while gazing out his side window.

Tillie warned me that Connor would have my pants off by noon with his charm if I were working with him. While I don't necessarily agree with her, I think I can see why she'd say that. He has an easy way about him, much like Jed has. Though Jed was never overtly sexual. Not with me, anyway.

I'm sure he's plenty sexual with his new girlfriend, Cammie.

I can't help but smile at Connor's cheekiness. "Yeah, I'll bet."

We round a bend in the road and the cabin comes into view, first in breaks in the trees, and then, as we get closer, the full looming building, cast in shadows from towering trees.

"That one's gotta come down soon." Ronan points to a dead birch.

"Tell Darryl. Wolf won't let us touch a single tree without permission. Kind of ironic, don't you think, given the forest raping he did down the road." Connor throws the truck into reverse and then, stretching his arm over the back of the seat behind me to navigate, his giant, firm body twists into me as he backs up toward the door. "All right. We're here." He shuts off the engine and both guys climb out.

I move to follow out Connor's side when he stops me with his hands on my knees, the heat from them searing my skin through my nylons. "Whoa. Not so fast. Do you want to lose your shoes?"

I look down to see the foot-deep ruts of thick mud where truck tires have torn the soft spring ground. Crap.

"Here. Let me help you." Before I know what's happening, Connor's hands are around my waist and he's lifting me up. I yelp as he pulls me to him, roping one arm around my hips. I fall into him, struggling to keep my balance and not shove my breasts in his face, an impossible feat. He hugs me to his body tight as he carries me toward the porch.

"Took you long enough." Tillie stands by the door, arms crossed over her chest, duster in her hand, with a pinched look on her face as she watches us.

"Had to move a lot of stuff to get to these," Ronan explains. He drops the tailgate on the truck with a loud clatter.

"By the way, I really like what you did with your hair," Connor murmurs, setting me gently onto the porch, the hand around my waist giving me a light squeeze. With a wink, he trudges back through the mud to help Ronan.

"You are takin' off those dirty ol' boots before you step foot inside here, ya hear!" Tillie warns in her heavy southern twang.

"Yes, ma'am!" they both parrot, the muscles in their backs straining as they hoist the first mattress.

Tillie turns to me. "Wolf finally untied you?"

I feel my face blanch. "What?" *How does she know?*

"We thought he had you chained up or somethin'. You've been scarce as a ghost."

"Oh!" I force a laugh as relief hits me. "Yeah. It's been busy."

"What are you doin' here?"

I shrug. "Mr. Wolf wanted me here to make sure things were on track."

She snorts and disappears into the cabin.

six

"How much more is there left to do?" I glance over my shoulder at Tillie and another staffer, Bellamy—Bell for short—as they stretch a crisp white sheet over the master bed.

"What's the matter? Not as exciting as watchin' the big, bad wolf fire people?" Tillie says, throwing a smirk over her shoulder. She's been casting off little snipes like that all afternoon. I can't help but feel like some of them are directed at me, simply through association. Or maybe I'm just overly sensitive to anything negative Henry-related.

"Starving," I murmur, dragging the duster along the dark corners where the walls meet the ceiling, catching any last remaining cobwebs along the way. I'm not exactly dressed for heavy-duty cleaning. I peeled off my jacket and untucked my blouse, making it a little easier to help.

"Well, it's no wonder. You shoulda eaten when they brought over dinner."

"I wasn't hungry then." I was too worried about Henry and what is happening back at the hotel. I'm still worried, but hunger pains are finally winning out.

"There are probably some scraps left, if those savages downstairs haven't devoured it all. Or you could make a run back to the hotel in the truck."

Driving alone on that road? No thanks. "I can wait a bit longer." I toss the duster into the cleaning supply bucket and scan my phone for a text from Henry that I already know hasn't come. I've been at this house all afternoon. It's now after 9:00 p.m. and the sun is beginning to set—Alaskan summers are still something to get used to—and Henry hasn't called or messaged me once. I've been managing his e-mail as best as I can from my phone, though I'd rather be on my laptop.

What did his father say after I left? Has the media heard about the wrongful dismissal suit yet? How fast do things like that spread?

I know nothing, I remind myself. Absolutely nothing, should anyone ask.

Which reminds me...

Pulling my personal phone out of my pocket, I open up the text thread from Jed. I really don't want to message him, but I told Henry I would and it's a good idea to get it over with now. Still, I won't acknowledge his last message to me, about how he's been thinking about me. So instead, I go for casual conversation:

Abbi: *How are things back home?*

I have no idea if he's still up, given Pennsylvania is four hours ahead. He has always been a night owl but he has a full-time summer job that he has to be up early for so I don't know if—

Three dots start bouncing on the screen.

Jed: *Same ol' Greenbank. Nothing much has changed.*

A second message comes shortly after:

Jed: *Way more exciting up there, I'll bet.*

I bite the inside of my mouth to hide my smile, even though he can't see me. *You have no idea.*

Abbi: *It has its moments. The grand opening is this weekend so there are all kinds of magazine reporters and other important people. Working lots.*

I need to do damage control for that text Henry sent on my behalf, but I don't want it to be obvious that that's what I'm doing.

Jed: *How are you managing with your boss?*

Abbi: *Fine. He's so busy, I barely see him. Honestly, I was just kidding about what I said before. I mean, he's an asshole but he barely even looks at me.*

I can't bring myself to add the last part, about how I was just trying to make Jed nervous. That makes me sound weak and like I want him back. I know now, without a doubt, that I don't want Jed back, ever.

Jed: *Oh, good. I'm glad. You had me worried. You're such a sweet girl, Abigail. I wouldn't want anyone taking advantage of you.*

I can't keep the snort from escaping me. *Someone like you, Jed?* Asking me to hold out and save myself for him, that he was just "sowing his wild oats." Now, seeing it from the outside, it makes me sick. It makes me grit my teeth with anger.

"What's up?" Tillie asks, dropping the pillows into their cases.

"Nothing." I put my phone away, no interest in carrying on the conversation. My purpose for texting Jed is over. I take in the bedroom now that it's dressed, so to speak. "This place looks amazing." The housekeeping staff that's been working here all day have done an incredible job, transforming the cabin from a dusty, desolate space to a cozy and rustic getaway. Yesterday, it was empty except for a few random dusty dressers and side tables. Today, each room has a bed—pulled from the excess supply room at the hotel. John, the old man who drives the ferry, showed up with a dark leather couch and armchair set and a harvest table around dinner time, hauled all the way from a furniture store in Homer. Between the new furniture, the crisp towels and bedding, a few new lamps and rugs and other accessories, you'd never know that it was all but abandoned only twenty-four hours ago.

"Paige warned us to bust our asses and make this place shine. God knows what would happen to us if we didn't. Probably be ridin' the ferry with our belongings, just like Rachel." Tillie fluffs the pillows with firm smacks before dropping them onto the bed to arrange them neatly, the bitterness in her voice obvious.

"It seems like a lot of people are angry about Rachel."

"Honestly? It's a great big ol' pile of bullshit is what it is. I mean, come on! This is the hotel industry for God's sakes! *Everyone* sleeps with *everyone*, especially round here. Put a bunch of hot-blooded men with attractive women in a village of cabins and what do you expect!" Tillie's southern twang really kicks in when she's passionate about something. I would probably enjoy listening to her, if it wasn't Henry's head on her pike.

"She didn't sleep with a coworker. She was with a guest."
Do not defend. Do not defend.

"And who do you think Wolf is sleeping with up here, because don't tell me he's not gonna get his dick wet the entire summer. If it ain't his staff, then it's the hotel guests, too. And how does that look? Man runs the whole damn chain and beds his paying customers, but goes all big brother on his staff when they're off shift. It all reeks of hypocrisy, if you ask me. 'Specially when his own assistant is using the spa and pissing guests off, and gets off with nothin'."

I feel my face turn bright red.

"Oh, you thought people wouldn't find out about that?" Tillie laughs. "Darlin', there are no secrets within these walls."

I'm guessing that's not entirely true, because if they knew what was going on within the walls of Cabin One, Tillie would flat-out say it. But still... this is what Connor meant when he said I was above the law. *Oh my God!* Do they know that Katie gave me a Brazilian wax?

I turn to gaze out the window at the peaceful water and empty dock, taking a moment to let my face cool. I'm going to murder Katie if she told people!

Clearing my voice, I offer, "I didn't get off with nothing. I got written up."

"Did you get put on a boat and shipped off after spending a pile of money on a plane ticket to get here?"

Point taken. It isn't fair that I got off, and the only reason I got off is because I'm sleeping with Henry. This is why Tillie's not entirely friendly with me today. I guess I can't blame her.

"So, is someone actually staying here?" Bell asks, fussing with the eyelet lace on the duvet.

I offer her a smile, a silent thanks for changing the topic. "No. It's all for the media this weekend. They want to see the history behind Wolf Cove and why Mr. Wolf chose this location to build the hotel."

"There are a lot of them comin' in. Talk about a dog and pony show. I guess with William and Scott Wolf coming in, too, it's only expected."

"What do you know about Scott Wolf, anyway?" I ask,

faking mild curiosity. If anyone knows anything, it'll be the queen of gossip, Tillie.

"Oh, he's a real piece of work. Has a major Henry Wolf complex. He's older than Henry and yet his baby brother gets all the love. Rumor has it Scott lost his everlovin' mind when their father told them that Henry would be takin' over the hotel chain. I guess he'd rather have that than the gold mine and thinks he should have first dibs. Spoiled brat, if you ask me."

Bell snorts. "Wow."

"Wonder why their father is handing it over. I saw him earlier. He doesn't look very old."

"Who knows. Doesn't want the headache, maybe?"

So Tillie doesn't know about the cancer. The only reason for that would be that they've kept it secret.

And yet Henry divulged it to me.

Tillie straightens the end table, eyeballing it against the other one. She's suddenly more chipper, which usually happens when she's dishing out gossip. "Either way, Scott has not taken it well. He owns a stake just like his brother, and I hear he's been fighting against Wolf Cove the entire time. Probably out of spite because his brother inherited all the land. Then again, I also heard that the strife is more about Scott's wife than it is about any mine or hotel."

"Scott's married?"

"*Was.* She's an ex now, and apparently Henry helped with that, if you know what I mean." She waggles her eyebrows.

Ugh. Please tell me that's wrong.

Tillie grabs the bucket of cleaning supplies, her sinewy arm flexing under the weight. "Come on. I think we're done up here."

I trail her down the rustic stairs—the steps made from

logs split in half—that overlook the grand room, doing my best to push away the uncomfortable conversation from upstairs. The crackling fire in the massive stone hearth helps.

"So? What do you think, boss?" Connor asks, stooped over to shift the burning log with an antique iron poker, his back muscles shifting beneath his t-shirt.

I think that, though I was drunk and it was dark the first night I met him, the weeks of outdoor work in Alaska have honed his body even more. But I don't say that. "It looks like it's actually usable." Everything is clean, the wood polished, the furniture rearranged. Once they close the windows that have been sitting open all day to air it out, and let the fire warm the place, it'll be cozy.

"Yeah?" Connor's eyes dip down to my blouse. "Here, you should come by the fire and warm yourself. You look cold."

Only five minutes after my last embarrassing moment, I find my cheeks flushing again. I cross my arms over my chest, silently cursing the lack of any padding in this bra. Had I thought ahead, I would have run back and changed, or at least grabbed a sweater. Thankfully I found a safety pin to secure my shirt, so I'm not flashing anyone anymore.

I wander over to stand next to him, holding my hands in front of the flame, because I *am* cold and I *do* need to warm myself up.

"We're done here, Connor," Tillie calls out. "Let's wrap it up."

"Yeah, well, you're gonna have to wait. Paige asked me to burn a fire for a few minutes. She wanted to give it that freshly used look and smell." He turns back to the fire. "We've got two trucks here. You and Bell go ahead with Ronan. I'll drive Abbi back with me."

Tillie's eyes narrow for just a moment before a wide smile stretches across her beautiful face. "No, that's okay. I can stick around for a bit. Abbi's the one who's starving, right, Abbi?" There's something decidedly insincere in her manner, something disingenuous behind those eyes.

"It's okay. I can wait. I'm supposed to leave with the last crew," I explain. "Mr. Wolf's orders."

"Well, we wouldn't want to anger Mr. Wolf. Connor, can you help me get these things into the truck?"

"Ronan's out there."

With a glare and a small huff, she spins on her heels and heads out the door. She's obviously pissed about something.

Connor seems oblivious or unfazed. To me, he says, "Pretty amazing, don't you think? It's kind of cool that the old man built—"

My work phone chirps with a text. It's an instant reaction, lifting the phone to my face. It's also incredibly rude. I smile an apology to Connor as I read the text from Henry:

Henry: *Take the morning off and meet Belinda in the lobby at 11. She'll prep you.*

I frown. Of all days to give me the morning off, I would think it wouldn't be on the day of the grand opening. I quickly type out a response:

Abbi: *Are you sure? It's going to be really busy. I can be there early to help.*

Henry: *I'll be tied up with my father and Scott all morning.*

Ugh. I think I'm okay with not facing either of them again, especially after today's introductions.

Abbi: *K.*

I hesitate, but then I quickly punch out:

Abbi: *Do you want to review the schedule one more time, tonight? I know you're stressed about it.*

I add a smiley face and then promptly erase it. That screams "code for sex" if someone were to read this.

Henry: *I'll be fine. See you tomorrow, Abbi.*

My shoulders sag with frustration at his refusal. I really wanted to see him tonight. But then I remind myself that he's been with his father and Scott all night. I don't blame him for not being in the mood.

"Trouble in paradise?" Connor asks, earning my wide eyes of panic.

"What are you talking about?"

He shrugs. "Just that look on your face. You look disappointed about something."

"It's nothing. I'm just... I can't seem to do anything right," I lie.

"Yeah. I've heard that about him."

Man, does Henry have a bad rep. How much worse is it going to get if people hear about Kiera's claims?

A horn blasts several times outside, followed by Tillie's, "Come on! We're waiting!"

Suddenly, I'm exhausted. Today has been a long day. Tomorrow is going to be even longer. "We should get going. I think this looks plenty used for Paige." I push the glass door shut and pull the lever to close off the chimney, cutting off the air circulation and effectively smothering the fire.

"Where'd you learn how to do that?" Connor eyes me curiously.

"Years of fires in the wood-burning stove at my family's farmhouse."

He stands taller, looming over me. "Damn, I sure do like a woman who knows how to handle a fire."

After an afternoon of overt flirting, I'm somewhat more comfortable around Connor. Enough to joke with him, at least. "Well, I just put your fire *out* for you."

Deep dimples mark his cheeks as he laughs. "You heading back to the staff lodge for dinner? I heard you were starving."

"Actually, I think I'm more tired than I am hungry. I need a good night's sleep." Something I haven't done since the day I stepped foot in Wolf Cove.

We hit all the lights and lock up—in case of who out here in the wild, I don't know—and head out the back door to find both trucks rumbling.

Ronan is waiting on the stoop. "Tillie's waiting for you, C. And you're coming with me and Bell. We'll have to come back in the morning to drop some plywood down over the mud for people to get across." I hold my breath as Ronan scoops me up without warning, carrying me across the thick mud to the flatbed truck in much the same way Connor did earlier. I'm forced to settle my hands on his firm, broad shoulders to keep myself upright.

"See you back at home!" Tillie calls out in that sweet drawl, already sitting in Connor's truck.

As luck would have it, I'm in the middle again, only the interior of the flatbed is much less comfortable and narrower. There's a giant gearshift jutting up from the floor that I can't really avoid straddling.

"It's *so* dark," Bell whispers from the passenger side as we move slowly along the laneway. "Do you think there's bears and stuff out here?"

Ronan reaches over to shift gears with his big, work-worn hand. Even without touching me, the simple motion somehow feels sexual, the gear sliding closer toward me. "Bears, wolves, cougars." Bell slams her hand over the pop-up lock, earning Ronan's deep laughter. "Don't worry. Nothing's going to get us in here."

I bite my tongue against the urge to tell them about the

grizzly bear we saw. That would mean telling them that I was out with Henry cutting firewood, and there's enough gossip around here, clearly.

I breathe a sigh of relief as we turn onto the main dirt road, a road built to truck wood to and from the clearing site. I can't even fathom how all this property is Henry's. I'm sure part of the tension between him and his brother has to do with his grandparents leaving this all to him. If I were Scott, I can't say I wouldn't harbor at least a bit of resentment.

Then again, he was handed a gold mine to run. He's not exactly hard done by.

We turn right onto the main road, toward the hotel. I expect to see the headlights that have been trailing us all this time come into view in the rearview mirror appear again. When they don't, I look over my shoulder to find the truck sitting idly, the distance between us growing. I frown. "Something's wrong. You should turn around."

"Nah. They're fine. They'll catch up with us in bit." There's just enough light in the truck to allow me to catch the sly grin on Ronan's face as he peers down at me, his gaze flickering to my mouth.

And it clicks.

Tillie's sleeping with Connor.

And he's been blatantly flirting with me all afternoon. No wonder she's been so pissy. My head falls back against the rear window and I chuckle at myself for not seeing it sooner. "Oh..."

"You're quick, red." Ronan changes gears again, his fingers doing a split-second graze along the inside of my knee on his way past.

It could easily have been an accident, but something about Ronan tells me it wasn't.

seven

It takes me a few moments to recognize the scent of Katie's spicy floral perfume.

And another few moments to realize that she's lying in my bed, next to me.

"Do you think I should talk to him about her?" she hisses, and I'm hit with a wave of alcohol off her breath.

I groan, reaching for my phone to check the time. It's 2:00 a.m. "What?"

"About Rachel. She's still in Homer. She hasn't been able to get a flight out yet, so she's just been touring around. When's the next time she's going to be in Alaska, right? But what if she manages to get a flight home tomorrow? So I was thinking, if I go to Mr. Wolf and ask him really nicely, and promise that nothing like this will ever happen, would he change his mind?"

I groan, finally clueing in. "I doubt it."

Her body tenses next to me.

"I'm sorry, Katie. But he can be a real asshole, you know that." He can also be very, very generous and giving, but in ways I never want anyone to experience. Anyone except me.

"I know. I was just thinking…" She burrows into my side. "What if you asked?"

"*Me?*"

"Yeah. I should have been fired too, but he didn't fire me because of you. So maybe he'll listen to you if you ask."

I sigh. "I don't know, Katie."

"Please? Can you just try?" Her voice has taken on that really whiny tone. She must be really drunk. "I can't imagine the entire summer here without Rachel."

Just like I couldn't imagine the summer here without Henry. But… I drop my voice to a whisper in case someone isn't wearing their earplugs. "She slept with someone else, Katie. She cheated on you. Don't you care?" I'm not sure how many people know about Rachel and Katie, besides me. And Henry, because I told him. And I only know because I saw them firsthand and, well, they're definitely *together.*

"What? No." Katie laughs. "Oh, you're so adorable and innocent. I know it doesn't make much sense to you. We're best friends first, and Rachel likes guys as much as girls, so I'm not going to tell her she can't be with them. That'll never work. She'll end up miserable and I don't want that. So we're open about things."

Open? "So you mean you're okay with her messing around on you?" People actually make those kinds of arrangements?

"We don't look at it like that. We're just enjoying life and our bodies while we're young and we can, you know?"

Not really, but I'm learning quickly.

"So, can you please just try?"

I sigh. Firing Rachel was definitely a big mar on Henry's reputation with his staff. "I'll ask him tomorrow."

She gasps. "Oh, thank you! Thank you! Thank you!

You're the best!" Before I know what's happening, her mouth is planted on mine in a hard kiss, the taste of alcohol lingering on her lips.

Pushing her off with an embarrassed chuckle, I warn her, "I can't promise anything, so don't get your hopes up."

"Too late! They're up!"

She's about to roll away when I grab her. "Hey, did you tell anyone about the other day? About giving me a *you-know-what*?"

"No? I don't think so?" A pause, and though it's dark, I picture her pretty face scrunched up in thought. "Well, I *may* have mentioned it when I was trying to convince Darian from over in cabin eight to do hers, because have you seen her in the shower? It's nowhere as wild as yours was but it definitely could use some tidying. Why?"

I sigh. No, I didn't notice Darian from over in cabin eight, but I don't have the obsession with ripping hair from bodies that Katie does. "No reason. Just something Tillie said."

She snorts out loud. "Tillie's got lots to say. So... how does it look?"

I hesitate, but then remind myself that there's no point in being modest around Katie. "Good. I guess?"

"Ha! Told you so. We'll have to buy a kit in Homer and do it here next time, so we don't get into trouble with the boss again."

"Yay. Can't wait," I mutter, though I have to admit I am happy that we went through with it, given how acquainted Henry has gotten with that part of me.

She rolls away and stumbles from my bed—the bottom bunk in a cabin of three sets—and into hers.

And now I'm wide awake, with the taste of liquor coating

my lips, staring at the bottom of the bunk on top of me where Autumn snores softly. I learned her secret to undisturbed sleeping: a face mask and earplugs. Apparently everyone around here sleeps with plugs and face masks. Everyone except me.

Not that either of those would help with my spinning thoughts.

What is Henry doing right now?

Sleeping, I'm sure. I wish I were lying next to him in bed. But that will never happen, not as long as I'm working for him here.

I sigh. How am I even going to broach this subject with him? And tomorrow, when he's already got so much on his plate. I could lie and tell Katie that I asked about Rachel and he said no, but I'd rather know that I genuinely tried.

If I can just get him alone for fifteen minutes, I could make sure he's in a *really* good mood before asking.

Turning onto my side, I close my eyes and let myself drift off with a smile of anticipation.

~

I DON'T KNOW why I'm so nervous. Maybe it's because my relationship—both work and otherwise—with Henry has been pretty clear-cut so far: Henry says "jump" and I say "how high?" It's not the other way around: me, asking him for things. Me, telling him what I want. Outside of the bedroom, that is. Though, even in the bedroom, he's pretty demanding.

After an hour of staring at my phone, contemplating my best strategy, I remind myself that while, yes, he's intimidating and we've barely scratched the surface of knowing each other, in some respects I probably know him better than anyone else here. With a deep breath, I open up a text thread to him.

Abbi: *I have a very important but quick question. Can I come by?*

I close my eyes and set my phone on my chest, my heart rate speeding up as I wait.

I jump at the vibration a minute later.

Henry: *Not a good time.*

My stomach sinks. He must be wrapped up with work. Or maybe he thinks "I have a question" is code for sex? Swallowing my unease, I try again.

Abbi: *Seriously. Just a question. It's important, and brief. I promise.*

A moment later:

Henry: *You've got me here, now. What's your question?*

I roll my eyes. Over text is not how I wanted to do this.

Abbi: *I think you should give Rachel back her job.*

I bite my bottom lip as I watch the three dots dance on the screen.

Henry: *That's not a question.*

No, I guess it's not.

Abbi: *Can you give Rachel back her job?*

Henry: *She went against company policy.*

Okay... so not a flat-out "no."

I purse my lips together, wondering if questioning him is smart. He's never given me reason to believe I hold any sway in suggesting anything business related.

Abbi: *So have others, and they weren't fired. I think you should give her a break.*

My phone starts vibrating with a phone call. My heart swells when I see Henry's name pop up. "Hello?"

"Why?" The single word as greeting, delivered in his

deep stern voice, throws me off, and it takes a moment to gather my thoughts.

I drop my voice to a whisper, though Katie's the only one here and she's dead to the world, her mass of bleach-blonde hair splayed around her pillow. "With everything going on right now, the last thing you need is people questioning why you fired her and you didn't fire me. Katie and I broke policy, too. Plus, people around here don't like you very much right now. Everyone's afraid to make a mistake and be shipped off. They spent a lot of money on plane tickets to get here."

Several long moments of silence hang between us.

In a last-ditch effort, I add, "You once said you wanted people to be happy working here."

"So?"

"So, if you really care about your staff, which I think you do, then you'll make choices to win their respect back."

There's a slight pause. "They don't *respect* me?" He says this like he's surprised by it. Maybe he is. It's one thing not to like the CEO of the hotel chain you work for because he's hard-nosed. It's entirely different not to respect him.

"Not exactly…"

"Why? What are they saying?"

"Right now? That you're a spineless dickhead." I hold my breath, waiting for his response, hoping he doesn't ask me who said that. I don't want to get Ronan in trouble or worse, fired.

"Fine."

I frown, not sure that I heard correctly. "Fine, yes?"

"Where is Rachel right now? Can you get hold of her?"

"She's still in Homer, trying to get a flight home. Katie has her number."

"Get her on the next ferry back. But she's on a short leash and I won't give her another chance. Make sure you tell Belinda when you see her so she can get her set up again."

I let out a sigh of relief. "Thank you."

There's a pause, and when he speaks again, his voice has dropped to that gravelly, intimate tone. "Thank me later."

My blood starts pumping through my veins. I don't want to hang up with him yet. "How are things? Were you with your father for long last night?"

He groans. "All night, and this morning. Him, telling me how to run things like I don't know anything, and then my brother throwing his useless two cents in any chance he can, to try and prove he knows better than me. I'll be so happy when they're both gone."

He's more candid than he has been in the past. I can definitely feel a shift in our relationship since yesterday. It's nice. "Hang in there. It'll be over soon."

"Gotta go. See you later." He hangs up, leaving me smiling.

"Katie!" I yell, no longer concerned about her obvious hangover or the fact that she's still sleeping. "Guess what!"

eight

I'm smiling as I push through the staff entrance at the back of the hotel, on my way to meet Belinda. I have no idea what to expect today, but I'm sure I can get through it. I can get through anything. Connor was right. I do have some power, after all.

I'm still smiling when I round the corner and plow right into someone, earning his grunt.

"I'm so sorry, I—" My words fall short when I see Scott Wolf's face. His eyes are more gray than blue, but just as steely as Henry's. "Excuse me." I take a step back to give him a wide perimeter, focusing on the long hall and not breaking out in a run to get away.

"Abbi, right?" he calls out.

My feet falter. "Yes. Again, I'm so sorry."

"No big deal. Are you heading to the lobby?"

"Uh..." *Say no! Say no!* "Yeah?"

He falls into step beside me. "It's a maze down here, isn't it?"

I smile politely. "It's easy once you figure it out."

"My people tell me that every time I go into the mine,

and every time, I swear," he chuckles to himself, "I say a small prayer when I make it out alive."

He's making small talk. I can handle small talk. "That'd be scary, being so deep underground like that."

"It is. You never really get used to it. At least, I haven't, and I've been going down in there for over ten years now."

Silence hangs between us as we make our way along the hall at the clipped pace that I have set. He doesn't seem to be struggling to keep up.

"So, how do you like Alaska so far?"

"I love it, truly. It's beautiful."

"It is, isn't it? The resort is nice. I've been wandering around all morning, scoping everything out."

Is that the truth? I can't tell. If it's not, he's very convincing. "There's a lot to see."

"Way more than there was when I was young, that's for sure. We used to spend our summers up here."

"Yes. Mr. Wolf mentioned that. At your grandparents' cabin."

"Have you seen it yet?"

"Yes. Actually, I was just there yesterday, making sure it was staged appropriately for the media."

"Good, good. I'll be heading over there later. It's been a few years since I've seen it."

"I think you'll be pleasantly surprised. It's been well-kept and they worked hard to clean it up."

"My grandfather would love to know that." Scott seems charming enough, and genuinely friendly. But after Henry's warning, the last thing I want is to be alone with him, which is why I speed up when I see the elevator ahead.

"So, where are you from?"

"Pennsylvania."

"Ah, the great state of virtue, liberty, and independence. My ex-wife went to Penn State."

Ex-wife. The one that became an ex because of Henry, as rumor has it? I clear my throat. "I've heard that's a nice school."

"Great school. One of the best. So, how'd you end up here?"

"A career fair in Chicago, where I go to school."

"Oh yeah? Which one?"

Talk about twenty questions, but they seem harmless enough, and nothing I shouldn't answer. "North Gate." When he frowns, I add, "It's a small Christian college. I'll be starting my last year there this fall." We reach the staff elevator and I hit the Up button. The doors open and he holds his hand out, letting me enter first before stepping in. A very gentlemanly thing to do.

Maybe Henry's just being paranoid.

Maybe he isn't so bad.

"So, has Henry fucked you yet, Abbi?"

I choke on my gasp. "What?" I manage to get out.

"You heard me," he says in a calm, cool tone, all semblance of charm gone.

"I did. I'm just..." My heart is hammering inside my chest, the walls of this elevator suddenly closing in on me as the doors shut. He lulled me and then, wham! Completely blindsided me. "I'm his assistant."

Scott hits the Stop button and the elevator comes to a jarring halt.

And now I'm trapped in an elevator with him. "So was the last assistant that he fucked. The one who's now suing our company and pressing charges for sexual assault against him."

I back away from him, genuinely terrified. "I don't... know anything about—"

"In case you haven't learned yet, my brother can't keep his dick in his pants, and he'll tell you anything you need to hear to let him under that skirt. So tell me, Abbi from Greenbank, Pennsylvania, population five thousand, daughter of Roger and Bernadette Mitchell, previously engaged to the reverend's son before he found a girl who *wasn't* saving herself for marriage," he turns to level me with a severe stare, his gaze flickering down to my chest for a long, uncomfortable second, "what lies did he tell for you to lie down on your back for him? I'll bet they were good."

His words suck the air from my lungs. "How do you know so much about me?"

"It wasn't hard. People love to talk, especially about their sweet Abigail Mitchell."

Oh my God. Henry's brother had me investigated?

"He's just using you. That's what Henry is: a user, a manipulator. So what did he say? That you're special? That you're different? That he's never felt this way about any woman before?"

My blood is rushing through my ears.

"Oh, come on. Smarten up, Abbi. He said the same thing to that journalist last night while he was over there, fucking her to make sure he gets a stellar review of this giant waste of money that we're all standing in."

I use the elevator wall to support myself, my knees suddenly weak.

"You may as well admit to it all now because Henry's days with Wolf Hotels are numbered. He's already confessed to everything, and after his last fuck-up, my father's done giving him chances. I'll be taking over everything, including Wolf Cove, within the next few weeks. It's already done. So if you want to keep your job, you better start showing your loyalty to me. Don't protect him. He doesn't give a shit about you."

Roshana Mafi?

I can't keep the shock from my face, his words like a swift punch to my gut. Is this true? Is this why Henry wasn't willing to let me come by last night, and this morning? Because he was with another woman?

No. It can't be. I just talked to him today. He agreed to let Rachel come back. He made it sound like he was looking forward to seeing me later.

"Use your head. I know you're a smart girl, with that 4.0 GPA. You have real potential. I'd hate to see it ruined when my brother's legal issues hit the media. It would be so easy for you to get dragged down with him. He's got a real appetite and I'm guessing a lot of women will come out of the woodwork to share details." Scott smiles, but it's not at all kind. "Imagine what that'd be like, sitting in the front pew of church while the good reverend and everyone in there picture all the dirty, depraved things you must have been doing with him."

I close my eyes against the threatening burn in my chest and try to calm my breathing. Henry warned me that his brother was a manipulative weasel who wants the hotel chain badly. Likely badly enough to corner his brother's assistant in an elevator and try to manipulate her into admitting to sleeping with him, which would guarantee William Wolf pulls the hotels away from him.

And if Henry already admitted to it, I wouldn't have to.

This is all bullshit.

It has to be.

Scott begins to laugh. "What did he do? Promise you a real relationship? Ask you to stick by his side? Of course he would. He needs to keep you happy and quiet while he tries to buy his way out of this mess."

Scott is hitting too close to home now. Steeling my nerve, I reach past him and hit the release button for the elevator, all while swallowing against the bile threatening to rise. "I don't care what Mr. Wolf does in his private life, and I don't know what he could possibly have admitted to because I can assure you, I have a strictly professional relationship with him. Now, if you'll excuse me." I bolt out of the elevator the second the doors open. I can't get away from Scott fast enough.

A wave of relief hits me at the sight of Belinda standing in the lobby, tapping her toe and glancing at her watch.

She frowns as I hurry toward her, but a quick glance behind me seems to give her the answer. "So I see you've met Scott," she mutters, venom lacing her tone. "What did he say to you?"

"Nothing." Only when I try to adjust my blazer do I realize that my hand is trembling.

Belinda grabs my forearm and pulls me into a corner. "Abbi? Tell me, now," she demands in a stern voice, her eyes all the more severe behind those heavy-rimmed glasses.

And suddenly more kind.

But what can I trust her with?

She seems to read my unspoken question. "Henry hired me and has given me every opportunity to succeed in this company where his father and brother would not. I'm loyal to him, not them. So you can tell me what that piece of shit said to you," she says in a calm, slow voice.

I swallow. "He had me investigated."

Her pretty face twists up, displaying the shock that I feel. "What?"

"He knows where I'm from, my parents' names. He knows... other things!"

"Fuck." She shakes her head. "But, I'm not surprised. Look, there's a huge power thing going on between those two, and their father isn't helping any. Scott wants Wolf Hotels and he's looking for ammunition." She hesitates. "He accused you of sleeping with Henry, didn't he?"

"Yes. And I told him I'm not but—"

"He doesn't care. Henry's in such deep shit with... this problem that I can't talk about, but needless to say, if Henry were screwing around with you, William Wolf would flip his lid. He'd see it as the last straw, a final sign that he can't trust Henry with Wolf Hotels."

So, Belinda knows about Kiera, too. I remember her mentioning something about it to Henry last week. I wonder how much she knows. "Scott said he's already made that decision."

"No." Belinda's head shakes vehemently. "That's bullshit or I would have heard about it already. Don't believe a word Scott says. Not a word! He's like a snake in long grass in a children's playground. And he's smart; he knows just what to say to get under your skin. He's done it to me before, too."

I exhale deeply, the first real breath I've managed since running into Scott. He's lying about everything.

About Roshana and Henry, last night.

She pats my shoulder. A strange, comforting gesture, and something I'd never expect from her. Maybe it's her preoccupation with all the media, but she's being civil with me today, seemingly unconcerned with whether I may be sleeping with the boss and trying to get me fired for it. Or maybe we've just done a good enough job at covering it up that she actually doesn't suspect anything anymore.

"Come on, we can't let him derail everything. That's

what he wants, to make Henry look bad. We're here to make him look good, and we have a lot of work to do before we can make sure that happens." She glances at her watch with a groan. "And forty-five minutes to do it before you need to be with him."

That's forty-five minutes too long.

I need to see Henry right now.

I need to know that *everything* Scott said was a lie.

~

"God, I can't wait until this weekend is over. I need a day off," Belinda grumbles under her breath as we speed through the hall, her heels clicking noisily on the tile. We're back in the underground part of the hotel, far away from the guests. I've been watching over my shoulder for Scott, but thankfully he's not lurking down here.

"What will you do on your day off?"

She snorts. "What *is* there to do around here?"

"I don't know. Go for a hike? Take the ferry into Homer? Borrow one of the staff kayaks?" What would *I* do on a day off? Get Henry to take me out for a drive, somewhere remote and beautiful, where we can take our clothes off and be as loud as we want without concern of observers. Ideally where there *aren't* grizzly bears to interrupt us this time.

Or maybe I'd just lock the doors, draw the blinds, and strip down and distract him from his work.

I bite the insides of my cheeks to quash the goofy grin from taking form on my face.

Luckily, Belinda doesn't notice. "Bugs and wilderness. My two favorite things." She jabs at the elevator button. "More like order room service and watch Netflix, and tell the world to fuck right off. I can't wait to get back to New York."

"You don't like it up here?"

"I'm a city girl. The quiet drives me crazy. You have the schedule, right?"

I tap the screen of my iPad, where the media and interview schedule that Belinda laid out is ready. Henry is booked solid from noon until four, where he gets a quick break to change for the ceremony and dinner event. Four hours of talking and charming people in one setting or another, and answering questions. Not exactly glamorous.

"There will be a lot of people floating around, trying to grab his attention for as long as he'll give it. He needs to be courteous and charming, but keep things flowing. He can't be looking at his watch and worrying about time, because it makes people feel like they're unimportant. He needs to give each person his undivided attention. Your job is to manage him. Keep him moving and on time. How good are you at interrupting people?"

Terrible. Absolutely awful. "I'll do what needs to be done."

"Good. I'll be floating around, making sure everything else is going off without a hitch. Flawless operation is everything today." She smoothes her hands over her business suit—yet another black jacket and skirt combo that's probably too provocative for a hotel manager, but Henry's not saying anything to her about it. She's immaculate as usual, her blonde hair down in smooth waves today. I wonder how long it takes her to do that.

"Has anyone ever told you that you look at lot like Sharon Stone?" I blurt out, followed quickly by, "The much younger version of her. You know, *Basic Instinct*?"

She smirks. "Aren't you like twelve? When would *you* have watched that?"

"Twenty-one. And it was on TV late one night." My parents were fast asleep upstairs. I clutched the remote tight, ready to switch the channel at the first sound of a stair creak.

"Hmm... Yes, I've heard that. Once or twice." She smiles to herself and I'm pretty sure I've just earned some brownie points with the Wolf Cove hotel manager.

My personal cell phone rings then. Crap. I never called my mother back after her timely interruption of my eavesdropping yesterday. I'm going to get an earful about what an awful daughter I am. I don't have the energy or time to deal with her right now.

With a sigh, I reach into my suit jacket pocket and set it to silent.

"Mother?" Belinda asks.

"How'd you know?"

"Because you look like the type to talk to your mom everyday. Oh, I almost forgot. William—Mr. Wolf to you—has his own limited schedule of interviews that his assistant will manage, so you don't have to worry about it. He's mainly here for photo ops, anyway. Everyone knows he's got one foot in retirement." She groans, hitting the button several times. "Come on! What's taking so long?" She glances at her watch again with a huff. This frazzled, impatient side of Belinda is so different from the calm and collected one I've seen up until now. I guess a lot of this falls on her if something messes up.

"It's all going to go perfectly," I offer with genuine sympathy.

"It had better. We need these magazines leaving here with rave reviews about how magical and luxurious Wolf Cove is, or William will do something stupid like give Wolf Hotels over to Scott, and then I'll be looking for a new job because I'm not working for that lecherous pig." Her voice seethes with disgust. She does a quick hair flip, giving her a chance to covertly scan the area around us for anyone who may have overheard. "Don't *ever* repeat it."

"Of course not."

The elevator doors finally open and we step in. "I can't wait until they're gone. Having all three of the Wolf men in one place is going to make my head explode. And don't even get me started on what it does to Henry. Don't take offense to anything he says to you."

What about the Wolf women? "Will Mr. Wolf's mother be visiting Wolf Cove as well?" I ask as casually as possible.

"Henry's mother?" Belinda frowns. "No. She's been out of the picture for years. She had enough of William and the entire Wolf family when Henry was about eleven, I think? I can't remember. Henry's not close with her. The boys went to boarding school for most of their lives. Oh, also, Henry asked that I bring in more formal attire for you for tonight."

It takes me a moment to process the rapid change of topic. Henry's mother basically abandoned him from the sounds of it. And Henry wants me in a formal dress tonight.

"I'll have it sent to your cabin. You won't have time to go pick it up. You'll be too busy managing his schedule. And him."

"Well, hopefully an entire night and morning with them hasn't put Mr. Wolf in a bad mood."

Belinda snorts. "He wouldn't have been with them all night and morning. Henry would have ditched them the first chance he could. He can't be in a room with Scott for more than five minutes without the two of them lunging for each other's jugulars."

I didn't think it was possible for my stomach to sink further, but I was wrong. Henry said he was with them all night and morning. So, is Belinda wrong or was he lying to me? Scott has definitely succeeded at one thing—making me doubt Henry.

"Don't worry. I'm guessing he's going to be in a *fantastic* mood today," Belinda mutters as the door opens and we step into the lobby, the buzz of laughter and chatter making the churn in the pit of my stomach worse.

I trail after her, the blood roaring in my ears once again as we emerge from the narrow hall and into the grand foyer, with its soaring ceilings and grand, rustic beams and glass walls. The place is filled with people.

And right in the epicenter of them is Henry, his beautiful face glowing with that charming laugh as he chats up an eclectic mix of people.

Including Roshana Mafi, who's standing directly next to him. His hand rests on the small of her back while she stares up at him, her eyes full of secrets and longing.

nine

I keep my eyes locked on Belinda's muscular calves and blink away the burn in my eyes. I can't rid my stomach of that smoldering discomfort I feel, realizing what I should have seen immediately.

That I'm the foolish farm girl who ate up every word he fed to me, right down to the part about us being different.

I guess Scott wasn't lying. Not about that, anyway. There's no reason for Henry to lie to me about being with his father and brother all night and all morning unless he was with someone else. Someone who is exotic and powerful and will tell him she wants him within five minutes of meeting. Someone he needs to impress to get a favorable article for his precious Wolf Cove hotel in a top travel magazine.

I'm so stupid. I shouldn't be surprised. The signs were all there. The personal note he wrote to her, requesting a cabin for her next to his.

I've just been too naïve to see it. Jed was right.

And here I am now, standing in the midst of this lobby, shocked and hurt. Two things I *can't* be right now. *This* is my job. I don't have time to be hurt or angry, or to even think about it. I have to get through this afternoon, and all I want to do is run. But if I run, the other employees will notice. They'll ask questions. They'll start talking, and guessing, and they'll put it together. And then everyone will be talking about me. With so much media here this weekend, there's a chance that someone will hear something, and then it's over. *Everyone* will know.

I have to make it through this afternoon.

Belinda stops so abruptly, I bump into the back of her, earning her glare when she spins around.

"I'm sorry," I offer weakly.

"So you know where he needs to be, right?"

I fumble with my iPad. "A casual lunch meeting in Rawley's with Maury Downing from *Travel Elite* magazine in ten minutes. A boat tour at one. Aerial tour at two thirty—"

"Okay then." She jerks her head in the direction of Henry. "He gave you this job, so go and do it, and do it well." With that, she marches in the opposite direction toward the ballroom, leaving me to fend for myself.

Taking a deep breath, I steel myself for an agonizing afternoon and make my way to the edge of the group as they chatter away. I'm supposed to be Henry's personal shadow, who goes unnoticed but swoops in when Henry needs help, or needs a time check.

A shadow who's not allowed to stand here and cry as she pictures Henry naked and lying with that woman standing right beside him.

I must be doing a good job because no one bats an eyelash at me, including Henry, the picture of simple elegance in a pair of dark-wash jeans and a fitted arctic-white shirt, an intentionally casual outfit to counterbalance the black tie event later.

He says something funny and Roshana tips her head back to give him a deep-throated laugh, her hand reaching for his forearm to squeeze it. It's such an affectionate move.

It's a kick in my chest.

Had he had this planned all along? Is this why he gave me the morning off? Was he in bed with her when he answered my text?

When he called me?

I am such an idiot. I was so eager to move on from Jed, so desperate to not feel the pain in my heart, that I dove heart-first toward Henry. He knew how easy a target I was, and he took the opportunity. He *is* a predator. Maybe not the kind that forces himself on women—can I believe him anymore about that?—but certainly one who preys on vulnerable women.

I gave him anything and everything he wanted. I believed everything he said.

He *did* tell me that what we have is different. I believed him when he said that, too.

Anger and embarrassment boils inside me. Anger with myself, for believing him so readily because I *wanted* to.

Now all I want to do is go back to the cabin and curl up in my bed, because this little fantasy I've been living in is over. It didn't even last four *days,* let alone four months.

I feel eyes on me. I pull myself back from my inner despair to find Henry's blue gaze on me. Despite my current pain, he still manages to steal a heartbeat or two.

I tighten my jaw, the urge to scream, "*You lying bastard!*" almost too much to control. But that would only swell my embarrassment. "I'm sorry to interrupt, Mr. Wolf, but you have a meeting to get to right now." Surprisingly, my voice isn't shaky or soft. It's wooden. Almost robotic.

A frown flickers across Henry's forehead and he pauses

for just a moment before turning to the group. "I'm so sorry, but I'm being summoned. Please feel free to find me later today. I'd love to finish this conversation."

A chorus of smiles and nods and "okays" ensue.

He's three steps away from the group when Roshana calls out in that husky voice, "Henry? Just a moment?"

I scowl as he stops and leans in to catch her murmurs, her smiles.

Her clawed hand on his forearm.

I can't hear her, but I hear him chuckle and say, "No problem. I'll have my assistant set something up for us."

Oh, will he, now...

"Great. I'm looking forward to it." She flashes that dazzling smile at him as he pulls away and falls into step with me.

And suddenly I want to get far away from him.

"Is there a reason you're making me run to keep up with you?" Henry mutters under his breath, just loud enough for me to hear.

I slow down, but only a touch. "I'm sorry. I just know you don't like being late."

He checks his watch. "Noon, right? We have time."

I don't answer. I can't. There's a giant lump in my throat and I'm doing my best not to cry, and that's only making me more angry at myself.

Honestly, what did I expect from Henry Wolf?

He smiles and nods at passersby on our way to the elevator. "I thought you'd be struggling to keep your appreciation for me in check after what I did for your roommate."

He didn't do that for me. He did that for him.

When I still don't answer, he edges closer to me. "What's gotten into you?"

"More like, what have *you* gotten into?"

"Excuse me?" Iciness creeps into his voice.

My cheeks flame. That wasn't supposed to slip out. "Nothing."

He hits the elevator button and it opens immediately. "After you. Please."

The longer I'm near him, the more it hurts, and I can't help it anymore. Now I'm rushing to brush away the tear that slipped out.

"Jesus Christ." Henry herds me in with a hand on the small of my back and hits the Close button to stop anyone else from getting on. "Is there a reason my assistant is standing next to me, *crying*?"

This is mortifying. "Noth—"

He slaps a hand over the elevator Stop button and the elevator comes to a jarring halt. It's the second time I'm trapped in the elevator with a Wolf within the last hour. Both times uncomfortable, but for different reasons.

"I don't have time or patience for evasiveness, Abbi. Spit it out."

"You weren't with your father and brother all last night and this morning!" I finally blurt out, hot tears burning my skin.

He opens his mouth but hesitates. "According to who?"

"Your brother. He cornered me earlier to ask me if you've... fucked me yet." My voice stutters over that word.

Henry's eyes flare with rage. "What did you tell him?"

"Nothing!"

He heaves an obvious sigh of relief. He's clearly more concerned about his brother knowing about us than about what *I* know of his night and Roshana. "What else did he say?"

"That your dad has decided to pass Wolf Hotels to him, and he'll be taking over in a few weeks."

That earns a derisive snort, so I guess that's not true either. "What else?"

"He had me investigated." My voice is wobbly. I hate when my voice is wobbly.

Henry's face twists with confusion. "What? What do you mean?"

"I mean, he knows all about me. Where I'm from, my parents' names, about Jed.... It scared me."

The Henry from yesterday morning, with his arms around me, telling me that we were different, would wrap his arms around me now. I'd like to think that, anyway. But this Henry's lips purse together tight. I can see the wheels churning behind his eyes.

"He also said that you'll use me and throw me away. That I shouldn't trust you." I hesitate, but only for a minute. I need to know. "Did you sleep with her?"

He blinks at me once... twice... before hitting the elevator release button.

What kind of answer is that? My stomach sinks. "Did you?"

"I've got way too much on my plate to deal with silly little-girl jealousy right now, Abbi."

"Are you kidding me?"

"Are *you* kidding *me*? I'm trying to run a worldwide hotel chain, that asshole is trying to sink me, and I can't have *my assistant* getting jealous around every pretty woman I meet with."

Getting jealous? This is beyond getting jealous. This is fact. This is him sleeping with other women the same day he's sleeping with me.

He hasn't even asked who I'm talking about. He hasn't denied it.

That's all the answer I need.

God, when Jed did this to me, I was completely blindsided. But Henry... shame on me. I should have seen it coming a mile away.

The elevator doors open and a dark look has taken over Henry's face. "Go clean yourself up. I'll expect you back within listening distance in half an hour." I watch his back as he passes the entrance to Rawley's, dialing someone on his phone.

~

I THOUGHT those few days after I caught Jed cheating on me were long and painful.

And they were.

But guiding Henry around today, tending to his every need while this thick fog of disappointment and hurt hangs over my head, unable to just hide out and do what I want to do—cry my eyes out—made for an excruciating afternoon.

And it's nowhere near finished.

I trail Henry as he pushes through the lobby doors, holding one open for me. "Be at my place in thirty minutes." I've only caught the faintest glimpse of a sour mood, buried deep beneath the ever-charming mask he wears so well when he needs to. It's like our conversation in the elevator never happened.

That basically gives me ten minutes to change and freshen up, given the time it takes to walk to the staff village. I mutter a "Yes. Mr. Wolf," on my way past.

"Abbi."

I pretend that I don't hear him. He doesn't call out, doesn't chase after me, not that I expected him to.

I count my steps all the way back to my cabin, focusing

on my breathing, on the dark clouds rolling in over the mountain range, anything to try to dull this ache.

This isn't what Alaska was supposed to be.

~

I STEP into the cabin to excited chatter.

"Look who's here!" Katie exclaims, her arm slung around Rachel's shoulders.

I smile because despite my mood, I'm genuinely happy to see Rachel again. "Welcome back."

Rachel pries herself away from Katie to pull me into a hug. "Katie told me what you did. Thank you," she whispers in my ear.

I shrug. "Glad I could help." And I'm glad I asked this morning, before I knew all that I know now.

"Belinda sent me home with a garment bag for you. I hung it up over there." Tillie points to the hook in the corner.

Right. The formal dress that Henry wants me to wear. "Thanks. I have about two seconds to change before I have to be back."

"Ugh. I don't envy you tonight, that's for sure. Those people are too much. I'm gonna have nightmares about the things I found in those rooms today."

"That bad?" Rachel begins pulling out clothes from her duffel bag. She must literally have just arrived off the ferry.

"*That* bad. I was assigned to the penthouses today. Well, except for Wolf's. You know, because he's a freak who doesn't allow anyone except Abbi in there to clean. But you know that woman from that magazine? The beautiful but bitchy-looking one?"

My stomach tightens.

"Ohh... I heard about her." Katie waggles her brows at Rachel, helping her unpack her clothes.

I distract myself from my bitterness and—yes—jealousy by unzipping the garment bag. A simple black dress and blazer hang inside. It's nothing exotic but it's nicer than the blouse and skirt combo, especially when everyone else will be fully decked out in formal wear.

"Yeah, well she's a beautiful bitch pig is what she is. She didn't even have the decency to make sure the condoms were put in the trash. They were all over the place. I found two stuck to the shag rug and one was on the nightstand. Ugh. The dried spooge took the finish right off."

"Gross!" Katie cries out with laughter.

"Right? But, damn, did she ever have a good night with whoever she hooked up with."

I blink back the burn in my eyes.

Three times with her, Henry? Once wasn't enough?

Who am I kidding? This is Henry. Of course once wasn't enough.

Tillie pulls her blanket over herself and then reaches back to pull the privacy curtain around her, face mask and earplugs already in hand. "Wake me up by eight. I feel the need to drink heavily tonight."

I keep my back to them as I peel off my day uniform and wriggle into the dress, doing my best not to start crying. Right now I envy Tillie. I'd do anything to be able to curl up in my bed and pull the curtain on my life.

"Do you need some help with that?" Icy-cold fingers make me jump. "Sorry." Katie pulls the zipper up my back.

"Thanks." I check the one full-length mirror on the outside of the powder room door, standing taller. "So? What do you think?" I smooth my hands over the soft matte black material of the sleeveless dress that ends just above the knee. It's nothing flashy, or intentionally provocative, but it hugs my curves all the same. I think it looks nice.

Katie's frown makes me think I'm wrong.

"What?"

"Something's off."

"Really?" I look at my reflection again. "Like what?"

"Shoes. Necklace," Rachel pipes in with her ideas.

Katie's nodding with her but still looks perplexed. And then she snaps her finger. "Boobs!" She rifles through her drawer. "You need a bra."

"I'm wearing a bra." I frown at myself in the mirror. Does it look like I'm not wearing a bra?

"36D, right?"

"Right." I'm not going to ask how she knows.

"Here." She tosses a lacy black bra at me. "It has superpowers. Trust me. Turn around." I do, and her hands are working to unzip and slip off the top of my dress before unfastening my bra.

I feel both Rachel and Katie's eyes on me but I put my self-consciousness away and slip my worn white bra off, quickly exchanging it for Katie's.

"See? Much better!" Katie exclaims when I'm redressed and checking myself in the mirror.

"You're right." I can't explain exactly what is different, because they still look huge next to my slender waist, but something is definitely different.

"Can you handle heels?" Rachel pulls out the pair of heels she was wearing the day she served drinks to Henry and those bigwigs in Lux.

"I can try." It's been a while.

Katie throws a silver rope-like necklace around my neck. "How much time do you have?"

I check my phone. "I should probably leave now."

"You can be a few minutes late, right?" She grabs her cosmetics bag.

The old me—the one who wanted to please my boss—would have said absolutely not.

But I'm guessing my days here are numbered anyway.

"Sure. Why not."

ten

Maybe passive-aggressiveness is my thing, because I arrive at Penthouse Cabin One seventeen minutes late with an odd sense of satisfaction. It doesn't completely erase the dread, though.

Taking a deep breath, I enter through the service entrance, as usual.

The door that leads into the main cabin is closed. It's never been closed.

Do I let myself in?

So much for my satisfaction. Now I'm just confused. Henry's probably pissed at me for being late, but I know he hasn't left because I hear a low muffled voice. I try pressing my ear against the door but I can't make out any words.

Setting my things on the desk, I wander over to the restroom to take another good look at myself; at the magic that Rachel and Katie managed to do with twenty minutes.

I hardly recognize myself. With smoky black shadow and a thick fringe of black lashes, my hazel eyes look gold. I suck in my cheeks and turn my face from side to side, admiring the contouring. I look older. Twenty-five or twenty-six. They decided to stick with a light gloss on my lips and I'm glad for it because this is already a big change.

And my hair.... They swept it up in this kind of fancy, smooth ponytail. When Rachel started teasing and spraying my roots, I panicked, afraid that they'd cause irreparable damage to my newly colored red hair that I love so much. But they promised it would all wash out and they knew what they were doing.

And they must, because I've felt the looks all the way here.

I offer my reflection a sad smile. At least I'll look good on the outside, even when I'm drowning in agony and disappointment on the inside.

I frown at the sound of the service phone ringing.

Henry's calling me from the cabin. We've never actually used this phone, not even once. I pause, contemplating what to say. Finally I decide on "Hello, Mr. Wolf. How may I be of service to you tonight?"

"Abbi, please come in here." He hangs up abruptly.

Rolling my eyes and dreading the inevitable, I open the door and step inside.

Henry's not alone. His father is with him.

"Hello, Miss Mitchell." At least William Wolf has a smile for me this time, one that doesn't seem entirely hostile. He's dressed in a classic tux, complete with black bow tie. His thick head of silver hair is combed back, much like Henry wears his, only he doesn't have the curly ends. All in all, he's quite dashing.

No one would ever think he has only three years left to live.

"Hello, sir." As much as I want to completely ignore

Henry, my eyes veer his way anyway, taking in the black-on-black tux he changed into. The coat hangs open to reveal the vest beneath, hugging his body so well. He looks incredible.

And he's staring at me. His face is impossible to read but his eyes roam over my body, and in them I see that same heated look he always gets right before he starts removing my clothes.

Three times, with Roshana. Three times, I remind myself.

A lump forms in my throat and I peel my eyes away, focusing on William Wolf. "Can I get something for you? A drink, perhaps?"

William Wolf holds up the crystal glass of amber liquid already in his hand, a smirk on his mouth.

Strike one. I offer him a sheepish grin. "Of course, I'm sorry. I somehow missed that. What else can I get for you?"

"I'd like you to tell me what happened in the elevator with my son today."

Which elevator?

Which son?

"It sounds like Scott behaved offensively with you?"

Oh, right. I clear my throat. "Yes. I'd say so."

The two men simply stare at me, and I realize they're waiting for me to elaborate.

"He—" My cheeks flush as I replay Scott's exact words. "He insisted that Mr. Wolf and I had a more than professional relationship. That, if I didn't admit to as much, I would not have a job here when he took over the hotel, which would be in a few weeks."

William Wolf's brow jumps at that but he says nothing.

"And what did he say? About *you*?" Henry prods calmly.

"It sounds like he had me investigated. He knew a lot of personal information." It still makes me want to shiver.

"That must have been shocking for you."

"Yes, it was. In fact, it was terrifying."

William Wolf tips his glass back before setting it on the table. "I apologize for my son. He crosses lines when he wants something."

Again... which son? Because the same could be said for the one standing next to you.

He turns to Henry. "I'll see you in the ballroom for the photo ops." His thick brow lifts, communicating something silently. "Keep me informed."

"As soon as I know for sure."

What's going on now?

Mr. Wolf drops a hand on his son's shoulder. "You've done an excellent job with this place. You'll run Wolf as well as your grandfather and I have." He drops his voice. "And we'll sort out that other problem. It was one mistake. We've all made them, myself included."

Henry offers him a curt nod as William turns and walks away, smiling at me on his way past.

The door closes with a thud.

And I have no idea what to say or do now.

Henry pours himself another drink. I open my mouth to warn him against it—he has to give a speech tonight—but I bite my tongue. If he wants to get drunk and make a fool of himself, go right ahead. At least then I won't be the only fool around here.

"We should probably get going now, so we're not late." I begin making my way back to the servants' quarters to collect my things.

"Abbi."

My feet falter, but I don't face him.

He heaves a sigh. "In this job, sometimes I have to say things I don't mean, and do things I don't want to do."

"Oh, you're saying you didn't *want* to sleep with her?"

"Would you please turn around." There's that edge to his voice, the one I've become familiar with.

I steel myself, and keep my back to him.

"Who *exactly* are you implying that I've fucked?"

A strangled laugh escapes my throat. Implying? Now I do turn around, so I can catch the truth in his eyes, even if he won't admit to it. "Who do you think! Roshana Mafi. Remember? The one you insisted should be right next door."

He says nothing for a long moment, simply staring at me with that intimidating gaze. "Why do you think I fucked Roshana Mafi? Because Scott, my brother who I warned you was a liar and a manipulator, told you so?"

I swallow against the rising lump. I don't want to get Belinda in trouble by mentioning her assumptions. "Your hands were all over each other today. And my roommate said—"

"Oh, well if Scott *and your roommate* say so...." An annoyed smirk touches his lips. He hides it behind his glass of scotch.

He still hasn't admitted to it.

But he also hasn't denied it. I'd love to hope that means it isn't true.

I would love to.

"You used me." I fight the tears threatening.

His brows arch. "And you haven't used me?"

"No!"

"No? You weren't desperate to get over your ex-fiancé?"

"This wasn't about him. I'm—" I cut myself off. Why am I doing this to myself? There's just no point. "You know, I'm not feeling well. If you don't need me for—"

"I *do* need you. You're my assistant and you're not bailing on me tonight." He takes a step forward.

I take five steps backward.

He drains his glass and carefully sets it on the table, his fingers resting on the edges for a long moment as his gaze disappears into thought. "Look, things between us may have gotten out of hand. I've been under a lot of pressure, and arrogant enough to think that I could do what I want behind closed doors. It's made me say and do things I shouldn't have." He sighs. "You're young and inexperienced, and I've made a few mistakes with you, and for that, I'm sorry."

Is that what I am? A few mistakes for Henry?

"I think it's time I start acting like the man my father thinks I am. At least I can be honest, going forward."

"What does that even mean?"

"It means you're my assistant and I'm your boss and we should take a step back and focus on that for right now."

He expects me to just pretend none of this happened? Come in here day in, day out? "I can't do this. I can't work for you anymore," I hear myself say, and the moment the words escape me, I know they're true. Painful, but true.

Henry levels me with a calm look. "You want to go back to the farm? To your controlling mother and your ex-boyfriend who's fucking his girlfriend in barns all over town? Go back to, what, baling hay and praying in church and being good-girl Abigail who sells soaps at the bazaar and pines over your lost love? You'll be miserable." He has the audacity to smirk. Probably because he's right and we both know it.

Just thinking about going back to Greenbank has tension cording my neck. "No. I don't want to go back there."

"I didn't think so. So, we'll just wipe the slate—"

"I can't work for you."

He frowns. "Everyone here works for me, Abbi."

"Move me to Outdoor." That's where I was supposed to be to begin with.

"No." Henry's denial comes hard and fast.

He doesn't think I can handle that department. "Fine, then Housekeeping or—"

"No. It's this job or no job."

"Why?"

He hesitates. "Because you're a good assistant, and I need a good assistant. I trust you. And because I'm the boss."

I grit my jaw against the urge to scream at him. How on earth am I going to show up here every day and pretend that nothing's happened between us? That he hasn't hurt me? So now I'm, what, going to trail him around, booking meetings and taking notes, and pretending none of this ever happened?

He's basically ending things with me a day after he said he wanted us to work out and then fucked around with someone else. I'm not sure which part I'm more upset about.

"I can't do it."

"Well, that's your choice. Either stay on at Wolf Cove as my assistant, or hand in your resignation and go back to Greenbank. It's up to you, and I expect an answer by tomorrow." He collects his phone and printed speech. "We should go. We don't want to be late."

What are my options here? Run to the cabin now, and I'm guessing the ultimatum he just delivered is off the table. I'll be on the first ferry home tomorrow morning. Stay and face Henry day in, day out, and pretend that he hasn't seen me naked, hasn't kissed me, hasn't been inside me, hasn't made me scream out with ecstasy?

Hasn't lied to me, hasn't hurt me?

He strolls past me, the smell of his cologne swirling past him in a tantalizing haze, his gaze sliding over my dress. "You look nice tonight."

For some reason his compliment feels like a slap, and I flinch.

Calm and collected Henry is back. Whatever connection we shared yesterday has been severed with the fine blade of betrayal, and it doesn't even faze him.

I don't know what the right choice is. Which choice I'll regret more. But right now, there's nothing I can do but follow him toward the door.

He pauses, his hand on the handle. "I'd tell you that I didn't fuck Roshana, nor do I have any intention of doing so, but it sounds like you've already made up your mind about me, and I'm not going to beg you to believe me. I don't beg."

He steps out into the cool spring evening, the Alaskan sun buried behind the thick, dark onslaught of storm clouds that spark with lightning and threaten a downpour, his fingers splayed to hold the door open for me.

This time I'm the one who keeps the healthy distance between us as we walk along the path, a good three feet of it.

"Henry!"

I look to my left in time to see Roshana sashaying down the path from her cabin in a flowing one-sleeve dress, her dark skin radiant against the snowy white of the silk material. She's obviously been at the salon because her blue nails are now tipped with white and her hair is styled smooth and long.

She looks like a bride in that dress.

"Walk with me." She shuffles her purse to her other arm, freeing her left hand.

Henry doesn't hesitate to offer her his arm, bending

down to lay a kiss on her cheek. "You look ravishing tonight."

Ravishing. Not simply "nice."

I fall into step behind them, steeling myself for a lot of pain.

eleven

"Not bad for the Alaskan wild, right?"

I peel my vacant stare away from the mingling crowd to acknowledge Rich, the main host from Lux, who has learned how to juggle Henry's constant dinner reservation changes like a pro, saving my butt more than once. "Hey, what are you doing here?"

"They needed a slave with fine-dining experience. I fit the bill." He scans me from head to toe. "You clean up well."

I offer him a weak smile. "Thanks. I had help."

"*Right.* I heard the Barbie dolls are back together under one roof again." A wry smile twists his lips. "Tonight should be interesting."

I assume he's talking about Katie and Rachel. Does he know about them? Does everybody? Probably. I guess I'm naïve about that, too. I hadn't even given thought to what might be going on in the bunk next to me with this unexpected reunion.

I really need to buy myself a pair of earplugs.

"Any guesses on how much tonight is going to cost Wolf?"

"No idea. A lot." I let my eyes wander over the room again. I listened to Belinda describe what would be done to the room but somehow I managed to walk in completely surprised. The room lends itself to a more rustic theme to begin with, with plenty of rich wood paneling along the walls and antler-cast candelabras. But the explosion of white flowers and simple white pillar candles along with Wedgwood china and servers dressed in old-fashioned butler uniforms turn the space into a high-end romantic cave.

When we arrived, it was still daylight and the view of the mountains framed within the glass wall of windows was awe-inspiring. The photo ops took close to an hour, followed by a few cocktails, followed by the official ceremony. The Wolf men shared the stage with various political notables for the idyllic ribbon-cutting ceremony, Scott standing stoically off to the side, his face unreadable. William, introduced as the owner of Wolf Hotels, gave a short speech about the history of the Wolf family, and how proud they are to have brought their legacy back to Alaska in the form of this majestic hotel.

But he quickly passed the microphone over to his son, applauding him for his business sense, his bold risk-taking, and his passion for Alaska.

I held my breath as Henry stood up there, enchanting the crowd of several hundred with his captivating form and his polished words, enrapturing the women—and some men—in the crowd with his very presence. There's just something magnetic about the man. Even though I've spent the night convincing myself that I hate him, I couldn't help but listen to him intently. To his genuine love of Alaska and the memories it has held, for his hopes for the future as president and CEO of the entire company.

That was hours ago. Now the orchestra is finished, the elaborate candelabras are burning bright, and a steady thrum of electronic music courses through the air. I've never actually been to a club, but I imagine this is what it is, the steady procession of alcohol sure to guarantee a night of debauchery. Where earlier women were moving gracefully, standing upright and sucking everything in, they're now throwing their heads back with wild laughter. Where men arrived layered in their tuxes, they've now cast away waistcoats and bow ties dangle from collars.

Except for Henry, of course. He stands statuesque, holding the same drink he started with after speeches, listening and smiling and occasionally grazing a woman's arm or shoulder, or the small of her back.

And every time he does, I see them catch their breath, and fire lights in their eyes.

And a pang of sorrow stabs me in the chest.

"I've heard these Wolf parties go late. Stick around if you want a good show. Should be fun," Rich murmurs.

"I'll keep that in mind." I shift my feet, the heels beginning to hurt. I'd love to kick them off. I haven't sat down in hours. I don't know how Belinda does it. I've watched her strut around all night in her stilettos without a hint of discomfort.

Scott has been conspicuously absent since the ceremony. At least, *I* noticed when the round of applause was over, the string of violins began, and William Wolf leaned into his ear, sending him off stage and out the door immediately after.

I can't say I'm not happy about it.

"Oh, looks like Wolf needs you. See you around." Richard takes off, offering a nod toward Henry as they pass each other. Henry merely glares at him before adjusting his sights on me, something he's done very little of all night. I've stayed within ten feet of him, a shadow that floats unseen, but taking in everything he does, aware of his every move, and I've barely caught his attention, even in passing.

Roshana has been watching him intently, too. I've found small consolation in the fact that she hasn't been attached to him all night, but she's been watching. With every hair flip, she takes the opportunity to mark his location.

Just like most women in here do.

Henry is a prize in their eyes. I guess he was a prize in my eyes, too. *Was* being the operative word. Now it just plain hurts.

"I no longer need you tonight. You can go home. Take the morning off and come to my place at one." He's his usual public self—detached, impersonal.

"Okay." I steal one last look at his impassive face and then head for the exit.

~

"Abbi!"

My bunkmate's voice carries across the narrow corridor by the lobby. I haven't talked to Autumn in days. Of all of us, the concierges have been working the hardest to please guests. I heard they're understaffed, which doesn't help.

She speeds over to meet me by the indoor water fountain—a dazzling sculpture of stone and logs, intended to represent a natural waterfall. "You look... *incredible*!" Her green eyes sparkle as they skate over my features.

"Thanks."

"Are you done for the night?"

"Yeah. You?"

"I wish. I have another hour to go." Her angular face,

highlighted by an adorable pixie cut that I could never pull off, scrunches up. "These media people are awful. My lips have been attached to their asses all day and night and I'm sick of it. Now they're drunk and even more demanding. I just spent fifteen minutes trying to explain to one of them that, no, they can't go for a two-mile hike in the middle of the night because there are animals out there that will eat them! So now we have to alert security to keep an eye out for any idiots heading toward the trails." She scoffs, making her annoyance somehow funny, and I start to laugh. It feels good.

"It's getting late. Maybe they'll be too drunk to do anything but sleep."

"Yeah." She rolls her eyes. "After they finish fornicating in public. You want a good laugh? Grab a drink and talk your way into the security room. Those guys see the full gamut of things on nights like these. People in stairwells, in hallways. Sneaking into banquet rooms. Apparently there were two people getting hot and heavy on this last night." She points at the log-carved bench next to us. "The woman was giving the dude a hand job. Security had to politely escort them to their rooms."

Oh my God.

"Yeah. Anyway, you should come to the staff lodge tonight. A few of us are going to de-stress with some drinks."

"I'll think about it." Apparently the staff lodge has become one big party most nights. There's always someone who doesn't have to get up early in the morning for their next shift, and the Outdoor crew doesn't care if they go to work hungover.

"The big bad wolf is running you ragged, isn't he?" She tsks. "I heard he's not easy to work for."

"No, he's not." That's an understatement.

"But, hey! I heard you had something to do with getting Rachel back here, so I guess you hold some sway." Autumn nods to something behind me. "Speak of the devil. Wow. Look at him."

My heart stutters of its own accord, simply because I know she's talking about Henry. Taking a deep breath, I glance over my shoulder. Henry strolls toward the lobby doors, flanked on either side by a rosy-cheeked Roshana and a willowy blonde in a crimson dress, the two women staggering slightly. His hands are settled on the smalls of their backs.

My stomach drops as I watch him step forward to hold the door for them. The blonde passes through but Roshana stalls, turning to brazenly grab hold of his belt buckle and pull him to her. He smiles down at her, coaxing her through the entrance with a nod toward the covered path.

I watch them walk cozily along until they disappear from view, heading toward the seclusion of their private cabins.

I don't think he saw me, but I wonder if he'd even care.

"I guess he's getting his freak on tonight. Not surprised, given what I've heard about him," Autumn jokes, oblivious to my anguish.

So I'm not the only one that sensed that's where the intimate touches and looks were heading.

It wasn't bad enough that he screwed her last night. He's about to screw her again, tonight, along with another woman. And I have the pleasure of knowing about it while it's happening this time. No wonder he gave me the morning off, again.

"Abbi? You okay?" Autumn frowns. You're a little pale."

"I haven't been feeling well all day."

She rubs my arm. "Go and get some sleep. We'll party at the lodge another night."

"Sounds good." All I want to do is put my pajamas on and curl up in my blankets and wish this awful, sick feeling away. "See you later." I don't hesitate, turning to dash toward the nearest exit.

"Oh, wait, Abbi. Let me get you an umbrella! It's—"

Her voice disappears behind me as I push through the door and into the cold rain.

twelve

I'm shivering by the time I reach the path to my cabin, the silky material of my dress clinging to my body, my face no doubt streaked with black mascara, from the tears or the rain, it doesn't matter.

Great. It sounds like there's a party going on inside. That steady beat of music is going to be a problem. Then again, maybe it'll help drown out my sobs.

The moment I step inside the cabin, I know I won't be curling up or sleeping any time soon. The smell hits me first; booze, clean sweat, and a muskiness that I now recognize as sex—arousal and slick bodies grinding against each other.

I gasp in shock as I take in the sordid sight of strewn clothes and tangled bodies.

Ronan is shirtless and standing with his back against Katie and Rachel's bunk. His jeans and boxers are pushed down his thighs and his fingers are tangled through a kneeling Rachel's bleach-blonde mane, his hands moving in time with her bobbing head as she sucks him off. Rachel is completely naked.

BREAK ME

As if that's not enough, Katie is sprawled out on top of pillows on the floor in front of me, her enormous fake breasts sitting perfectly upright, her legs spread and her bare pussy on full display. At least, I'm pretty sure it's Katie. I can't actually see her face given it's buried between Rachel's legs, her fingers gripping Rachel's hips as she tongues her best friend's slit.

My roommates are having a threesome in the middle of our cabin, and they clearly don't care who might walk in and see it.

Ronan's hooded gaze meets mine but he makes no attempt to stop Rachel, his lips parting with his ragged breaths. He even scoops her hair off to one side to, I think, give me a better view of his erect cock, sliding in and out of Rachel's mouth.

I'm frozen, wanting to turn around and run, but unable to move.

The music must have drowned out my entrance because Katie and Rachel haven't stopped, or covered themselves up. I would think they'd stop out of respect, had they realized they were being watched.

Then again, they probably shouldn't have started this here, out of respect.

I'm still frozen, still telling myself to turn and run.

Still staring at them like a pervert.

Ronan's heady gaze hasn't left me, either, and he begins thrusting his hips with each bob of Rachel's head, his hands gripping her hair in tight fists. He clearly enjoys having a spectator.

Rachel pulls away from him with a loud moan, her fist wrapping around his erection to continue what her mouth isn't doing, her free hand stretching over Ronan's firm, heaving chest, decorated in ink, as she looks down at Katie between her legs. "God. Yes. Almost there. Yes!" Rachel's moans grow louder as Katie's fingers disappear into her, and Rachel begins grinding her hips. Moments later she cries out in ecstasy as she comes against her friend's tongue.

And I am *still* standing here, watching this!

Rachel aims her mouth for Ronan's hard, protruding cock again but he steps back, reaching for a foil packet that waits for him on the bed, ripping the package with his teeth. "Turn around."

He slides the condom on as she obeys, getting to her feet.

And that's when she sees me, and Katie sees me, and both their eyes flash with surprise.

"Abbi, I didn't think you'd be back so—" Rachel begins, but Ronan cuts her off.

"Don't worry, she's been here a while. She's enjoying this. Aren't you, red?"

I can't respond, because I don't know. *Am I* enjoying this? Is that why I haven't bolted yet?

Ronan guides Rachel to her knees and, shoving his pants to his ankles, he kneels behind her. With his hand on the back of Rachel's neck, he gently pushes her face between Katie's thighs. And offers me a wry smile. "You're welcome to join."

Rachel looks up at me once more, just as Ronan thrusts into her from behind and the sheer ecstasy of it splays across her face.

The same look I saw in my own face yesterday, when Henry thrust into me.

Henry.

My initial shock of walking into this debauchery has faded, replaced by the raw realization that *this* must be what Henry is doing with those two women right now.

It's a gutting reality.

I turn and bolt out the door, down the slick path, fighting my tears, no clue where I'm going. I can't go to the lodge, or the hotel—not the way I look right now. I run without aim, lost and alone and heartbroken.

Right into someone.

"I'm sorry!" I try to fumble past him, keeping my head down.

"Abbi?" He pulls his hood back to reveal his face.

"Michael?" Henry's masseuse.

"What are you doing out here?" He pauses, frowns as he takes in my face. "Are you okay?"

Three simple words. A simple question. But for some reason it crushes my resolve, and I break out in a fit of sobs.

Michael quickly wraps an arm around my shoulders, pulling me into his broad chest. "Come on, let's get you back to your cabin."

I shake my head frantically. "Can't.... My roommates.... Sex.... Ronan....." I can barely get the words out.

"Okay, okay. Shhh.... Come on. My place is just over there. I can't promise mine aren't too, but they're probably doing it somewhere else right now."

Cocooning me against his body, Michael leads me along the path to a cabin on the opposite side of mine, swiping his key card to unlock it.

The cabin's empty.

I hear a soft "Thank God," under his breath. He pushes the door shut and leads me to the far wall. "Bottom bunk is mine. Here, let me get you something. You're shivering." Michael rummages through a drawer while I do my best to stifle my sobs. He hands me a plush white towel. "Just did laundry."

I press it against my face to smell it, inhaling the scent of the fabric softener. That's always been a calming scent to me. Only when I pull it away do I remember my face is streaked with makeup. "I'm so sorry!" I cringe at the black marks I've already left.

He reaches over his head to yank his sweatshirt off, his t-shirt lifting just high enough in the process to show me his stomach, the ridges of his abs hard and defined, the trail of blond hair turning darker as it disappears below the waistband of his black dress pants. "Don't worry about it. It's just a towel. That's what bleach is for."

Still, I must look a disaster. "Do you mind if I use...." I gesture toward the small powder room.

"Of course, go ahead. But I make no promises about what shape it's in. There are six guys and who knows how many girls using it."

My eyes drift around the cabin at the strewn about clothes and shoes, trashcans overflowing with candy wrappers, and the empty beer bottles stacked next to them. "I'll keep that in mind."

"I don't have much that will fit you, but you really should get out of that dress before you get sick." His eyes drift over my frame, and I instinctively tug on the skirt, wet and clinging much higher on my thighs than it should. Ducking his head, he rummages through the dresser again, pulling out a t-shirt and boxers. "Best I can do, but it'll be more comfortable."

I collect them from his hands with a small "thank you," and make my way into the small powder room, trying to quell my shivers as I close the door behind me.

A homely girl stares back at me from the mirror, her face streaked, her hair clinging to her scalp, her eyes bloodshot, her teeth chattering noisily.

The dim lighting in here sure doesn't help.

Stripping down to nothing—everything is soaked right through—I quickly towel myself off and wash my face with the bar of soap, doing my best to ignore the condom wrappers that spill out over the trash can. At least the makeup comes off easily enough, leaving me with a fresh, albeit puffy face. My hair is an entirely different story. Nothing short of a hot shower and conditioner is going to tame this mess, but I pull the elastic and pins out, and finger-comb the tangles.

Thankfully it's still just us when I emerge. Michael has kicked off his shoes and socks, and changed into track pants, and is sitting on the edge of his bed, resting his elbows on his knees. He's turned on the small reading light affixed to the side of the bunk to cast some light into the little nook.

"A little bit better, at least?" He nods toward the clothes I slipped on. The t-shirt reaches midthigh and I have to hold up the boxers to keep them from slipping off.

My smile is weak, but genuine. "Yeah. Thanks. Do you have somewhere I can hang this?" I hold up my wet things.

"Right behind you." He's on his feet and coming around to help me, reaching over me to get the wire hanger off, the faint smell of soap and cologne wafting from him. "We'll hang it above the heater."

I quickly hook my dress and undergarments. There's no hope for modesty with my panties and Katie's bra dangling, but Michael doesn't say anything. I guess he's learned how to be respectful of people's vulnerabilities, given his profession.

"You're still shivering."

I fold my arms over my chest, trying to still my body. "I'll be okay."

"Get under my covers. That'll help."

I merely nod and comply. After the day I've had, I'm

beyond caring that I'm crawling into a guy's bed. I pull the blankets up to my chin, reveling in how safe and comfortable they feel.

"Do you mind?" Michael gestures toward the bed.

"Of course not. It's your bed."

He eases in beside me with a groan, forcing me close to the wall to fit both of us. The bunks are wider than the ones I remember as a child, but they definitely weren't designed to sleep two grown adults comfortably.

Silence hangs as he stares at the top of the bunk above us and I stare at his profile. He's really handsome in that high school sports-star way. Short blond hair and a wide easy smile, framed by dimples, a jutting Adam's apple to define a long, thick neck. His jaw is coated with just the slightest amount of blond stubble, which I'm sure will be shaved off before his shift tomorrow.

If I weren't so enthralled by Henry, Michael is the kind of guy I would have noticed walking by. Probably would have watched shyly.

Henry....

I clear my throat, trying to dislodge the lump that's flared once again. "Where are your roommates?"

"A couple of them are working the night shift. The others are probably partying in the lodge." He turns to settle big blue eyes on me. "Is whatever you walked in on in your cabin what made you so upset?"

I shake my head.

"Do you want to talk about it?"

"About what I walked in on?" It was shocking, yes. It was depraved, yet, if I'm being honest with myself, I wasn't completely turned off by it. Ronan's naked form doesn't elicit feelings of disgust, that's for sure.

But that's definitely not something I'm admitting to Michael.

He chuckles. "I was in the lodge earlier, with Katie, Rachel, and Ronan. The three of them left together after a bunch of drinks and I have a pretty good idea about what you would have walked in on back there. So, no, not that. Do you want to talk about what had you burst into tears like your heart's been broken?"

My heart *is* broken. Again. Because I'm a stupid farm girl who can't see things that are right in front of me.

I shake my head. I *can't* talk about any of it, because it would mean divulging details about Henry.

Michael heaves another sigh. "Okay, I understand. But if you change your mind, I'm here to listen. And you can stay as long as you need to."

"Thanks." I offer him a weak smile as one of those ragged post-sob sounds escapes from my lungs. This feels like the safest place for me to be right now.

Voices flare just outside the window.

"Shit," Michael mutters, reaching behind him to grab hold of the privacy curtain. He has it drawn all the way around the bunk just as the door opens to loud laughter.

"Dude, I wouldn't last ten seconds with that girl's lips wrapped around my cock."

I recognize that voice but I can't place it.

"Like you're gonna get a chance. She's been polishing Buckey's knob every night for the last week. Bastard. They went into the tool shed last night and she let him go bareback in her ass."

"Lucky fucker. I need to find myself one of those. I've been yankin' it too hard lately, with all James's pussy comin' through here."

Michael's body tenses beside me. "Guys.... Watch it."

"Yo." One of them calls out, and a moment later. "Oh! Sorry."

They must have seen my clothes hanging by the window. At least they have the decency not to talk about women like that while one of them is here.

There's some whispering, and then feet shuffling, and then the door opens and closes.

And we're alone again.

Oh my God. My cheeks flush with realization. They left to give us privacy. They think we're having sex.

Michael smiles apologetically. "Sorry about that. Miguel's got a foul mouth but he's harmless."

Miguel? "The line cook in the staff lodge?"

"Yeah. You know him?"

That's where I've heard his voice before. "I met him on my very first night here." I smile. "Seems like so long ago."

"The days here are long, aren't they?"

I sigh. "The longest."

Michael shifts to his side, propping his head up by an elbow. "Here. Roll onto your stomach."

"Why?"

I tense as he reaches over to prod the muscles in my back with his strong fingers. "Because your muscles are tight. I can help with that."

He once offered to give me a massage. I declined, all because Henry asked me not to go anywhere near him. A tiny spark of anger flares in the pit of my stomach. Henry doesn't get to demand things like that. Not anymore.

"You don't have to do this," I say, rolling over to face the wall, tucking my arms along my sides.

He sweeps my long, damp hair over and begins gently kneading between my shoulders with one hand, ignoring my words. "Are you happy you came to Alaska?"

A soft, embarrassing moan escapes me, the strength of his fingers against my muscles soothing. Thankfully, he doesn't comment about it. "Yes. No. I don't know."

"Working directly for Mr. Wolf can't be easy."

I don't want to think about Henry Wolf, or what we had and don't have, or how he used me, how he lied to me. How he's screwing those two women right now.

"Relax, Abbi," Michael murmurs, his voice deep and soothing. "You're as tight as a wire."

Henry liked to tell me how tight I am.

I close my eyes and focus on Michael's large, strong hand instead. "This must be the last thing you want to do right now, after doing it all day."

"Normally I'd say yes, but that's definitely not the case with you."

Is that his way of saying he's interested in me? If so... it's flattering, but I just have no energy to even think about being with another man right now. So I stay quiet and revel in the feel of his skilled hand as it works along my shoulders and down my back, the pressure perfect, the motions rhythmic. Even one hand is heaven. What would both feel like?

Michael seems like a genuinely nice guy. I eye the small ledge on the wall—a design feature for each bed in each cabin, to house your personal items. He's tossed his wallet and phone up there, next to a small box of tissues. And a strip of condoms.

Has Michael slept with someone here?

In this bed?

Do I even really care?

"Have you warmed up enough now?"

"Hmmhmm," slips from my mouth, my eyes still glued to those condoms.

He tugs on the cotton t-shirt. "Would you mind taking

this off? It's easier against bare skin." He must sense my hesitation because he quickly adds, "I do this with clients every day, Abbi."

"You lie in bed with clients every day?"

The bed shakes with his laughter. "Okay, maybe not that. But I'm not going to try anything on you, if that's what you're wondering."

He *does* massage naked bodies all the time. I take a deep breath and, before I can think too much about it, I'm lifting his t-shirt over my head and setting it next to me on the pillow.

Goose bumps erupt all over my back and I want to pull the covers up to my neck.

The weight in the bed shifts and Michael's suddenly moving and tugging at the covers, and I feel the soft cotton of his sweat pants brush against my bare legs as he slides in next to me. "There. Now we can pull them all the way up and keep you warm." His fingers smooth over my back from under the blankets and he continues kneading. "Perfect. I can get deeper this way."

My blood stirs at his words, even if I don't want it to.

Thankfully, he doesn't say any more, seemingly content to work away all the stress and tension in my back and arms in silence, his hand touching every square inch of my skin, his fingers never once wandering too far down to graze the sides of my breasts, pressed against the mattress.

But this silence is a dangerous place for me.

Because in the silence, with Michael's skilled hands on me, I'm thinking of Henry.

Of what he's doing right now.

Of what went wrong.

Of what, if anything, was ever real or true.

I can't spend the rest of the summer around him, at his

beck and call. I just can't do it. But I won't go home. I won't be stuck spending the summer in Greenbank with Mama, listening to her go on about Jed and how I need to win him back.

Why would Henry refuse to let me move to another department? Is it a power thing? Why would he want to hurt me like that, when he's already hurt me so badly? Is he that heartless?

A fresh wave of tears stream down my cheeks again, these ones silent.

But somehow Michael knows immediately. He slips one of his long muscular arms beneath my head and, with a gentle hand on my shoulder, rolls me onto my side, until my back is against his chest. Adjusting the blankets so they're covering my bare front, he ropes his other arm around and folds both in front of me, loosely hugging me. "It'll be okay. Whatever it is, you'll be fine," he murmurs into my hair.

I don't know if he's right but it feels good, hearing him say that. "I'm so tired." I really am.

"Then shut your eyes and go to sleep." He reaches above us to switch off the small reading light. The night-light that's plugged into the wall socket next to the shelf kicks on, casting a glow in the small space. Not annoying, just enough to know where I am when I wake up.

I begin to believe that maybe I can just fall asleep here, in the comfort of Michael's arms.

That's when the door bursts open and a woman's giggle carries through the cabin.

Michael heaves a deep, irritated sigh. I gather he's not happy about the additional company. "I can ask them to leave, if you want," he whispers.

"No. It's okay." He shares this cabin with five other guys. They have a right to be here, too.

There's a series of stumbles and "ouches" and "shits" and more giggles—they're obviously drunk—before a bed creaks and a privacy curtain draws.

"James! Stop!" The girl whisper-giggles. The sound of a slap follows, then zippers being unfastened, and then the very distinctive smacking of lips. Low music starts playing—over a phone speaker, probably. Not nearly loud enough to drown them out.

"Do they know you're here?" I whisper as softly as possible.

"I doubt they care." Michael's sigh skates over my neck. "And I'm sorry."

About five seconds later, the girl lets out a guttural moan and I understand what Michael is apologizing for. We're about to lie here and listen to his roommate have sex.

thirteen

"No! It's your turn first this time," the girl whispers.

"I can't. I've been watching your ass in those tight jeans all night. I won't last through it. But I won't take long, I promise. And then I'll be ready again by the time you're done. *Please*," James negotiates.

He must have convinced her because a moment later he lets out a low, "Fuck, yeah. All the way, baby."

The muscles in Michael's arms begin to cord, but otherwise he remains silent and still as we listen to some girl suck his roommate off.

I'm now wide awake, and suddenly feeling the urge to giggle, the reality of my night just too much.

"Shhh," Michael whispers into my ear, but I can hear the amusement in his tone. He wants to laugh, too.

"How often do they do this?"

"A few times a week. That's the problem with this setup. I mean, come on. There's no privacy, so people either abstain for months or relax their need for privacy. Guess which option most people are leaning toward?"

I don't know that Katie and Rachel have ever had a need for privacy to begin with.

James's moans and whispered instructions are growing louder and more frequent as the minutes pass, and Michael's heartbeat against my back is speeding up. He's breathing heavier, too, and has shifted his lower half away from my body.

He's turned on, listening to his friend get a blow job. I guess I can't blame him for it. Listening and watching to Katie and Rachel in bed together affected me, too.

Finally, we hear James groan a warning of, "I'm coming." It's followed by a series of primal grunting sounds that sparks a tingling between my thighs, my own breaths coming harder and faster, my body naturally tensing.

The bed creaks loudly as they shift positions.

And the girl lets out a soft gasp.

I close my eyes and grope for Michael's hand in the dark. He takes it, weaving his fingers within mine, tightening his hold as she moans.

I remember what that feels like, to have Henry's face there. The first swipe of Henry's tongue over my clit, the delicious burn of his stubble against my skin. It was excitement, and nerves, and anxiety, all mixed together.

All that time Michael spent working the knots out of my back seems pointless now, as tension seeps into my body once again, the knowledge that I'll never feel Henry's touch like that again excruciating.

The realization that his face is between someone else's legs tonight, agonizing. I fight against the urge to begin crying again, focusing instead on the girl's pants, picturing their naked bodies—tangled; imagining what it would feel like to be on my back, feeling that right now.

If this attractive, nice guy, who I would probably be

fantasizing about had I never crossed paths with Henry Wolf, who is holding me tightly, had his face between my legs.

My chest is rising and falling with quick breaths, and a deep throb grows between my legs. I can't relieve the pain in my heart, but I can relieve that discomfort, at least.

And why shouldn't I?

Henry doesn't care.

There's a voice in the back of my mind, screaming at me to stop, to rethink this, to think about my values and what I've already given up. I force it aside, because neither that voice nor my values will help ease the emotional ache.

Steeling my nerve, I tighten my grip over Michael's hand, and I move it toward my chest, pulling it under the covers, down along my curves, his knuckles skating over my nipple as I drag his hand farther down, all the way to the waistband of the boxers I borrowed from him, so loose they've practically slipped off me anyway.

I hesitate, but only for a second, until I remind myself that I want to not think about Henry and what he's doing right now.

Michael tenses behind me, and for just a moment I worry that he's going to refuse.

But then he shifts his body to press his long, hard erection against my backside.

I close my eyes and hold my breath as I drag his hand farther down, pushing the boxers down and unfurling my fingers from his to settle his hand on my smooth mound.

His shaky sigh skates across the side of my cheek, but he doesn't hesitate, slipping a long finger through my wet folds, slowly and gently, the arm that my head is resting against curling, pulling my head tighter against his. Over and over, his finger slides back and forth, skating over my clit, never pushing inside me.

Making me grow incredibly wet with anticipation.

I've tuned out the girl next to us, my lips pressed firmly together to keep my own moans from escaping as Michael teases me mercilessly. I'm torn between staying still and rolling onto my back to give him better access.

Finally, on one of those lingering strokes over my opening, his finger doesn't glide past, instead slipping inside me. My stomach muscles clench with the intrusion. "Is this because of me? Or them?" he whispers, his mouth pressed against my ear.

"Both," I answer honestly, shamelessly.

I guess he's okay with that answer. He tugs my boxers down, stretching to push them past my knees. I easily kick them off the rest of the way. With a hand on my inner thigh, he guides my leg up to curl over his, pulling my body back into him, opening me up to him. And then his hand is back between my legs, and he's plunging two fingers deep inside me, as far as they can go. He finds my clit with the pad of his thumb, and he begins circling it with the same skill he used to work the knots in my back.

I close my eyes and lose myself in both Michael's hand and his lips, now trailing wet kisses along my neck, making me shiver.

Next to us, the girl lets out a deep, guttural moan, followed by a cry. That's two girls I've heard come tonight.

I'm going to be the third.

The sounds of a bed creaking and foil tearing tells me they're moving on to the third act next to us. It doesn't bother me much, now that I'm minutes away from coming myself. "*Oh, yeah,*" James groans deeply, and I know he's just pushed himself into her. My muscles clench against Michael's fingers.

The repetitive squeak of the mattress and skin slapping begins. Michael grinds his hips into my ass, pressing his hard length against me. He's practically panting, his warm breath kissing my skin in little puffs.

I begin to feel guilty. Everyone in here is about to get off, but him.

So I reach back and, with tentative fingers, slip inside his track pants, under his boxers, and wrap my hand around his girth. He's big. Not as big as Henry, but still impressive. And *so* incredibly hard.

"Abbi," he whispers against my ear as I slide my hand up and down his cock, the angle and the fact that he's wearing pants making it awkward.

"Yeah?"

He hesitates before whispering, so quietly, "You can say no, and it'll be okay but... I *really* need to be inside you."

My hands stills, his request stealing my breath. Sex? With Michael? Just days ago, I was still a virgin. How did this happen?

Because I met Henry Wolf. That's how this happened.

A pang twists my heart.

"Okay," I hear myself whisper without thought. Because I don't want to give room to focus on consequences or regrets or anything but my physical needs right now. Because I have this deep throb between my legs that I want relief from. Because I do like Michael and I find him attractive.

We quickly adjust our bodies, me shifting to my back and him kneeling between my legs. The blankets have fallen off me, leaving me completely naked and exposed, but thankfully only as much as the low glow of the nightlight allows.

He's fumbling with his things on the ledge, knocking stuff over. "Fuck, I know I have one somewhere here," he mutters. He switches on the reading light.

Suddenly our little nook is flooded with light.

I tense, the urge to cover myself strong. Michael pauses in his search, his eyes flaring with desire as they take my body in, drifting from my breasts to my stomach, to the bareness between my legs. "God, you're beautiful."

Reaching over his head, he yanks his t-shirt off, and then pushes his track pants down past his thighs, letting me take in his naked body, his chest firm, his torso long and lean but layered with defined muscle, his erection standing tall, a bead of moisture resting on top. With another quick top-to-bottom look at me, his eyes like finger trails along my body, he focuses on the small ledge by the wall again, seizing a condom.

Ripping the wrapper with his teeth, I watch him roll the condom over himself. They're still going strong next door, both of them grunting and moaning, completely unconcerned with us.

And I'm going to do this. I'm really going to have sex with Michael tonight.

"Can I?" I reach for the lamp, switching it off before he can deny me the option.

In the dim light, I watch Michael climb on top of me, my thighs spreading wide apart to accommodate his hips, and his cock, which is now sliding along my slit, the tip lining up with my entrance.

One quick thrust will get him inside me.

But instead of thrusting in, he leans down to cover my lips with his. His touch is soft, the gentle tentative strokes of a first kiss, as if we're not seconds away from having sex. I open my mouth for him, and welcome his tongue against mine, tasting Michael for the first time. He eases my nerves with each pass of his tongue, his kisses growing deeper until the stubble from his chin scrapes across my skin.

He's propped up on one elbow, but his free arm moves down my body to fill his hand with my breast, the pad of his thumb rubbing over my pebbled nipple in small circles. A thrill shoots down to my stomach, straight to my clit.

And so suddenly, he thrusts himself into me.

I cry out with the odd mix of pleasure and pain.

"You're so tight," he whispers against my lips, drawing his hips back and then pushing in again, sliding in deeper. I'm only somewhat conscious of the fact that James may be able to hear him say that, *if* they're listening.

With each thrust, he moves deeper, until I'm stretched and completely full.

I've now officially had sex with two men. It's an odd mental declaration to make. I wonder if every woman does this at that pivotal moment of a guy entering them for the first time, or is it just inexperienced women like me?

Michael's so different from Henry. Where Henry took and demanded, Michael has tested and hesitated and waited. Up until now. Now there's no hesitation, the bed creaking with each one of his thrusts, competing with his roommate. Two couples having sex no more than ten feet apart. I should be mortified but right now all I can focus on is how good this feels.

My hands slide all over him—over the stubble coating his jaw, over his broad, strong shoulders, tensing with his exertion, over the ridges of his sweat-slicked back—as my head falls back and I revel in the feeling of being joined with such an attractive man.

Of Michael wanting *me*.

"Oh, fuck! Yeah!" Next to us, James yells as he comes for a second time tonight.

A few hard, quick thrusts and Michael follows his roommate quickly with a deep moan, pulsing inside me.

That's it?

"Shit. I'm so sorry," he whispers against my mouth, his words between ragged breaths. "I tried to hold off, but I couldn't help it."

"That's okay." I swallow my disappointment, the heaviness in my belly still there but quickly morphing to a dull ache.

"Finish her off, man!" James hollers. "Come on, let's race. Winner gets to watch."

"Fuck off," Michael growls.

"Fine. But still, race you."

Michael chuckles. Planting a deep kiss on my lips, he whispers, "Just relax," and then calls back, "You're on," as he slips down my body, taking the covers with him once again.

Oh my God. This isn't happening, is it? They're not *actually* going to—

A gasp escapes my lips as Michael's tongue swirls around my clit for the first time. A second later, the girl echoes me.

This is actually happening.

Michael pushes my thighs apart as far as they can go and then, slipping both hands under my body, he angles my pelvis up, opening me up even more. I can see the glint in his eyes as he pushes his tongue into me.

As much as I want to stay quiet, I can't. I revel in his talented mouth as he alternates between sliding it through my seam and sucking on my clit, the sound echoing through the cabin along with my whimpers and moans.

That now familiar burn begins to build in my lower belly again, the one that tells me I'm going to come soon, the one that makes me no longer care about who can hear or see what. I reach down to run my fingers through his short hair, using the leverage to pull his face tighter to me.

He answers by slipping first two, then three fingers in me, turning them sideways to stretch me, rubbing my inner wall, while his tongue laves over my clit, over and over and over again.

I'm moments away from coming and I've spread my legs wide. I wouldn't care if we lose the race and earn an audience as James threatened. I buck against Michael's face, my orgasm coming hard and fast. I let myself cry out, I let them all hear me come. Because there's no point hiding it. And because I've already heard all of them come so we're in this together. And because tonight, I just don't care.

The girl orgasms seconds after me, maybe from sheer luck, or maybe because hearing me set her off.

Either way, all is suddenly and eerily quiet in the cabin.

Michael pulls his fingers out and kisses the insides of my thighs. He reaches for a tissue from the ledge. I quietly watch him slide off the cum-filled condom from his still-erect cock. "I'll be back in a sec." Tugging his pants up, he slips off the end of the bed, pushing the curtain open a touch. I listen to his feet pad softly along the floor to the powder room directly across. Light floods over me a second before the door shuts, leaving me alone with my thoughts.

And a sudden onslaught of guilt, something I don't understand. Henry doesn't care, so why would I feel guilty?

Maybe it has nothing to do with Henry. Maybe it has everything to do with becoming this person I never thought I'd be, who has casual sex, who listens and watches others having sex.

Who am I becoming?

I pull Michael's t-shirt over me and tell myself that this isn't a big deal. That Michael is a good guy who Mama would probably approve of, and if I was going to have sex with anyone tonight that wasn't Henry, it should be Michael.

It's *really* not a big deal.

The toilet flushes and a moment later the door opens again, giving me a great view of Michael's taut stomach.

"Leave the light on," James calls out. I hear his bare feet hit the wood floor.

"Dude! Come on!"

"What?"

A second later I see get my first look at James. Or, James from the waist down and buck naked, his semi-flaccid dick bobbing with his step. I close my eyes. I've seen three dicks tonight. Three!

James's voice drops to a soft whisper, but I can still hear him when he asks, "Who?"

"Good night."

"Fuck. Come on!"

"Night, Lorraine! Always a pleasure."

I hear a muffled "Night," and my mouth drops open. Lorraine? My roommate, Lorraine?

Michael pulls the curtain closed behind him and crawls into bed with me, resuming our precoital spooning position with a kiss along the back of my neck. He clearly wants me to stay the night. And, truth be told, I don't want to be alone tonight.

"Did that make you feel better?"

I smile, and nod.

And close my eyes as the heavy weight settles on my chest once again.

BREAK ME

I WAKE, my body draped over Michael's, my head resting against his chest.

"...the fucking guy was so damn drunk, he pissed all over himself. And me!" A guy complains. "He couldn't even remember his name. We had to carry him to his room. Fucking guy reeked of piss. So, yeah. Shitty night. I hate working foot security at these events."

"Don't blame you," another guy mumbles, and I instantly recognize the Australian accent. That's Andy, the guy assigned to be liaison to Roshana.

Damn her. Between Tillie cleaning her room and now Andy, Michael's roommate and her liaison, I feel like I'm always two degrees of separation between knowing what she's doing with Henry.

The security guy chuckles. "What the hell happened to you, anyway? She lock you up all weekend?"

"Dude. I don't even know where to begin with her and her multiple personalities."

"Yeah. Jerry said she's prime-grade bitch. She returned a hard-boiled egg three times, yesterday? Something like that, anyway."

Andy groans. "I think I've slept all of five hours since Friday. She made me sit in that little room and listen to her fuck all night on Friday."

"Who?"

Andy snorts. "Who do you *think*?"

"Of course. Chick like that goes straight for the top dog."

The top dog would be Henry Wolf.

I flinch, the brutal reality opening the emotional gash wide again. I feel sick. But not just sick. Anger is stirring deep within me. He had the nerve to deny it! To make me feel like not believing him would be *my* fault!

"At least you could tug one off in the privacy of your own little room, unlike this fucking place."

Andy chuckles. "Yeah, there's that. Still, she should have let me go home."

A zipper unfastens somewhere in the cabin. "Maybe she was hoping you'd go a round with them. She looks like the type that'd take two dicks at once."

"Two of something, anyway. Last night she came home with this smokin' blonde and the boss, and—hey..." Andy's voice drops. "Did Aspen finally hook up with someone?"

Aspen. It takes me a minute to clue in that he's talking about Michael, who works at the Aspen Wolf during the winter.

Andy must have seen my clothes on the hanger.

The curtain shifts at the foot of the bed and Andy's handsome face peers into our space. Thank God the covers are pulled over me to cover my naked bottom half.

"Fuck off," a groggy Michael calls out. I didn't even realize he was awake.

Andy ignores him, grinning at me. "Oh. Hey."

I feel my cheeks flush. "Hi." Great. Now Andy knows I slept over. How long before this gets around?

Andy climbs the ladder. The frame creaks as he stretches out in his bed. "I'll be sleeping 'til Tuesday if anyone needs me."

"Yeah. Hittin' the showers. All this fucking piss," the other guy mutters. The door opens and shuts, and all is silent in the cabin once again.

"Hey." Michael's fingers slide under my chin, lifting my face to his. He lays a light kiss on my lips, and his arm tightens around my body. "Are you feeling better, today?"

I offer him a weak smile.

No, I'm not. This all feels wrong. Being here, in Michael's bed. In his arms. I should never have slept with him last night. I used him. Like, really and truly used him, and he doesn't deserve that. He's a nice guy, and I think he may like me.

His fingers graze over my cheek, pushing strands away. "What are you thinking about?"

Henry.

Going to Henry's house at 1:00 p.m. Telling him... what? He demanded an answer today on whether I'm staying or going. I don't know yet. All I know is that I can't work for him anymore.

Why is he doing this to me? Isn't it better for him if I'm not there every day? Maybe he doesn't want to outright fire me, though. Me quitting to go back home would probably look better than him firing me and looking for a new assistant.

But, heck, I'd think he'd want to appease me. I'm a risk to him now, all emotional and hurt. He has that mess with Kiera to deal with. The last thing he needs is me around, telling people that he screwed me, too.

A thought strikes me.

Maybe I need to remind him of that.

I wriggle free of Michael's arms. "I've gotta get to work."

fourteen

My mind is lost beneath the stream of hot water as I weigh my options.

Am I insane for even considering staying? I'm hurt, and angry. Probably as hurt and angry as Kiera was when "they decided it best that she resign." That's what Henry said. Did he give her an ultimatum, too?

Maybe that explains why she'd blackmail him, why she'd want to hurt him back for the pain he caused her. Thinking back on it, the e-mails noted her leaving Wolf Hotels three months earlier, and the severance offer coming only a month or so ago. Plus, there's the "incident" that led to her having Henry's DNA on her panties three or four weeks ago. That can only mean one thing—that Henry slept with her as recently as three to four weeks ago. Why did he sleep with her then?

Was it because something was still going on between them? Or because he was trying to convince her to sign the gag order? Did he tell her all kinds of things that night? That she was special, and they were different, and he just had to be careful because of his father. That they needed to wait until Henry had control of the company?

Who knows anymore.

All I know is that I don't think I can be that vindictive as to try and blackmail Henry to get what I want. And honestly, I don't want *anyone* knowing what went on behind closed doors while I was supposed to be working. While some women around here would revel in having everyone know they were sleeping with him, I'm not one of them.

"We are *so, so, so* sorry, Abbi."

I jump at the sound of Katie's voice directly behind me. She's wrapped in a towel and standing in my shower stall. Again.

At least this time she's not getting a full-frontal view.

"We were *so* drunk and caught up in the moment, and Rachel thinks Ronan's hot. Tillie and Lorraine were partying in the lodge, and Autumn texted to say she was on shift until midnight." She's rambling, her pretty face scrunched up with a pained expression. "Honestly, we should have at least locked the door or something, but we really weren't thinking. Those parties go until late and we figured Wolf would make you stay." She finishes the rant with, "I'm sorry. Please don't hate us."

I stick my face under the hot stream of water again, acutely aware that she could be staring at my ass right now. Does that even bother me anymore? Being naked in front of Henry and Michael has definitely shed some of my shyness. "It's okay."

"Seriously? You're not mad at us?"

Oddly enough, I'm not mad. In fact, a part of me envies them for their freedom. It doesn't seem like they're weighed down by the kind of guilt or confusion that I woke up feeling this morning.

"No. Not at all. Just... maybe next time give me a heads-up, if you can?" Even if I were mad, I wouldn't say a word. The last thing I want is for there to be tension in a cabin of six women. That would make for a *long* summer.

"Definitely." She hesitates, dropping her voice to a whisper. "And it's okay, you know."

"What's okay?" I glance over my shoulder at her again, to see her biting her plump bottom lip.

"I mean, if you want to watch. Or more. It's okay."

"I... don't," I stutter, feeling heat crawl up my face. Her perfectly manicured brow arches, as if she's calling my bluff. She knows I was hiding in my little corner, spying on her and Rachel. "I like guys."

"That doesn't mean you don't like to watch." She shrugs playfully. "You're curious. And we're hot. And Ronan is *really* hot. It's normal."

Is it?

I heave a sigh of frustration. Nothing feels normal about Alaska.

"Just thought you should know that we'd be okay with it." She winks and ducks out of my stall, humming softly.

~

IT'S two minutes to one when I approach the service entrance of Penthouse Cabin One, this odd mixture of guilt, and hurt, and anger, and dread weighing down each step.

I still have no idea what my answer is going to be—go back to Greenbank? Or face Henry, day in day out. Feel *this* every day as I approach this door. Will it get better?

I'm ten feet away from swiping my key card when the main door flies open. Scott barrels out, the back of his hand testing his mouth where his lip has been split and blood trickles down his chin. More blood leaks from his nose, and his left eye is red and puffy, the beginnings of a bruise already evident.

I can't keep my mouth from dropping at the shocking sight. Someone has punched the hell out of him.

Did Henry and his brother just get into a fistfight?

Scott slows when he sees me, a glower filling his eyes. "You may want to come back in an hour or so," he mutters, passing by me and heading down the path toward the main lodge.

I frown after him. Why?

Oh my God. Did he hurt Henry?

Panic hits me as I rush through the entrance, visions of him lying in a pool of blood by the dining table making my heart pound in my chest. The interior door is propped open this time, so I don't hesitate to run into the cabin, holding my breath for fear of what I might find.

I quickly zero in on Henry. His back is to me and he's standing in front of his desk, his focus beyond the window

Relief overwhelms me. He appears fine.

"Fuck!" He explodes suddenly, picking up a glass and whipping it clear across the room. It hits the fireplace and shatters. Countless pieces of glass scatter in every which direction.

A small shriek escapes me, pulling his head slightly to the left, toward me. But he doesn't turn to acknowledge my presence with a glance.

What the hell happened in here?

One of the side table lamps lays in pieces, scattered over the hardwood. The crystal decanter has been knocked over too. It's not broken, but amber liquid has spilled everywhere, and the pungent sweet smell of liquor hangs in the air.

Finally I gather enough nerve. "Henry?"

He looks down to his right hand, flexing it open and closed. "Get me some ice." After a pause, he adds in an unsettlingly calm voice, "Please."

I grab the ice bucket and fill it with ice from the freezer compartment, then snatch a towel from the powder room, and bring it over to him.

The softest "thanks" slips from his lips. He still hasn't met my eyes, his calm and somber mask unexpected given he just delivered a pummeling to his brother and threw a glass in anger.

Uncomfortable silence hangs.

Finally, I can't take it anymore. "I just saw Scott."

He sticks his hand into the ice bucket, a slight wince curling his lip. "It's been a while since I've hit anyone."

At least three times, from the looks of it. "Do you want to talk about it?"

His jaw tenses and I figure he's not going to answer. "The last time I saw Kiera, we left things on good terms. I told her she could come back to Wolf and work elsewhere, but she thought it best to start fresh somewhere else. So I was... surprised that she'd be so vindictive." He finally turns to settle a cold blue gaze on me. "Scott's the one who convinced her to go after me with the false accusations."

My mouth drops open. "Are you serious?" His own brother, trying to get him thrown in jail? "How do you know?"

"When you told me about what he said to you in the elevator, I started to wonder how low he'd go to have me cut out. So I had the PI that my lawyer hired to deal with Kiera look into his corporate phone records and the jet travel logs. Turns out he was in New York about a month ago without any of us knowing. He went to meet her, and start filling her head with bullshit. A lot of the same shit he fed to you, about how I had used her all along, how I was fucking around with other women.

"It was right after that Kiera asked me out for a drink and seduced me in my car. It was a moment of weakness on my part, because we had ended it months before. That's how she ended up with my DNA on her panties. The ones she decided to hold on to."

That answers my question about why they'd slept together so recently. "Are you sure?"

"She's admitted to it all. She told us everything. About how, when Scott visited her that first time, he told her I was looking for another attractive assistant to use in Alaska. She knew enough about Scott to not accept what he was trying to reel her into. Still, she was angry and hurt.

"It wasn't hard for him to call up Wolf Cove and find out that I'd brought you in as my assistant. That's when he contacted Kiera again, with your picture and some story about staff speculating that we were basically living together in the cabin. It made her crazy, and upset, and he coupled that with the choice of claiming sexual assault or having her husband find out about the affair. He told her that I'd pay the money in a heartbeat just to shut her up, and that all she needed to do was keep the lie about the assault going until they pressed charges. He knew that was all it would take to force my father's hand. She could recant after that and wouldn't get into any trouble because the police won't ever charge a potential rape victim, for fear of deterring others in future."

My mind is swirling with all this new information, with the extent that Henry's own brother would go to take over the business. It's impossible to comprehend, but I don't come from this world. Is *this* what it's like to be a part of the

Wolf family, to be surrounded by so much greed and wealth that you'll do anything, hurt anyone? Maybe this is why their mother ran off!

As angry and upset as I am with Henry, I'm also relieved for him. "So, she's dropped the charges?"

He pulls his hand out of the bucket and takes a look at his knuckles. They're red but they don't look too bad. "Yes. And taking the severance package we offered her. Her husband now knows that there was no sexual assault, so I'm not sure where that will leave things with them. But that's not my problem. If she had just come to me in the first place, I would have informed my father what Scott was up to and we could have avoided all of this."

"So, what happens now?"

"Now, my father gives me controlling power of Wolf Hotels. He's not waiting until the end of June. He's having the paperwork drawn up today."

"All because of Scott?"

"To spite Scott, or because he knows I'm the right choice...." Henry shrugs. "I don't really care. I get what I want and it's what's best for the company."

"Well... that's good. I'm happy that it all worked out for you." It doesn't change what happened between us but I do mean it.

"Are you?" He levels me with steely blue eyes, and I instinctively tense. There's something behind that gaze, as if he's restraining himself. And I remember that he smashed a glass. He's still *very* angry about something.

"Of course. I wouldn't want you to be accused of something you didn't do."

His lips twitch. "You mean, like being accused of fucking the key media contact who's doing a write up of my hotel?"

Is he seriously *still* going to deny it? I swallow my anger, but it's impossible. "I know what I saw." The looks, the touches....

Henry folds his arms over his chest, ignoring his sore fist. "And what exactly did you see? Because I know what *I* saw on the security footage, when I reviewed it to see what the fuck went on that made you think I was with her—me, leaving the main lodge late Friday and heading back to my cabin, fighting the urge to demand that my assistant come here so I can bury myself in her."

My heart skips a beat but I don't get a chance to even process that because Henry's still talking.

"My brother, appearing at the bar the moment I'm gone to lubricate Roshana with enough martinis that she willingly brought him back to her suite."

My stomach drops. "Scott?"

"My idiot brother knew how important Roshana is to Wolf Cove, so he decided it'd be a brilliant idea to fuck her on Friday night."

Wait. What? Scott was with Roshana Friday? Not Henry? All those condoms from Friday night weren't on account of Henry? I frantically wrack my brain with everything I know and think I know. Scott's the one who told me that Henry and Roshana were together Friday night, but he's also convinced there's something going on between us. So Scott lied. But of course he lied. He figured he'd get a reaction out of the poor dumb assistant who's head over heels for her boss. To get me to confess to our inappropriate relationship. And he's been around the hotel industry all his life; I'm sure he knows what staff is like. He probably made sure to leave her place littered with condoms just to spark gossip through the housekeeping staff.

My heart begins racing.

If that's true....

Henry's voice has turned icy. "What's wrong, Abbi? You look *guilty*. Did you do something that you're perhaps ashamed of?"

I feel the blood leave my face. "No," I whisper.

"Really?" I swear I hear Henry's teeth crack from his jaw clenching so hard. "How was Michael this morning?"

Oh my God.

Henry knows.

How the *hell* does he know?

Tears sting my eyes, because I *do* feel guilty. I *am* ashamed.

But... no, it doesn't matter, I remind myself, as I wipe the teardrops from my cheek. "I saw you last night, leaving the lobby with Roshana and that blonde in the red dress."

"You saw me walking her back to her cabin, which is directly beside *my* cabin, and so you just figured you should go and fuck someone else."

"I know what I saw."

Anger radiates from him. "Well, I hope it was worth it because Michael is on the ferry as we speak."

"What!" Did I hear him correctly? "You *fired* him? You can't do that!"

"And yet I did."

"But he didn't do anything wrong!"

"You let him fuck you!" All calm composure is gone as Henry's booming voice fills the cabin and his face contorts with rage.

Is he kidding me? "You were off screwing *two* other women!" I know I sound hysterical now but I don't care. The tears have begun to slip unbidden again. I don't think I cried this much even after Jed hurt me.

Henry dips his head away from me, studying the hardwood floor, trying to calm himself, I presume. When he finally looks up again, I see something floating in his gaze that I can't read.

But that steely face that I now see, I know well. "You're right," he says in that overly calm, cool voice. "I did fuck two women. Right over there." He nods toward the living room, where dirty drink glasses litter the coffee table and the cushions are all out of sorts. Housekeeping hasn't been in to clean up because Henry doesn't allow housekeeping in here. "I sat in that chair with a scotch and watched the two of them tongue fuck each other, and then I took turns shoving my cock into first one, then the other." Each new detail is like a needle-sharp blade poking at my already aching heart. I don't need to hear the specifics. It only brings it to life in my head. "It was nice, you know, being with two women who knew what they were doing."

I recoil at the well-timed insult. Now he's *trying* to hurt me.

But Henry doesn't let up, his face twisting with a vicious smirk. "Don't you dare play the wounded fawn, Abbi. You do play it so well, don't you? But you didn't waste any time spreading your legs for another guy."

How did he turn this into *my* fault? "You can't fire Michael."

"Well, that's where you're wrong. I can do whatever I want." He examines the cuff of his dress shirt and, noting the spots of blood on the crisp white material, he begins unbuttoning this shirt.

"No you can't," I hear myself say, taking a step back, away from him. "You *can't* just do whatever you want."

"I will own 61 percent of Wolf Hotels by Tuesday, so you are very wrong about that."

"Does your father know about us?" It's a simple, innocent question.

And yet the flare in Henry's eyes tells me he sees the underlying threat immediately. Of course he does. A good predator is always five steps ahead of their prey.

I clear my throat, trying to sound more confident, even through the tears and the shakiness. "I'm guessing he asked and you convinced him that nothing happened between us. You lied right to his face."

He's lost interest in his soiled shirt, turning to face me head-on. "What are you trying to get at, Abbi?"

I won't let him punish Michael. "That you need to give Michael his job back." *Or else.*

I don't need to say it out loud. By the tightness in his jaw, he gets it. "Are you threatening me?" He takes a step forward.

I take three back, suddenly wondering exactly how bad an idea this was. "I'm trying to make sure you do what's right."

"And let me guess, letting you stay at Wolf Cove and work wherever you want is also the right thing to do?"

Yes.

"And if I don't give you what you want, you're going to tell my father that I fucked you, after I swore up and down that I didn't?"

I swallow my wariness.

He peels his dress shirt off, tossing it to the chair, his casual persona back. "That sounds an awful lot like blackmail, Abbi. Did you not just learn anything from the situation with Kiera? Did you not learn about how I deal with these kinds of situations?"

That he doesn't go down without a fight.

And here I am, threatening the one thing he wants more than anything: Wolf Hotels.

What the hell was I thinking?

Suddenly, the thought of staying at Wolf Cove no longer appeals to me. I'd rather deal with Mama and Jed than what Henry will do to me. It really is the devil you know versus the devil you don't situation, and I suspect making an enemy of Henry would be the worst decision of my life. "I'll hand in my things to Belinda and be on the next ferry out today." I turn to leave.

"You're not leaving Alaska."

I squeeze my eyes shut. "You said I had to stay and work for you, or quit and go back to Greenbank. So, I quit. Have a great life, Henry." I wish my voice wouldn't waver so much.

"That was then." He steps right through the spilled scotch, tracking the liquid toward me, stopping maybe a foot away, his towering body looming over me. "You know, Kiera was going to drop the charges and the lawsuit. I knew that, even before I knew what Scott had done. I knew she would make the right decision because the PI was going to show her the video I had of her spread-eagle on a table. The one I've been keeping, just in case."

My mouth drops open.

"The camera never gets a good view of my face but Kiera... well, her family, her husband, anyone who clicked on that link after we leaked it over the Internet would get a good view of *all* of her. And I promised her that I'd make sure everyone she knew would see it. I'd say she made the right choice with backing off, don't you?"

My heart is hammering in my chest.

"To be fair, she had no idea that a video like that exists. Had she, I'm sure Scott wouldn't have been able to manipulate her into all of this in the first place." His eyes drop to my mouth. "Most women would think twice before blackmailing a man if they knew he had something as revealing as that on them. Wouldn't you think so?"

Prickles run down my back. What is Henry saying, exactly?

Has he videotaped *us* having sex?

My eyes skate around the cabin's rafters, looking for evidence of a camera. It could be anywhere.

As if my mind and heart haven't been reeling enough over the past few days, he's sending me into a new tailspin. Who is this man? Not that I ever mistook Henry for an angel, with his dirty mouth and brash style, but he's telling me that he videotapes himself having sex with women, without their knowledge?

How could I have been so wrong about him? How could he be the Henry I fell for—gave myself willingly to—only to then so quickly morph to *this*? Was he always *this*, and I was just too blind to see it? I can't keep the tears from trickling out my eyes. "Please don't do this."

His mouth opens but he hesitates, squeezes his eyes shut. The chiseled lines of his jaw clench as he hardens his face. "You can go now, but don't even think about getting on that ferry. Be here at 7:00 a.m. sharp tomorrow morning."

I rush out the door.

~

"Abbi, aren't you going to grab dinner?"

"No. I have a terrible headache that I'm trying to overcome," I lie to Katie, pulling my covers to my neck. Here, curled in a ball within my hidden cocoon of a bunk, curtain drawn, I feel safe. If I go out there, people may ask questions.

Does Katie know that I slept with Michael last night?

Does she know that Henry fired Michael because of me?

She hasn't said a word to me about Michael, but I figure the gossip must be running rampant.

I almost went to Michael's cabin. Henry said Michael was already on the ferry but I hoped he was wrong. I wanted to talk to him, to apologize to him. But then I started to worry that he'd somehow figure out why he was fired, and then one thing would lead to another and the whole town of Greenbank would get to see me having sex on some video that Henry leaked because I was stupid enough to try and blackmail him. So I ran straight here.

I don't even have Michael's number to text him and see where he is, how he's doing.

"Do you want me to bring you back something?"

"No. I'm okay, thanks." I won't be eating tonight. I won't be sleeping either.

I'll be too busy dreading the rest of my summer in Alaska.

fifteen

The sight of Penthouse Cabin One sparked a wild thrill in my body before.

Now, the moment I round the bend in the covered path to see it, my stomach flips with unease.

A housekeeping cart sits outside of the main door. I guess Henry called them to clean up all the broken glass and booze. Good, because I'm not doing it. I don't want to be here. I dragged my feet all the way from my cabin after a night of tossing and turning.

I hate him, I tell myself over and over again. Because if I can be angry, and hate him, then it distracts me from how hurt I am, I'm learning.

Taking a deep breath, I swipe my key card and enter through the service entrance.

"Hello?"

"Yes?" Bell dumps a dustpan full of glass into the bucket before looking up to see me.

It's strange to see another staff member in here, even if I know her. I've been the only one to step foot inside since I started working for him, besides that one visit from Belinda and then Michael, of course. "Oh, hey." I do a quick glance around. "Do you know when Mr. Wolf will be back?" Maybe I'll luck out and only have to deal with him through abrupt text messaging.

"No idea. They just told me to clean the place out and get it ready for rental."

Rental?

That's when I notice that his laptop isn't on the desk anymore. And the checkered jacket he wore to cut wood isn't hanging on the hook.

And his hiking boots aren't sitting on the doormat.

In fact, all of his personal possessions seem to be gone.

A strange sinking feeling hits my stomach as I wander into the bedroom.

The bed's been stripped and remade. And the closet is empty of all his designer suits and casual clothes.

Henry's gone.

I wander out the door with an absent "Thanks," to Bell, and pull out my phone to see if maybe Henry texted me and I somehow missed it.

Nothing.

Not a single message from Henry.

What the hell? What does this mean for my job?

~

"Hey."

Belinda peers up over her glasses at me. "Good, you're here. I'll need your iPad and your work cell phone now." Her tone is clipped and businesslike. She's back to her normal, overly calm persona.

My stomach sinks. *So that's it? I've been, what, fired?*

"You can change in your cabin, or in the restroom near

the cleaners, up to you, but you better hurry." She glances at her watch. "The crew will be starting their shift soon. I'm sorry I don't have a proper uniform for you here yet, but Mr. Wolf didn't exactly give me much time to prepare."

I frown. "The crew?"

"Yes. The Outdoor crew. That you asked to be reassigned to now that Mr. Wolf has to go back to New York." She's speaking to me slow and loud, as if I'm hard of hearing.

Henry has gone back to New York?

Clearly Belinda thinks I was aware this was all happening. Why shouldn't she? That would be the normal thing to do: tell your assistant that she won't be needed anymore and that she's been reassigned.

But Henry didn't tell me that. Instead, he demanded that I stay and used the threat of a pornographic video to keep me from getting on a ferry and going home. Why put me through all that anxiety if he planned on leaving and letting me transfer out anyway?

Other than to toy with me.

To punish me.

To exert his power and control over me.

Maybe he's still screwing with my head now. Giving me what I asked for, only so he can take it away.

My stomach twists with hurt and anger.

"You're going to be reporting to Darryl Sykes, and you'll be working on a team with twelve guys. *Twelve guys,* Abbi. You're the only female. You'll be expected to carry your own weight around there, but Mr. Wolf seems to think you'll manage." Belinda's lifts her brow knowingly. "For the record, I think you're insane for wanting to work in the crew. You and them," she shakes her head to herself. "Let's just say I hope you've developed a thick skin. And if you haven't... just come and tell me and we can move you to Housekeeping, okay?"

"Okay." There was a time, just weeks ago, when she wasn't being anywhere near as accommodating, but I guess she was stuck playing whatever game Henry was leading.

She holds her hands out, waiting for the electronics still within my grasp.

I hand them over to her absently, still in shock over this unexpected turn of events.

"Mr. Wolf asked that I remind you of the confidentiality agreement that you signed. I've forwarded a scanned copy of it to your e-mail address for your records. You should review it."

I pull my personal phone out and see the notification from her sitting on my screen. I click on it and the attachment opens up. There's my signature at the bottom of the attachment. The day I signed this, I had no idea what kinds of secrets I'd be keeping. This is clearly his way of reminding me that nothing has changed.

"I didn't mean review it right now!" She glances at her watch irritably. "You should really get going. Darryl will be in shortly. He'll be waiting for you at the gates, and he doesn't like to wait."

I spin on my heels, ready to make a mad dash for the cleaners, where I can pick up whatever scraped-together uniform they managed to find for me.

But first....

It's the last thing I want to do right now, and yet I'm compelled to get answers so I don't spend the entire day in my head, concocting scenarios, none of them with happy endings for me.

I step into the stairwell where I can gain more privacy than out in the hotel hallways. Pulling out my personal phone, I find where I programmed his number—something I did the first day I started with him, for no other reason than because I wanted Henry Wolf's phone number on my personal phone—and I hit Call.

And I hold my breath.

He's not going to answer. Why would he answer? He's probably already on a—

"Wolf."

My heart stutters.

"Make it quick, Abbi. My plane is about to leave."

How does he know it's me calling? Does it show in the display? "I was just.... You're leaving."

"Is there a question?"

"Why are you leaving?"

"Because I have a hotel chain to run. I can't do that from the wilderness."

"But you said you were staying for the summer."

"Things changed." I can't help but hear the sharp edge in his already abrupt tone.

"I'm on my way to work with the Outdoor crew."

"Good. You got what you wanted."

"What I *wanted*?" What I wanted was for Henry *not* to break my heart by sleeping with another woman. I want to not feel like my insides have been torn out of my body, leaving this hollow ache behind.

He sighs. "You're young and inexperienced and naive, Abbi. I knew better. I was just so overcome by stress, and you were there. And *so* easy."

"Fuck you." I can't believe those two words slip out my mouth. I don't think I've ever actually said them to anyone, not even Jed. But what's more, I can't believe the real, raw anger that laces them.

"Take care of yourself and enjoy Alaska, Abbi. Go and fuck a few more people. I know I will." The line goes dead.

A sob tears out of my throat, and only then do I realize that I'm actually crying. God, I hate to admit it but Mama was right. I've seen Henry's teeth now, and he delivers one painful bite. A one-minute phone call with Henry and I'm bawling in a stairwell.

Furiously wiping away my tears, I rush down the stairs to change my uniform.

For the first time truly aware that, for all its vast, rich wilderness, Alaska feels completely empty.

sixteen

"Miss Mitchell."

The moment Darryl Sykes lays soft gray eyes on me, the moment I see the slight shake of his head and hear his sigh, I know what he thinks of this entire arrangement. Fortunately for me, he chooses not to share that opinion with me. "Get on into the truck. But spray yourself with this first." He tosses a can of bug spray in the air. I fumble with it before dropping it into the mud.

Darryl sighs again, this one louder and full of exasperation.

I offer him a smile of apology and then quickly douse myself from head to toe.

Mercifully, the uniform department had one pair of women's steel-toe boots available. They're two sizes too big and I feel like a clown, but they'll work. So will the pair of men's small pants that are loose but fitted enough not to fall off my hips. My Wolf Cove t-shirt fits, and if I roll up the sleeves of the Cove outdoor jacket, it'll do.

All in all, I look like a little girl dressed in her daddy's uniform, but I just have to grin and bear it until a size that fits me arrives. They said they're shipping a few sets up from Seattle. Thankfully some Wolf Hotel locations believe in equal opportunity between sexes when it comes to outdoor maintenance.

We ride in complete silence, and I'm okay with that. Darryl doesn't seem like the kind of guy who talks much. I'm guessing he's in his late forties, wiry, with shaggy salt-and-pepper hair and a thick mustache over his lip. I've seen him leave on a fishing boat after shift every day, so I'm pretty sure he doesn't live on the resort. He looks like the type of guy who sits in his living room alone with a bottle of Bud in one hand and TV remote in the other, happy not to deal with other humans.

It takes me a minute to realize that Darryl's taking me to the exact clearing where Henry brought me that one time, and the second I do, a sharp pang stirs in my chest, of the fantasy I wish I could go back to, to forget the bitter disappointment that has followed.

Three trucks are lined side by side, and six big, muscular guys are busy chopping and stacking wood into the back of them. There's clearly a "type" when they hired staff for the outdoor crew: strong and rugged.

A stir of nervous flutters spark in my stomach. *Do they know I'm coming to work with them? What are they going to think?* I wish I didn't care so much about what other people think.

"Grab yourself a pair of gloves. You'll be helping to stack wood today. We have a lot to replenish after the busy weekend and they're calling for rain for the next few days, so we'll be out here for most of the day." Darryl eyes me warily. "Hope you're up to it."

I collect the pair of workers' gloves, too large for my

childlike hands, and slide out of the truck without a word, because it doesn't matter what I say. Darryl has already made up his mind about me.

Connor sees me first, and it seems to catch him off guard because his face twists up in shock. Ronan, standing over a hunk of wood with an ax in hand, his jacket already peeled off despite the cool morning air, freezes midswing.

I don't think I can deal with them today. Especially not when Ronan watches me with easy eyes and a relaxed smile, not an ounce of embarrassment. As if I didn't walk in on him having sex with my roommates. As if I don't know what he looks like beneath those clothes of his, how big his dick is when it's erect, the kinds of sounds he makes when he's turned on.

My cheeks flare with heat.

"Listen up, everyone. Abbi Mitchell will be joining us in the crew for the rest of the summer, or as long as she decides she wants to put up with you idiots." A round of soft chuckles surrounds me. "I expect you all to treat her with respect. I better not hear anything different. Especially about you two." He gestures at Ronan and Connor.

"Best behavior, Scout's honor!" Connor promises, but that grin on his face makes me believe otherwise.

With that, Darryl climbs back into his truck and rolls away.

Great. That's exactly how I want to be introduced to these guys. And now they're all staring at me. Thank God for these baggy clothes.

I duck my head and trudge over toward the pile of chopped wood, my feet suddenly weighted down by my oversized boots.

"So, you got your sabbatical?" Connor hoists two large pieces of wood, one in each hand, seemingly with no effort.

I sigh, reaching down to grab a log. "Something like that."

"You don't look too happy about it."

"I'm...." What am I? This *is* what I asked for, after all, when I foolishly tried to blackmail Henry. So, did I succeed? I still don't know what's happened to Michael, and I'm afraid to ask anyone. "I'm surprised is all. I didn't really get much warning about the change." I glance at the other guys, who I've seen around the lodge with Ronan and Connor, but I've never actually spoken to them. I can only imagine what they'll be saying about me when I'm out of earshot.

Connor throws an arm around my shoulder, pulling me into his side. "Well, don't worry. Ronan and I'll do all the hard work. You can just sit and watch if you want."

When Ronan winks at me, I realize they're not talking about crew work at all, and Ronan must have told him what happened in my cabin. Do they all think I like to watch people have sex now?

I shrug his arm off, my cheeks burning with embarrassment. "I can handle the hard work. I've worked on a farm all my life."

"Oh, really." Ronan chuckles and holds out the ax.

Seeing the challenge in his eyes, I march over and yank it from his grasp, silently thanking my asshole boss for having the decency to teach me how to swing one of these while he seduced me into giving up my virginity.

Remembering the details from Henry's lesson—how to stand, how far apart my feet should be, where to aim—I try to ignore all the doubting eyes on me and I bring the blade down on the line once, twice. The third time, two pieces of wood tumble off the platform.

"Damn! She can put out fires and split wood. I think I'm

in love," Connor bellows from behind me, followed by a round of claps and hollers.

I'm so proud of myself, I can't keep the stupid grin from my face. I level Ronan with a look. "Where's the next piece?"

He simply lingers there for a long, silent moment, a mixture of surprise and newfound respect reflected on his handsome face, before he heaves over another chunk of wood and sets it up for me. "Well, all right then."

"And Ronan?"

"Yeah?"

"Leave me the hell alone, today. Please. It's already been a bad day." I beg with my eyes, hoping to appeal to his more basic human emotions, buried somewhere deep within that deviant body of his.

He says nothing, but the flicker that passes through his eyes makes me believe he might understand.

seventeen

"Those green things, they don't get any better when they're cold."

I drag my eyes up from the brussels sprouts on my plate to see Miguel's wide grin. He's making his rounds with a bin, loading in dirty dishes to take to the back.

The smile slides off when he sees my sullen expression. "What's the matter?"

"Nothing. Just tired."

"Right. I heard about that. So, you're part of the crew now? Crazy. How'd that happen?"

I've seen the look on his face plenty of times already today. A lot of surprise, even more doubt. I sigh. Everyone's been asking me that exact same question, along with "Why didn't you go with Wolf? Doesn't he need an assistant?" I give Miguel the standard answer that I've given to everyone else. "I knew my job as his assistant would only be a temporary one."

"So, this is really what you want?"

"I like being outdoors. It's what I originally applied for, so yes." So, so long ago, it seems now. Back when all I wanted to do was get away from Jed and Greenbank, sure that I'd never get over him. Unable to so much as imagine looking at another guy.

Boy, was I wrong on so many counts.

"Well, then, I guess that's good." He pauses. "It's a good look for you. It's hard though."

"Yeah." I reach up to rub my shoulders. A full day of swinging an ax and loading wood, then unloading and stacking has reminded me how inactive I've been through the school year. I'm going to have a hard time getting out of bed tomorrow morning.

I could *really* use a massage.

"Hey, do you know—" I begin to ask about Michael but then stop myself abruptly. Miguel knows that Michael was with a girl two nights ago. If I ask flat-out, he may put two and two together, and I can't risk anyone putting two and two together to equal Abbi was sleeping with Henry Wolf.

Henry has turned me into a paranoid freak.

But I need to know exactly what happened with Michael because no one has said a word about him being fired and shipped off yet.

Deciding on a more roundabout approach, I toy with my steamed rice and ask casually, "So, what's the latest gossip? Anything interesting happening around here?"

Miguel shrugs. "Rachel came back."

"Yeah. I know. She's my roommate."

"That's right! I forgot. A cabin full of beautiful ladies."

I stifle the urge to roll my eyes. After hearing how he refers to those "beautiful ladies" when he doesn't think they're around, his charm holds no power over me. "Anything else?"

"Nah. Same ol' shit."

I just don't get it. Miguel would have heard about his roommate being fired, wouldn't he?

Unless he wasn't fired?

Do I dare hope that Henry was lying? Or maybe he changed his mind?

"You still eating?"

I offer Miguel a weak smile. "I might. Thanks." My phone rings then, and I'm torn between relief that I can end my conversation with Miguel and annoyance that I have to deal with a call from home.

"See ya around, sweet Abbi." Miguel winks and moves off to the next table with that swagger of his.

With a sigh, I answer. My day has already hit rock bottom. She can't possibly make it any worse. "Hey, Mama. Sorry I didn't have a chance to call back."

"What on *earth* have you done to yourself, Abigail?"

I frown, unease sliding down my spine like a trickle of cold water. "What are you talking about?"

"There I was, mindin' my own business at Sunday service and Mary Jane shows me a picture of *my daughter* looking like a jezebel!"

I don't even know which Mary Jane she's talking about—we know at least five—but now I'm panicking, especially given Henry's threat. "What are you talking about?" For Mama to refer to me as a jezebel—a name that up until now has been reserved for Jed's girlfriend—is serious.

"Some big event at that hotel you're working at. There were pictures posted on that Tweeter thing."

Oh. I heave a sigh of relief. "You mean from the grand opening?"

"Alls I know is you were in a skimpy black dress and those ridiculous shoes, and I could barely recognize you under all that muck on your face. And what on Gods green earth did you do to your hair! You've ruined it!"

I roll my eyes. I expected as much from her. "Mary Jane, who?"

"Lucy's little sister."

Of course. Lucy. The one who e-mailed me, asking about Alaska. I taunted her with a link to a picture of Henry, mainly so it would get back to Jed, so people would stop saying I'm heartbroken and want him back. "Why are they looking at Wolf Hotels on Twitter?" I already know the answer to that, before she gives it to me.

"They're all obsessed with what you're doin' in Alaska and this boss of yours. And stop trying to change the subject."

Of course they are. Because they don't know the real him, like I so unfortunately do now. "I was required to wear that dress." I stubbornly add, "And I don't think I looked bad."

"You had everyone's tongues waggin' around here. I can't believe I had to defend my own daughter. What kind of employer would require you to dress like that as his assistant, you tell me that!"

She doesn't really want to hear the answer to that.

And I don't want to talk about Henry—or what I've been doing up here—with anyone, including Mama. "How are things in Greenbank? How's Dad?" I haven't talked to him at all since I got here, which isn't entirely unusual. He's not much of a phone guy and he's hardly actually at home. I'll have to call when I know he's around. Basically, at sunrise, at lunch, or at dinnertime. Otherwise he's in the fields or sleeping. The time difference is making it hard.

She heaves a sigh. "The usual. I haven't been sleepin' much, worryin' about you."

I hear the sound of her sucking back a sip of something. "You're drinking coffee?"

"Just my usual cup."

I roll my eyes again. "It's almost ten at night over there, Mama. You're not sleeping because of caffeine. Don't be trying to give me a guilt trip about that."

"I'm not givin' you a guilt trip. If you feel guilty, then it must be because you're doing something you shouldn't be doing."

Good old manipulative Mama.

The crew strolls in then, all freshly showered and changed, and my spirits sink. I was hoping to avoid them for the rest of the day, to be honest. Not that they've been anything but civilized. Ronan was decent enough to leave me alone, and Connor made only a few mild sexual innuendos that actually made me chuckle.

But I'm exhausted and sore and all I wanted to do was grab a quick bite to eat in peace and then go back to shower and curl up in bed.

Ronan and I lock eyes for a split second, but I avert my eyes quickly.

"Abigail! Are you even listening?"

"Yes!" I totally wasn't listening.

"That place and those people are obviously no good for you. You've had your time to do whatever it is you needed to do, and now it's time to come home, before you have major regrets. I'm sure Reverend Enderbey doesn't like seeing his future daughter-in-law splashed all over the Internet, especially not dressed like that."

I let out a loud groan of frustration. Every conversation with her is the same. She is relentless and delusional. She's one of those people who thinks that if she keeps harping on a topic, she'll eventually get her way. The worst part is, she usually does.

"For the last time, Mama," I manage to get out through gritted teeth. "Jed and I are *not* getting back together. I don't care if you're right and he gets bored of Cammie. I don't care if he changes his mind. I don't want him back. I will *never* want him back." It's time to lay down the law, because I can't keep dealing with this. I'll go insane. "You want to know why I don't call home more often? Why I avoid your phone calls? For this exact reason. I'm sick and tired of the broken record. I love you, but from now on, every time you bring Jed up, I will hang up the phone."

"Abigail Margaret Mitchell, I am your mama and you do not speak to me like that."

"Too bad, Mama. You're not respecting my wishes and you won't let me move on!" I'm not bothering to be quiet. I don't care who can hear me anymore.

A strangled gasp fills my ear. "After all your daddy and I have done for you, paying for your schooling, raising you right, giving you everything you have, you have the nerve to speak to me like that."

Here we go, the second stage of Mama's guilt trip. "I appreciate all of that, but that doesn't mean you get to make my decisions for me. I'm an adult now."

"I don't try to make your decisions. I simply try to guide you in the *right direction*!"

The *right direction*—to spend the rest of my life with my cheating ex-fiancé because it looks good for the Mitchell family that he's the reverend's son. It took me a while to realize that this is what it's really about: our standing in Greenbank. Our standing with the church. She's so caught up in that, she can't see anything else.

The guys head toward the cafeteria. Except for Ronan. He's weaving through the tables, on his way toward me.

"I've gotta go. My boss is calling," I lie. I can't deal with her anymore. Not today.

"And your boss is more important than me?"

No, nobody is more important than you, Mama, because you're a narcissist.

"Talk to you later." I hang up before she can respond, dropping my phone into my pocket just as Ronan stops next to my seat, the smell of fresh soap enveloping me. While I wasn't sweating today, I know I'm far from clean. I really should just get up and go right now. "Aren't you getting dinner?"

"Connor's grabbing a tray for me." He spins a chair around to straddle it, his knee bumping into mine. "You okay, red?"

I tuck my legs in tighter and stab my roast beef with a fork. "I'm fantastic."

"Good. I was afraid you weren't, the way you ran out of your cabin that night."

Is he actually going to bring that up, right *here*? I glare at him, hoping my warning is clear—that I never want to talk about that night with him, especially now that I'm going to have to work with him every single day.

"Hey, boss." Connor comes up from behind to set his tray down on the other side of me. He hands one to Ronan. He eases into his seat. "Long-ass day, huh?" He shoves a slice of roast beef into his mouth, then washes it down with beer, before winking at me.

"Yeah. But I liked it." I will not show these guys my physical pain, I promise myself as I quietly eat my cooled plate of food.

Other guys begin trickling in from the cafeteria line to take seats at our table.

"I'll get you a beer," a guy in a security uniform says to another. The badge clipped to his shirt reads Corbin.

"Fuck that. You'll need to buy me a case for me to ever agree to swap with you again," the guy trailing him says. He's also in a security guard uniform, with a badge that reads Mark. I immediately recognize his voice as the security guard roommate from Michael's cabin. He looks exactly like the burly teddy bear I imagined when I heard his voice.

Does he know what happened to Michael?

"Come on! It's *a bit* funny," Corbin says, smiling.

Mark drops his tray onto the table. "Nope. It's not."

"Why would you want to sit in a room all night and watch monitors, anyway?"

"Same reason you do. So I can watch people screwing in the stairwell. And *not* get pissed on."

Right. He's still angry about that.

"Watching people screw. What would that be like? Hey, red?" Ronan murmurs under his breath, knocking my arm with his elbow.

I don't think anyone heard but still, my face explodes with heat. I stuff a brussels sprout into my mouth to avoid having to answer.

"So, how many cameras are there around this place, anyway?" Connor asks.

"Dude..." Mark groans, cutting into his meat. "So many. Unless you're inside your room or the showers, assume you're on camera when you're on this property."

Cameras, everywhere. Does that mean that the Wolf security watched my mini breakdown in the stairwell this morning?

"Seriously? Fuck... Can't get away with anything," Connor mutters.

"No. *You* really can't." Corbin points his breadstick at Connor and then laughs, like he's already caught Connor on camera doing something untoward. I wonder if that something untoward is with Tillie. Though I doubt she's dumb enough to get caught on video.

Not like me.

"Not unless you know where the blind spots are, and there aren't many," Mark adds.

There's a round of ketchup-passing and salt-tossing back and forth around me, as the guys trade comments about hot guests and hot coworkers through mouthfuls, not in the least bit concerned that they may offend me.

"He's alive!" Mark announces as Andy takes a seat. "Thought you were going to be incapacitated for a few days." He laughs when he says that, like there's some funny story behind it. Obviously he knows something that I don't.

"Yeah, that was the plan," Andy mutters in his throaty Australian accent. "But my shoulder's acting up again."

"Get Aspen to work on it. It's his damn job. What the hell else is he good for?"

"I wish. Aspen's gone. Left yesterday."

My heart skips a beat. *And... finally*. Confirmation that Henry wasn't lying and he really did fire Michael for sleeping with me.

"Gone? What do you mean, gone?" Clearly, Mark had no idea.

"I mean packed up and on the ferry, gone."

Mark's face pinches up. "Like, *fired*?"

"Dunno. He just said he had to go."

"But isn't he, like, Wolf's *guy*?"

Andy shrugs. "Wolf's gone so why keep him up here?"

"Nah. That doesn't make sense. He's one of the favorites on staff. He must have done something to piss Wolf off."

"Like I said. Don't know anything." Andy's gaze flickers to mine for a moment before focusing on his dinner.

Andy does know something: that I slept with Michael the night before he was shipped off.

I drop my focus to my plate.

"Wonder if it has anything to do with what happened with Wolf's brother. You guys heard about that, right?" Corbin asks.

"Right, I saw him storm through the lobby all bloodied. He left on his helicopter right after," Connor says, clearly unconcerned. "Sounds like Wolf and him got into a fistfight. I would have loved to see that." A pause, and then he turns to me. "Hey, were you there to see that?"

"No. I came after." I stuff another sprout into my mouth and chew slowly.

"Damn... his own brother. That's pretty cold. Wonder what that was about?" I feel Ronan watching me as he takes a sip of his beer, and it prickles the hairs on the back of my neck.

And here I was, thinking guys didn't gossip.

Ronan thinks that fight was about me. But it wasn't. It was about his brother trying to have Henry framed for rape and pushed out of the family business, I want to say.

Then again, why am I even defending Henry?

"Probably has something to do with finding out he got his brother's sloppy seconds," Corbin says through mouthfuls.

"Which chick?" Connor asks.

"The one in Penthouse Two."

"Damn." Connor nods his approval, while my chest tightens. I'm not going to sit here and hear details of what these guys may have caught on a security camera. I quietly gather my dishes, hoping to duck out without notice.

No such luck.

"Hey. Where are you going? We're just getting started. It's your inaugural night as part of the crew." Connor scrapes the last forkful of food off his plate, having inhaled his dinner. Ronan's not far behind him.

"I have to call home and then shower," I lie. I'm getting so good at lying.

"You must be sore after working so hard all day. Need any help in the shower?"

My cheeks flush. There are at least ten guys within ear shot. "No."

Connor's rich blue eyes peer up at me. "I'm serious."

"So am I. Where's Tillie, by the way?" And why would she put up with a guy who so openly flirts with *everyone*?

"Probably working. I don't know." His gaze drops to my chest. "We have an understanding."

An understanding. I roll my eyes. What I'll never understand is how these people treat sex so casually.

"We'll be here if you change your mind!" he hollers after me as I drop my tray on the counter.

"I won't," I mutter under my breath as I leave the lodge, intent on a quick shower and then bed. But when I hear laughter as I approach my cabin, I'm forced to continue on past it. *Great*. I can't even hide out in peace.

eighteen

I spot the staff beach, a small sandy inlet with a couple of canoes and kayaks and a paddleboat. It's empty at this time of day, which means I won't have to talk to anyone.

I stroll down the dock, a single stretch of three four-foot sections—tiny compared to the one that receives the ferries and other boats—and perch myself on the end where I can wallow in my own misery.

Curious to see what Mama found so offensive about that picture, I pull my phone out of my pocket and open up Twitter to check the Wolf Hotel account. I'd never been on Twitter before coming to Alaska, but Autumn got me on it, insisting that any good assistant should keep an eye out for things posted online about her boss, when her boss is Henry Wolf.

Sure enough, several media outlets posted pictures from Saturday night's gala, including plenty of Henry in his tux, looking as dashing as he does in real life.

If only people knew what a complete asshole he can be when you piss him off.

It takes a bit of scrolling, but I find the picture that must have Mama all up in arms. I'm standing behind Henry and to the right. I could easily pass for mid-to-late twenties in this picture, my hair a glossy deep red with auburn and gold highlights, my cheekbones high and defined so nicely. Katie's super-bra makes my breasts stand front and center and my waist even tinier than it normally looks next to them. The skirt is a few inches above my knee, which would irk Mama some, but it's not like my butt is hanging out. And my legs look incredible in the heels I borrowed from Rachel, my calf muscles straining just like hers were the day I admired her.

I don't think I've ever looked at a picture of myself and truly loved the way I looked. And I've never looked sexy. Not until now.

No wonder Mama thinks I look like a jezebel.

I'm just sliding my phone back into my pocket when it rings, startling me. I close my eyes and heave a sigh, dreading the number from home showing up on the screen again. I swear, if Mama is calling to give me more grief, I'm going to scream.

But it's not Mama.

It's Jed.

I don't know if that's worse or better.

"Abigail! Hey. I wasn't sure you'd answer."

I instantly pick up on that apologetic tone—low and soft, and contrite. The one Jed always used on me when he had upset me.

"What's up?" I'll bet Mama just got off the phone with the Enderbeys, recapping our entire conversation.

"Nothing much. I just realized how long it's been since I heard your voice. It's been forever."

"Yeah, it has been." *That's because you cheated on me.*

"So what have you been up to in Alaska? Making friends and stuff?"

I haven't really made much of an effort, to be honest, so wrapped up with Henry. Kind of sad, really. Not that I'm going to tell Jed that. "Yeah. I've made some decent friends."

"And you changed your hair?"

Great. First Mama, now Jed. "I saw the pics and I think I looked great. So if you're calling to tell me I look like a jezebel, I'm going to hang up on you, Jed."

"Whoa! Whoa, relax." He chuckles. "You didn't look like a jezebel. You looked good. Like, *really* good. Just... not like the Abigail I remember."

"I'm not her anymore." I'm not sure who I am.

"Yeah, I'm getting that feeling." There's a hint of something in his voice. "So... are you, like..."

"Just spit it out, Jed."

"Are you seeing someone?"

I hesitate, so tempted to lie. But then I'd no doubt be dealing with another phone call from Mama tonight. "No."

He heaves what sounds like a sigh of relief. "That's what I told your Mama, but she's all worried."

Why? Why is Jed so sure I'm not with anyone?

And why the hell is he calling me?

Suddenly I want to make him uncomfortable. "So, how's Cammie?" We've never talked openly about her. I've never so much as uttered her name to him. It's been like a curse word.

He stumbles over his words. "Fine. Uh... we take turns driving back and forth on weekends to see each other. It's a long way. A lot of gas. And she doesn't really love Greenbank or spending so much time around the church, which is kind of a problem, seeing how involved our family is." He pauses. "She's not you, Abigail. I miss you."

A month ago, I was dying to hear him say that. To give me hope that this was all a terrible nightmare that I'd wake up from eventually. But now I hear it and it just reminds me how pathetic I was for not whipping that promise ring at his head the day I caught him cheating on me.

I still have that stupid thing sitting in a box on my little ledge by my bed. I'm going to chuck it into the water the first chance I get.

I don't know if this call is his first step in trying to gain a reconciliation, or keep me on the leash he thinks he still has me on, but either way, I won't let him worm his way in, not when I'm so vulnerable. "No, she won't ever be me, but that was your choice and now you're stuck with her. Or you can find someone else. It doesn't matter, because we're over."

I imagined saying something like that in my head more than once, but it always ended in what-if questions. *What if I regret it? What if I say it and I can't ever take it back?*

But now I've said it out loud and I haven't crumpled with instant remorse. In fact, it felt oddly liberating. Jed has all but vanished from my thoughts since I've come to Alaska.

All because of Henry.

The man who has left me brimming with a full range of emotions. Who I began to care for deeply. Who has lied to me, hurt me, threatened me.

Who I have blackmailed.

Who maybe, just maybe, I may have hurt. Because why else would he so swiftly fire Michael? Why else would he so quickly turn so cruel?

It will never excuse the fact that he slept with Roshana and her friend on Saturday night, and that's the only reason I was even in Michael's bed that night. He probably thought I wouldn't find out. He, of all people, should know how word spreads around here. Cameras, everywhere. Eyes, everywhere.

Or maybe he just plain didn't care if I ever found out, because he also assumed I'd accept it, the same way that I basically accepted how badly Jed treated me.

If there is one positive outcome to this entire mess with Henry, it's that my small-town farm-girl naivety has been effectively squashed.

"Come on, Abigail."

So lost in my thoughts, I forgot that I have Jed in my ear. "Come on, what?" I wipe away the tear that trickles down my cheek. Not for Jed. For the cruel disappointment that is Henry.

"You know we're meant to be together."

I watch a family of ducks float along the edge of the water, weaving in and out of the rocky shoreline, three of the four little ducklings following their mama in a row while the fourth veers off course, earning a loud squawk of annoyance until it gets back in line. Only to veer away again, like it wants to go on its own path. "We *were* meant to be together, and then you broke us. And honestly? I think I'm glad you did. Otherwise I'd still be floating along in the line like that duck, going exactly where Mama wants me to go." I'm in a world of hurt and anger right now, and yet for some reason I still don't regret coming to Alaska, or falling for Henry. I probably should.

Maybe I've gone from being pathetic to just plain screwed up.

"Duck? What duck?"

"The family of ducks on the water! The ones—" I roll my eyes at myself. Why am I explaining anything to Jed? "Nothing."

"Don't tell me you don't still love me. We'll be more than

friends again one day. You'll see. You're just being stubborn but, whether you realize it or not, you're waiting for me."

Jed always was a bit too confident for his own good. I'd grown so used to it that I never really noticed it anymore. But now I do, and it sparks the fit of rage that should have hit me when he told me to wait for him—to save myself for him—all those months ago.

"I am *not* waiting for you! And it's Abbi, *not* Abigail!" My voice echoes across the cove, sending the ducks speeding away and likely disturbing guests at the hotel. I hang up and stick my phone into my pocket before I do what I really want to do right now—pitch it as far as I can into the water so I never have to talk to anyone from Greenbank, Pennsylvania, again.

"So she *can* get angry."

I gasp and jump at the deep male voice before heaving a sigh. "What do you want, Ronan?"

His boots scrape across the dock. "You're in my spot."

"*Your* spot?"

"I come down here every night after dinner. So, yeah, it's my spot." He eases down beside me, crossing his legs beneath him. In one hand he has a beer, and the other a cigarette, which surprises me because I never saw him smoke at work.

"Fine." I make to stand.

"I'm kidding. Stay for a bit." He sticks the cigarette between his lips and flicks the lighter to it. When he peers over to see me glaring at him and it, he merely shrugs.

We sit in silence, me staring out at the water and trying to memorize the beauty of this peaceful night, the sun still high in the sky, the water calm and blue, while Ronan quietly puffs away, the stench of the smoke wafting through the air.

"You're polluting Alaska."

"Yeah, I know, but it goes hand in hand with the beer." He adjusts himself and his leg bumps against mine.

I instinctively pull back, tucking my knees up under my arms, to rest my chin on and bring some warmth to my body. The evening chill is already in the air, and I'm wishing I brought a warmer sweater.

"Who was the guy on the phone?"

"Nobody."

"Nobody that you're not waiting for?"

"Exactly."

He takes another long drag. "So, he cheated on you?"

I frown and replay my conversation.

"Cammie," he offers.

Great. Ronan was standing there and listening for awhile.

I don't answer.

"How long were you two together?"

"Why?"

He chuckles. "You don't trust me, do you?"

"Why would I trust you?" I turn to take in those haunting green eyes of his, amusement sparkling in them. "I know what *you* want. I've seen firsthand what you want, so don't sit here and pretend to care while you look for my weak spots."

"I never said I cared, and don't worry—" A wry smile touches his lips. "—I can already peg you inside and out, including all your weak spots."

I'm pretty sure I don't want to hear what Ronan thinks of me, and yet I can't stop myself from provoking him. "I doubt that."

He smirks as if hearing the challenge. Pausing to take a long sip of his beer, he unleashes his thoughts on me.

"You've been a nice girl and a good daughter all your life. You use your manners, you look for ways to help people, you're constantly looking for approval from everyone around you, always listening to what your parents and teachers and church ask you to do, never wanting to piss people off. The thought of being away from your family for an entire summer was never something you would have imagined.

"But then something happened—something to do with that guy on the phone, I'm guessing—and you decided to run as far away as you could to get away from it. That's why you're in Alaska. Am I right so far?" He breaks to take a puff of his cigarette.

And I struggle to keep my mouth from hanging open.

"What I can't figure out is if you were a virgin before you let Aspen in you, or not. I'm guessing whatever you had with the guy back home was PG-13 or straight lights-off, missionary style."

I keep my gaze on the ducks, unwilling to give him any answers with my eyes, even as my cheeks burn. How does he know about Michael?

"Oh yeah. What'd you think was going to come up a second after you left the dining table? You thought the Aussie was going to keep your little secret?" Ronan chuckles and it makes me want to punch him. "Then again, it wouldn't make sense if you gave it up to Aspen after holding out on someone special back home. I mean, I know Aspen was hung up on you; he wouldn't stop talking about you since he met you at Wolf's. But you're not the type to just run into a guy, go back to his place and fuck him, no matter how upset you are over walking in on me with your roommates. How'd you like watching that, by the way?"

"I.... You're depraved." I wonder what kind of home life

he has. It can't be good. His parents are probably criminals and drug addicts.

He smirks. "You think that now. But when you stop being ashamed of what you want, you'll see that there's more than one kind of friendship."

"*That* won't be happening." I move to get up.

"I saw the look in your eyes, Abbi. You can keep lying to yourself but don't bother lying to me. You were more than just curious. There's no way seeing that is what made you so upset. Something else—or someone—did something to you. To hurt you bad."

I don't like the edge in Ronan's voice. Like there's a secret lingering on the tip of his tongue.

He takes another long puff of his cigarette. "Must have been something, working with a guy like Wolf day in, day out."

And there it is.

My stomach drops instantly.

Ronan's not fishing for information. He actually knows. Or strongly suspects.

I squeeze my eyes shut against the panic, biting my tongue to keep me from begging him not to voice his suspicions. Waiting for him to add on his price for silence. Something sick and corrupt, no doubt.

"Don't worry, I'm not going to say a word about it. To anyone."

Liar. This is horrible. Will Ronan be my undoing?

"Look at me, red."

When I don't respond, rough fingers land on my chin and lead my head toward him more gently than I'd believe Ronan capable. Finally I dare face his eyes.

"I'm not going to say a word about it."

I won't acknowledge his promise, because acknowledging it would mean he's right, and maybe he's still unsure. Maybe he's like Scott, trying to trick me into admitting what he can't otherwise prove.

"Man, he did a real number on you, didn't he?"

They. They did a real number on me. I'm pretty sure I'm going to swear off all men—handsome or not—from now on.

Especially this one.

"Live and learn, right?" I'm learning. Boy, am I learning. I climb to my feet. "You've got your spot back." My footfalls make a hollow sound along the dock as I retreat to shore.

"Hey." His back is still to me. "I'm not as bad as you think I am. We'll be friends one day." All traces of humor are gone from his voice.

"I'm not so sure. Remember, I've seen what you do to your friends."

He turns to peer over his shoulder at me. "Give yourself some time. You'll learn to trust again."

"Maybe."

Ronan's right. He did do a real number on me.

And I'm not talking about Jed.

nineteen

July

"Abbi!"

I glance up in time to see Autumn hop over a row of small boxwoods.

"Look!" She holds up a stack of magazines, but then pulls it away, eyeing my dirty gardening gloves with a wrinkled nose.

With an eye roll, I pull them off and brush the streak of soil on my thumb onto my t-shirt. I peeled off my sweatshirt and jacket about half an hour ago; the late-afternoon sun too hot for layers. "What am I looking at?"

"Articles about Wolf Cove."

I flip through the first one, until I come to a full-page spread of Henry, his piercing blue eyes staring out at me. I instinctively take a deep, calming breath, as I always do whenever the topic of "Mr. Wolf" so much as touches anyone's lips.

I remember these pictures. They're the ones Hachiro, the tiny and inappropriate Japanese photographer, took of Henry. It was during those very brief few days of bliss, after I discovered his attraction to me and before I learned what a cruel bastard he can be. "Where'd you get this?"

"In the lobby. The hotel shipped a box to us."

"Huh.... Great pics." I flip through them, feigning disinterest, even as I secretly plot an excuse to get to the lobby and steal myself a copy.

It's been six weeks since Henry left. I haven't spoken to him once. Haven't heard a word from him. All that I know, I hear either through Tillie's passion for gossip or from what's posted online.

The official handover of Wolf Hotels from William Wolf to Henry happened immediately following the grand opening here, as Henry said it would. The newspapers reported it around the same time that they divulged William Wolf's dire health situation as potentially one of the reasons for the accelerated change in ownership.

Henry's not just officially a billionaire anymore. He's now a billionaire many times over and one of the most eligible bachelors in the world, as this magazine so aptly calls out.

I don't think most wealthy business guys get this kind of media attention, but most don't look like Henry. Plus, he's really been putting himself out there as of late, spotted at movie premieres and celebrity-type events with this model or that actress on his arm. Tillie has nicknamed him Bruce Wayne, because he's now flamboyantly acting like the playboy that everyone has apparently known him to be.

I try to let it not bother me. Every day, I try. I keep telling myself that it'll get easier, that I'll clue in like I did about Jed, and truly stop caring. After six weeks, the only thing getting easier is being able to compartmentalize the pain.

"And look at this other one." Completely clueless to my personal struggle, Autumn shakes the *Luxury Travel* magazine in my face. "Remember that evil woman? Well, she wrote a rave review of Wolf Cove. Said it was one of the best experiences of her life."

I'll bet.

"Since this article dropped last week, our reservations desk has been going nonstop. Next year is nearly sold out. Can you believe it?"

"That's great." I'm not good with faking amusement, and it shows.

"Hey, red! You almost done with those? I've got another one for you and we need to get them in before we can break for the day." Ronan steps over the bushes in his work boots and sets another flat of summer annuals in front of me to plant.

I could kiss him right now for interrupting this conversation.

"I'll let you go. See you in the lodge later?" Autumn says, collecting the magazines from me. I know she's going to tuck them away in her cubby. Unlike me, she and most other women here still live in fantasyland as it relates to their CEO and hotel chain owner.

"For a bit, yeah."

Autumn flashes a polite smile at Ronan, but I know it's fake. She doesn't much like him. She doesn't know the real him. She only knows the version that I knew early on, and I didn't much like him then, either.

But things have changed.

"What'd she want?" Ronan leans down to grab the old

trays as I pull my gloves back on. While I love the days when I get to garden, I'm covered from head to toe in dirt, and I have only three uniforms to last me through the week.

"Nothing. Just showing me some magazines."

"About Wolf?"

I hesitate. "Yeah." While Ronan knows—or strongly suspects—my secret, he's kept his word and never mentioned it once. In fact, we've stayed far away from any topic involving Henry.

He sighs under his breath, but I think I hear him murmur, "He's an idiot" as he walks away, his cargo pants hugging his impressive backside well.

It makes me smile. I know Ronan doesn't harbor a secret crush on me, for no other reason than I just know. But I also know he'd gladly sleep with me if I suggested it. That's something else I just know.

Because I've gotten to know both Ronan and Connor well over the past six weeks.

Every day is the same—I roll out of bed, throw on my uniform, and spend the day sweating and slaving and shrugging off their inappropriate jokes. We work long hours and I'm sore by the time I stagger in to the lodge for dinner, usually followed by a few drinks, until warmth begins spreading through my limbs and I can forget for just a while that Henry is gone and hasn't bothered to call. Not even once. Then I repeat it all the next day.

Ronan, Connor, and I work together most days, paired up to do trash runs, firewood collection, and a lot of gardening, me planting and pruning while those two do the heavy lifting. The odd day that we're not together, I don't have nearly as much fun.

Plus, we eat most of our meals together, and on our days

off, we usually grab a ferry to Homer with the other guys from the crew.

Really, the only time I'm not with Ronan and Connor is when I'm showering or sleeping, and they've both joked plenty about how we may as well do those things together too.

We've formed an odd friendship of sorts, where there is an underlying and unspoken physical attraction—how can there not be when the guys look like Connor and Ronan do—but we're all happy just hanging out and laughing while we work.

All day, almost every day. That's a lot of time to spend with two guys. You get to see beyond the facade.

Like, for example, Connor loves to toss casual sexual innuendos at me tirelessly, but when someone else in the crew besides him or Ronan tries to join in on the teasing, their hackles instantly rise.

And, while Connor impersonates the true player who won't commit to one girl, he actually hasn't messed around with anyone other than Tillie in the almost two months since they started seeing each other. Or whatever it is they're doing, that he won't officially acknowledge.

On the other hand, Ronan is the quiet player. Everyone knows what happened between Katie, Rachel, and him, but I'm pretty sure that's because of Katie and Rachel. He may like to kiss, but he's not one to tell. I've caught one or two comments about something that had happened the night before at the lodge with a girl, but it's never outright disrespectful.

And they've both sort of taken to watching out for me. Connor always saves a seat in the lodge next to him, and Ronan always brings me a second coffee in the morning, because one is never enough. They both know my affinity for sweets, and they take turns surprising me with a chocolate bar or a freshly baked cookie.

It's kind of sweet.

And, though I doubt they realize it, it has been my saving grace while I wait for my broken, angry, untrusting heart to heal.

∽

RONAN and I are pulling up to the gate with the garden tools just as Connor pulls in, slamming his truck door shut. Darryl had him doing something with the electric fencing today and he's scowling. It's a rare sight. "You guys ready to go? I could use a drink."

"Yeah. How was your day?"

"Fine." He lets out a heavy sigh and then, throwing his arm around me, he pulls me into his sweaty, dirty side.

I push hard against him, prying myself away, fake-gasping. "God! You need a shower!"

Connor lifts his arm up and smells himself. "Dude, you're right. I do. So do you. Let's help each other get clean."

"No."

"I'm serious." His eyes rake over my body as if to prove a point.

"So am I." I smack him in the chest. "No!"

"You're missing out." He speeds up to join the other guys. That's how the crew always travels—in packs.

"What's up with him today?"

Ronan hesitates. He's not one for talking about other people. "Him and Tillie got into it last night in the lodge, and whatever that was, it's officially over."

"Really? I had no idea." She's my roommate but to be honest, since I started working with the guys, there's been a noticeable rift forming between us. Maybe it's because I've gotten so close to them. Autumn thinks it's because she's jealous. Tillie does get very jealous, very easily, and she's not the typical southern belle who's good at hiding her bitterness behind a fake smile while she talks behind your back.

"Yeah. She wanted a label, and he didn't. So now...." Ronan rubs the muscles in his tattooed forearm. "Tonight should be interesting because he's going to want to get laid."

"Shit." Something else that I never used to do pre-crew and now do almost constantly is cuss.

But this night may deserve it because I have a feeling I know who will get an extra heavy dose of Connor's attention.

"Drink up!" Connor shoves another shot into my hand.

I lick the salt sprinkled on my wrist and tip the glass back, anticipating the tequila burn before it even hits my throat. It's even worse than the first time. I cringe as I reach for the slice of lime in Connor's hand. But he raises it above his head, a sly grin on his face. "Open up."

I'm desperate for that lime and he knows it. I eagerly part my lips and he slides the slice between them, the soft pad of his thumb lingering on my bottom lip. His heated gaze is locked on my mouth as I bite down, the sour lime combating the aftertaste of the tequila. "That's a good girl. Now suck hard."

I punch him in the arm for good measure, but he just chuckles, reaching over his head to yank his t-shirt off, revealing that ripped body of his. Every guy in the crew has a body like that, to one degree or another. Even my body has hardened, my arms taut and shapely, my abs more defined.

"Alright. On that note, I'm out." I always leave—to shower and get a decent night's sleep—around the time that the debauchery begins. Which, by Connor's level of intoxication, was a few minutes ago. I don't know how these guys do it day in day out and still manage to get their butts out of bed for a 7:00 a.m. start. As it is tonight, I've only stayed this long because I wanted to make sure Connor was truly okay with breaking things off with Tillie.

Tomorrow is going to be a rough morning.

"No way. You need to stay and protect me from making a fool of myself." Connor slings an arm over my shoulder and pulls me into him, until I'm pressed up against his hot skin. "Come on. Pick any spot on my body and give it a good lick. It's a helluva lot more fun than licking yourself. Well," His gaze drops to my mouth, and his voice drops a few octaves along with it. "I enjoy watching you lick yourself, but I'd rather you lick me. And I won't expect you to call me in the morning. We'll never even talk about it," Connor taunts with a grin.

I roll my eyes, but there's a point in the back of my mind that wonders if maybe I should. It would be very easy to fall for his charm, especially if I was drunk. He's attractive, and it'd be nice to feel something again. Physically, anyway. I know I wouldn't have to worry about developing real feelings for him.

I'm pretty sure Henry's broken that part of me.

"It's late and I still need to shower." I punch him in the stomach as I squirm away, earning a fake grunt of pain.

But he holds on tight. "Please?" Earnest eyes beg me. He holds a shot up.

"Come on, red. Just one," Ronan goads.

"You're not helping," I mutter.

"Sure I am. I'm helping him." He nods toward his partner in crime.

I heave a sigh. "If I do one, will you leave me alone?"

"Promise. For tonight, anyway." Connor grins mischievously. "Tomorrow's a brand-new day."

"Give me that." I reach for the shot.

"No way. First. Pick a spot to lick."

"Fine. Your forearm."

"What?" Connor's face scrunches up. "That's not sexy."

"I'm not trying to be sexy with you!" I giggle nervously, feeling curious eyes on us from all directions. Maybe this isn't a good idea. If Tillie hears about it and gets upset....

"Ronan, pick a spot for the Abbs." Another nickname that Connor has started using on me.

"Stomach." No hesitation.

I roll my eyes; though, given it's Ronan, it could have been a lot worse. And Connor's stomach, well... I'm staring at it right now and it's perfect. *Everyone* around here talks about how sculpted it is, with his eight-pack of ridges and that V-shaped cut of his pelvis.

And now I'm going to lick it in front of everyone.

I'm deciding how best to tackle this when Ronan kicks a chair over with his boot, a silent indication for me to sit. "Makes it easier for you."

"Thanks." Clearly, Ronan has done this before.

Connor steps forward to stand in front of me, straddling either side of the chair, reaching back to scoop my hair into a tight ponytail. It's hard for me to focus on his stomach when his crotch is basically in my face, too.

It looks like I'm about to give him a blow job.

I'm guessing this was intentional on Ronan's part. I shoot him a dirty look but he merely smiles and winks, nodding toward the shot in Connor's hand. He's enjoying every minute of my embarrassment. *Jerk.*

"Let's see what you've got, little one." I peer up and into Connor's face, staring down at me with heated eyes, his fist tightening its grasp of my hair. It would be easy to catch his skin with just the tip of my tongue, to get this over with quickly, to play up the naïve, innocent, inexperienced girl that Henry accused me of being.

I don't want to be her. So I lean forward and flatten my tongue against his stomach above his belt, just like I would have done to Henry's cock when I was sucking him off. And then I take a long, leisurely lick upward, coating my tongue in the taste of his skin.

"Here." Connor's smiling as he hands me my shot, only temporarily distracting me from the hard outline of his erection, directly in front of my face. He loosens his grip of my hair but doesn't let go as I tip my head back and down the tequila, the overpowering taste worse this time around because there wasn't much salt on his skin. Ronan tosses a slice of lime, which Connor catches effortlessly. Instead of handing it to me, allowing me to quell this bitterness in my mouth, he slides it between his teeth, flesh side-out.

And then he stoops down and leans forward to feed the lime to me with his mouth. I'd argue with him if I wasn't afraid that I may vomit from the tequila.

Our lips graze as I bite down, but I ignore it, reveling in the sour juice as it explodes into my mouth. I sigh with relief, milking the slice for every last drop, until I can't get anymore. I release it, and expect Connor to back off. Only he doesn't. He lets the chewed up fruit fall from his mouth and then he pulls my mouth to his to lay an unexpectedly sweet kiss against my lips.

It doesn't last more than four seconds but it feels like an eternity because it's been an eternity since I kissed anyone.

And I'm not exactly sure how I feel about Connor kissing me.

"Thank you." The smirk on his face when he pulls away is nothing short of victorious.

Clearing my throat, I grab my sweater, offering a mumbled "Night," on my way past Ronan.

~

I LET the hot water soak into my back muscles, soothing the ache in them. It's times like these that I wish I could show up at Michael's cabin, lie down in his bed, and get him to rub my back like he did that night.

I rarely think of him anymore, which just proves how messed up I was—and still am—over Henry, and how much I was just looking for an escape from my pain. In some ways I'm glad Henry shipped him back to Aspen. It's made me not have to deal with the mortifying aftermath of using a guy like that.

A shower starts a few stalls over, and it brings me a degree of comfort. While the women's shower room is big and bright and well-maintained, being the only one in here this late at night is a little unsettling.

I'm halfway through working the shampoo through my hair when the first deep moan carries over the running water.

My hands stall as I listen. Nothing but silence and running water responds.

Until I hear it again.

There's no mistaking that kind of moan.

I should ignore it. I should quickly finish washing up

and leave. But I've had three shots of tequila and Connor kissed me so sweetly, and my curiosity now overtakes my surprise. So I crouch down to look under the stall. I see two sets of feet—one male, one female—both facing the showerhead, the male standing behind the female, the female's feet spread fairly wide apart.

Oh my God. Someone's having sex in here. I've heard rumors of it happening—people will go anywhere for a bit of privacy—but I thought it might be just that, a rumor. Clearly it's not.

There's no way they don't know I'm here, so they must not care.

I take my time, running my fingers through my hair to work the shampoo out, all while keenly aware of what's happening just a few stalls over. Listening intently, hoping that a word or a sound might tell me who it is

Their soft pants grow louder, along with a few grunts and indecipherable whispers. If I close my eyes, I can imagine the guy thrusting harder and faster into her from behind.

That familiar sensation begins to build in my core.

I'm getting turned on listening to them.

It doesn't help that I'm standing naked in a shower, I guess. Or that I was treated to several days of mind-blowing sex, only to have it yanked away abruptly, leaving me with absolutely nothing for the past six weeks. Plus I've been the subject of constant flattery and brute charm by two attractive sexual men day in and day out for those six weeks. *And* I've had three shots of tequila and Connor kissed me tonight.

I'm sure all of that plays a role in why my breasts are growing heavy and my nipples are pebbled and when I run my soapy hand between my legs, my fingers are stalling on my clit.

Biting my bottom lip with hesitation, I peek under the stall again like the pervert I obviously am. The woman now has one foot raised beyond my view. I can judge each thrust by the movement of the guy's feet, spread out farther

Closing my eyes, I imagine myself in her position, with a man behind me, filling me like that.

But who? I don't trust anyone.

Except for maybe Connor or Ronan.

It's so wrong and dangerous to even let these thoughts enter my head, but I can't help it. I trust them more than I trust anyone else. I like them, I'm attracted to them, and I'll never get caught up in anything more than feelings of friendship toward them.

And I'm so damn horny right now.

Enough that I wish I'd taken Connor up on that offer of a shower.

"Oh, God, James. Yes!" A woman cries out in a deep southern lilt.

I bolt upright, wide-eyed, any thought I may have had of getting myself off while listening to them dead.

That's Tillie!

And James. Which James?

I only know of one—Lorraine's James. I saw them walking hand in hand along the path just this afternoon, so I'm pretty sure they're still together.

This must be another James.

A part of me wants to towel off and duck out of here right now, because otherwise our paths may cross and they'll know I stayed and listened to them have sex.

And yet I don't leave.

I grab my razor and take my time, dragging the blade

over every square inch of my legs, hoping I don't accidently cut myself with my shaky hands. Tillie or not, there's something about listening to two extremely attractive people having sex that stirs my blood. Or maybe it's because I'm simply envious of them.

Either way, I'm sure that whoever Tillie's with is hot.

"Yes. Yes. Yes!" Tillie moans just like I'd expect a southern belle to moan—deep and throaty—as she comes, closely followed by James shouting, "Oh, fuck! Yeah!"

And in that moment, I know that this *is* Lorraine's James, because he said the exact same thing the night I overheard him and Lorraine, when I was with Michael.

Oh man... this isn't good. But maybe Lorraine and he broke up after I saw them today? If not... am I a bad roommate for not telling Lorraine about this?

I'm pretty sure several of Jed's and my "friends" knew about Cammie before I found out. Their decidedly calm reactions when I told them what happened indicated that.

But Lorraine's going to find out anyway. Nothing stays secret around here. And then living in that cabin is going to be a nightmare. I sigh, debating what to do. This is the longest shower I've ever had in my life. My fingertips have turned prunish, and the water isn't as hot as it once was.

I really want to leave, but I absolutely don't want to come face-to-face with either of them, so I huddle under the water until I hear James say, "Catch you later." I peek through the side of the curtain in time to see him stroll out with a towel wrapped around his waist.

I wait another minute and then I shut the water and duck out in record time, leaving Tillie humming to herself.

This place....

It's definitely not Greenbank, Pennsylvania.

I REACH over my head to shut off my reading light.

And then I do the same stupid girl thing that I've done every night for the past six weeks—pull my phone out, crossing my fingers that my Internet connection is working, and I refresh the search engine for "Henry Wolf" to see if anything new about him has been reported.

Most nights, it's the same old stuff. Articles about Wolf Hotel, about the eligible Wolf bachelors. There are articles about the Wolf gold mine, and forecasts for how long it can be mined before the cost of increased diesel fuel consumption with mining so deep outweighs the profits and effort. Apparently there was a small accident five years ago when one of the tunnels collapsed. When I read that, I found myself wishing that Scott had been in that tunnel. I of course immediately felt guilty for thinking that, even if he deserves it.

Every night I brace myself for a picture of Henry with a woman. There have been a few, and on those nights I feel sick to my stomach and spend the night tossing and turning and, occasionally, crying quietly. I hate letting myself cry over him, so I usually fight it.

Tonight, a new article pops up. Wolf Hotels is opening a location in Prague.

I sigh, imagining what it would be like to hop on a plane and fly over an ocean to Europe. Maybe I'll do that next year, once I'm finished my last year at North Gate. I never thought I'd end up in Alaska this summer, so who knows? I don't even have a passport.

According to the article, the company is set to begin remodeling a historic building shortly, in time to open next year. My heart jumps at the picture set in the inset, of Henry in his suit, his dark hair combed back, the curls rolling at the nape of his neck, visiting the location just last week. Another picture follows it, of him stepping into a famous local opera house, his arm around a beautiful and glamorous brunette identified as Czech-born supermodel Luciana Boren.

This is the third picture I've seen of them together.

Tears sting my eyes as I read through the rest of the article.

Clearly, Henry has moved on.

I really need to, too.

twenty

"We need to load this all into the compost bins before lunch. You almost done in there?" Ronan calls from outside.

I lean over the work-bench and stretch onto my tiptoes to hang the shears onto the hook, admiring the tool shed. Everything is new and clean and well-labeled, and the scent of cedar wafts through. It's so different from the drafty old barn where my dad stores our farm equipment.

"Come on. Hurry up!" Ronan's hungry. I can tell. That's the only time I've ever seen him grouchy.

"Hold on!" I holler back, annoyed, shifting a box that's hindering my reach.

Suddenly, something leaps out of it, grazing my neck on its way past.

With a loud shriek, I drop the shears and jump back, just in time to see a brown and black striped body disappear behind some bags of mulch in the corner.

Ronan comes barreling in, his face stricken with panic. His strong arms instantly rope around me and he pulls me into his chest protectively. "What happened?"

"A chipmunk."

"A chipmunk?" The tension releases in his arms. "Are you kidding me? Jesus Christ, I thought you were being mauled by a bear or something."

"A bear, just sitting inside a garden shed?"

"Well, the way you screamed!" He defends himself.

"It *touched* me!"

"It *touched* you." He heaves a sigh, and then chuckles. "Fucking lucky chipmunk."

"Shut up." I'm laughing now too. Of course he's turned this into something sexual.

I'm still in his arms. He peers down at me thoughtfully, but says nothing.

"What?"

His eyes sparkle as they drift over my mouth, and farther down, to where my chest presses against his. "You should give me a chance."

"A chance? For what?"

The heated gaze that lifts to meet my eyes answers me immediately.

"I can't."

"Why not? I've seen you looking at me. I know you want me."

My cheeks begin to burn. "No, I don't." I *do* look at him a lot. And Connor. It's hard not to—they're both lean and cut and gorgeous. "And that doesn't mean I'm going to sleep with you."

His smile falls off as his hands begin to wander, sliding up to settle on my shoulders, his thumbs grazing along the collar of my t-shirt at my collarbone, just touching my skin enough to send a thrill down to my breasts. "I'm serious."

"So am I." I sigh. "I don't want to mess things up by complicating them."

"It won't. We both know where we're coming from." He says it so matter-of-factly.

I'm already shaking my head. "I can't."

"Yeah, you can. I'm telling you that you can." He pushes a wayward strand of hair off my forehead. "As unbearable as it will be for me, I'm giving you permission to use my dick for your amusement."

"Oh my God. Stop it!" I laugh as I push against his chest, my palms reveling in his firm muscles. He has never so overtly propositioned me before. Is it because of what happened last night with Connor? Is he jealous and getting competitive?

I gain some space between us, only to lose it when Ronan steps forward. "Does it make you uncomfortable to know that I'm hard for you right now?"

I can't keep my wide eyes from dropping down to his pants. Sure enough, I can see the outline of his erection. Does it make me uncomfortable? No, I don't think so. But I don't tell him that.

He smiles and under his breath, I hear a soft mutter of, "God, you're beautiful."

A nervous laugh escapes me. "Come on! You've slept with my roommates!"

"And you fucked Aspen. So what?"

"He wasn't your roommate. And I *watched you* with Rachel."

He rolls his eyes. "Once, like, forever ago."

"That's not the point!"

He steps in closer and I don't back away this time, even though I know I should, my entire body suddenly alive with adrenaline, reacting to the potential pleasure that Ronan is offering, even while the voice inside my head is screaming, *no! no! no!*

"The point is that you just stood in a shower for twenty minutes by yourself last night, listening to your roommate bang some guy. Don't tell me that didn't turn you on."

I groan. "I'm *really* regretting telling you about that." The only reason I brought it up was because I felt like Connor should know. He didn't seem to care much, but they were both very interested in the fact that I stayed to listen to the act in its entirety. And whether I touched myself.

I sure as hell didn't answer that question honestly.

"Do you want me to watch Connor fuck you? Would we be even then?"

Maybe this isn't about competition or jealousy, after all.

But... *oh my God*. "Do you *really* want to watch me have sex with Connor?" Just the thought has me blushing furiously.

"What, like you've never thought about it?"

Just last night, actually. "Thought about you watching me have sex with Connor? Uh... no!"

"Would you do it if Ronan *isn't* watching?" Connor pokes his head in, sliding his aviators down over the bridge of his nose to eye us. He's obviously been listening. "What the hell are you two doing in here?"

My cheeks burn even brighter. "Sorry, I was attacked by a chipmunk."

"Oh, come on. You know Ronan's dick is bigger than a chipmunk. A squirrel, maybe."

The two of them burst out in laughter and I just shake my head at them.

Connor steps into the shed. "So where'd this killer chipmunk go?"

I point to the corner, and he wanders over to kick the bag of mulch with his work boots. "We have to get the little bastard out. Can't have them nesting in here."

I watch as they begin dragging out the various boxes and bags tucked in beneath the table, the muscles in their arms and backs straining, the crew work pants stretching over hard asses.

"Fuck! There it is!" Connor shouts, and a second later a furry little body scurries past us and out the front door, earning my shudder.

"Hopefully he's smart enough not to come back." Connor dusts his hands off as Ronan shoves a barrel back under the desk. "So, back to the topic of us together. Is Ronan just watching? Or do I have to share you? At least let me have first dibs. I'm so brokenhearted over Tillie." He emphasizes that with a fake pout.

I spin on my heels and bolt out the door to climb behind the wheel of the flatbed truck. I crank the engine in an attempt to drown out their laughter. It seems I've somehow given them the green light. The innuendos are gone. Now it's straight proposition.

Connor rounds the truck, resting his arms against the door in the open window, amusement splashed across his face. "What? You think you're gonna drive?"

"I never get to drive."

"This isn't a Honda Civic, Abbs. Do you even—"

I throw it into first gear and release the clutch. Connor jumps back just as the truck lurches forward. I take off down the road, leaving them in a cloud of diesel fumes.

The composting site is a quarter mile up the road.

That should give all of us time to cool off.

~

LORRAINE'S HAND flies through the air, making contact with Tillie's cheek. The slap echoes through the staff lounge with an audience of at least twenty-five, most of us standing around the fireplace to watch the catfight unfold.

Connor tsks. "That's not good. She could get canned for that one." Nudging me with a soft elbow, he whispers, "Did you squeal, little piglet?"

"No! I haven't said a word to anyone but you two!" I'm actually offended that he'd even suggest it.

"Security cameras would have caught him going in," Ronan murmurs, downing his beer. "I swear, Corbin has a pussy the way he gossips."

Tillie has the nerve to look appalled at Lorraine's tear-filled violent reaction to finding out that her roommate slept with her boyfriend, while James has the decency to appear at least a little sheepish from his table.

Thanks to the three beers and one shot I've already downed, I feel the sudden urge to walk over there and slap *him* for his cheating part in all this.

"Come on." Ronan grabs my arm and pulls me toward the exit.

I'm not at all surprised that he wouldn't be interested in watching the emotional fallout. I don't want to watch it either, so I happily follow him. Not until we reach the side door do I realize that Connor's in tow as well.

"What? I want nothing to do with that either," he murmurs.

The three of us head down to the staff dock, our quiet gazes on the sun as it hangs in the sky, just beginning to set. "I don't think I'll ever get used to these long summer days."

"I hear the winters here are even longer. Six hours of daylight, or something like that." Ronan pulls out a cigarette.

Ronan and I sit out here almost every night after dinner, so much that I'm used to his bad habit. I'm pretty sure that when my summer in Alaska is over and I want to transport myself back to these peaceful nights out on the dock, all I'll need to do is light a Camel and close my eyes.

A full can of beer appears in front of me. Connor pulls two more from his pocket. He must have poached them from the crew's table on his way out.

"I shouldn't." I say this even as I sit down and crack the top. I'm much too relaxed for my own good. This one might put me over the edge.

"That a girl." Connor throws an arm around my neck and pulls me backward against his chest, his legs stretched out on either side of me. "Why can't every chick be as cool as you?"

"I'm a cool chick?" I roll my eyes but smile, torn between elbowing him in the stomach so I can pull away, and staying exactly where I am. I end up staying put, sipping my beer and looking out over the water as I lean against his chest. "You know, this isn't as bad as I thought."

"What. The beer?"

Ronan chuckles. "Connor's hard dick pressed against your back?"

I stretch my leg to give him a playful kick. He's quick, grabbing me by the foot and pulling my leg to dangle over his lap.

"What's not as bad as you thought?" Connor nuzzles his face against my neck.

Again, I know I should stop this right now. But I close my eyes instead. "No. Alaska."

"Fuck. Alaska's awesome! Why would you ever have thought it wouldn't be?"

"I don't know. I just did," I murmur, catching Ronan's thoughtful gaze. He slides his hand over my calf with affection, but says nothing.

He understands exactly why.

But that's our secret.

~

"Abbi!"

"Abbieeeeeeee!"

"Oh my God, would you shut your two fuck boys up! Some of us have to be up soon," Tillie snaps from behind her curtain.

It's three in the morning, and Ronan and Connor have been standing outside our cabin for the past five minutes, calling my name. Someone's going to alert security soon if they don't shut up.

"They're not my fuck boys."

"You sure about that? Because they sure seem to *love* you." Bitterness seeps through her voice.

"At least she waited to get with her roommates' boyfriend, whore!" comes the equally vicious retort from the top bunk.

I'm honestly not sure how we're going to get through until the end of August without them killing each other.

I ignore them both, sliding my shower flip-flops and a jacket on before I step out into the cold.

"Abbi!"

Their shouts aren't coming from the path. They're coming from behind our cabin. I wander over, a little panicked that something's wrong. Ronan and Connor stand with their backs against the wall, just under the window.

"What the hell are you two doing out here?" I hiss.

"There she is!" Connor reaches out to pull me into his chest with no effort. "We missed you."

"I was with you a few hours ago." I'm hit with the smell of beer. "God, you two are *really* drunk!"

"Nah. Well, maybe just a little bit." I can't see Ronan's face in the dark, but I can hear the sly smile in his voice. "But we had to see our girl."

I roll my eyes, but I laugh. "You two are idiots."

Connor squeezes me tight. "Endearing idiots, though."

"Endearing. Dude. That's a big word."

Connor lets go of me to punch Ronan in the chest.

"Go to bed, you two. We have to start work in a few hours."

"You're right. Okay. Let's let our girl sleep." But Connor doesn't release me right away, instead pulling me flush against his firm body. He dips his head into the crook of my neck like he did on the dock earlier, his mouth against my ear. "Good night, sweet girl." It's not a kiss but it may as well be, the shivers his lips send down my spine, making my nipples tighter than they already were from the cold.

Releasing me, he strolls away with ease, staggering only slightly.

Ronan scoops me into his arms and settles a hand on the back of my head, weaving his fingers through my hair. He gently tugs until my head falls back.

I know he's staring down at me, searching the dark for my eyes. Even though we can't actually see each other, I can feel that haunting gaze on me, boring into me. It's intense.

A soft gasp slips from my lips as he grows hard against my stomach. "Why did you two come here tonight?"

He leans forward and smacks his forehead into mine.

"Ow!"

"Sorry." He adjusts until our foreheads simply lean against each other. "Well, I can't speak for Connor but *I* wanted a fresh memory of you so I can take it back and jerk off in my bed."

I should be shocked that he admitted to that, but I'm not. I should be utterly disgusted by that prospect. But instead I find myself giggling, and warmth blooming in my core.

"God, it's becoming impossible to resist you, red," he whispers, leaning down to place the softest kiss on my jaw.

I shouldn't let him do this.

I shouldn't let either of them get away with anything they've been doing lately.

And yet I don't pull away, reveling in the closeness, in the smell of him, in the heat from his body, in the knowledge that he wants me.

His lips find my ear. "Now, go be a good girl and touch yourself, thinking about us." Peeling away from me, he heaves a sigh and wanders away.

Us. He said *us.* Not simply him.

I duck back into the cabin and crawl into bed as quietly as possible. I count the slow, heavy breathing of five people. The cabin's full tonight, but at least they're all asleep again.

And I'm wide awake.

And smiling at the bunk above me, thinking about those two.

I'm sure Connor is already facedown and snoring by now. But Ronan, I'm not so sure. Could he actually be lying in bed, rubbing himself, thinking of me? I close my eyes and try to picture what that would be like. I have a pretty good idea, given I've already seen him naked and in the throes of passion.

Heat stirs between my legs. I haven't come since the night with Michael.

My phone, on silent, lights up on the shelf beside me with an incoming text.

Oh my God.

My cheeks flush as I take in the picture of Ronan, lying in bed, naked and smiling up at the camera. It cuts off at his pelvic bone where the tuft off dark hair begins, but the way his arm is stretching down leaves little to the imagination of what he's doing.

He really is beautiful.

And he really is jerking off right now.

I should have known. Ronan's not one to exaggerate or outright lie.

A second later, a second text comes in:

Ronan: *Where's yours?*

I stifle my laugh, afraid of waking others up.

Abbi: *Not a chance.*

Ronan: *Come on...*

There's no way in hell I'm sending a picture like that to him, or anyone, *ever*.

Abbi: *Good night.*

Ronan: *At least let me see your face.*

Chewing my bottom lip with indecision for all of three seconds, I quickly hold my phone up in front of me and snap a picture of just my face. Deciding it's flattering enough, I send it.

Abbi: *Now leave me alone.*

Ronan: *Perfect. Thank you.*

You realize what he's doing with that picture, Abbi. Right?

Another wave of heat flushes between my legs. I flip to his picture again, admiring his chiseled body—it rivals Connor's, in my opinion—and his handsome face. And his candor. There's no confusion or head games with him.

Another text comes through:

Ronan: *Did that pic offend you?*

I frown at his question. Now he's worried about offending me?

Abbi: *No.*

Ronan: *Good.*

Another picture follows ten seconds later.

I gasp at the hard dick that fills my phone screen, gripped in his palm and smeared in cum.

Ronan: *All for you, babe. Night.*

Oh my God. I cover my mouth with my hand as I stare at it in shock, my heartbeat pounding in my throat. He really wasn't kidding.

And it's turning me on.

I shut my phone off and set it on the ledge, wondering if I should keep the image or delete it.

An hour later, still lying in bed with an uncomfortable buildup between my thighs, I reach for my phone to study the two pictures. Settling on the one with Ronan's face, I slide my hand into my pajama bottoms.

twenty-one

"How are you two feeling this morning?" Considering neither of them showed up for breakfast, I'm guessing not well.

I hold out two black coffees. Connor texted me, asking me to grab them for them. At least they showered before they got here, so they don't reek of stale beer.

Connor grins up at me from beneath the San Diego baseball cap he's donning today. "Fan-fucking-tastic. You?"

"I'm tired."

Ronan shoots me a sly grin as he takes my cup, his fingers grazing mine in the process. The ones he likely used to stroke himself with last night, seeing as he's right-handed. "Yeah. Sorry about that. Hope it didn't take you too long to get back to sleep." He watches me through a sip of his coffee as my face heats up.

Like he knows what I did.

"Okay. Listen up!" Darryl claps his hands, earning Connor's wince. "With this wedding ceremony tomorrow, we've got to change things up a bit."

I hear someone murmur, "Don't do it, man. Run while you can!" and a round of chuckles floats around the group.

"Alright, alright. Connor, you're with Pegs and Brody on tent set up."

Connor groans but Darryl ignores him. "Abbi and Ronan, you two do the weekly check on the Wolf Cabin, and then be back for landscaping around the site. Abbi, you lead on the planters. These morons couldn't make a garden look good if their lives depended on it. The rest of you... the usual."

Ronan and I together, and alone, all morning. It's not the first time, but after last night, after the tension that's been brewing....

My gut tells me this isn't a good idea.

The look on Ronan's face says the exact same thing.

∽

THE AIR within the cab of our maintenance truck hangs thick with unspoken words and undeclared intentions.

"No one's stayed in this place for three years and they still want us checking it week after week," Ronan mutters, steering around the worst of the potholes along the narrow path.

"It's important to them." *To him.* I keep a firm grip on the door handle, my eyes ahead, waiting for that bend where the cabin suddenly comes into view. I haven't been back since the day we staged it, the weekend of the grand opening ceremony.

The day Henry told me we *were* different. The last time I felt him inside me.

"You're doing it again."

I glance over to find Ronan switching his glances between the narrow road and me. "Doing what?"

"Disappearing into some deep, dark place where your face turns all sad."

Ronan is way too observant. "You should watch where you're driving. You know, in case of animals."

That buys me about ten seconds of silence. And then he asks so softly, "What did he do to you?"

Familiar hollowness blooms inside me. It's not even eight in the morning. I'm not sure I can face this. "He fooled me. He told me lies that I believed, because I was stupid and naive." I've never actually talked about it with anyone. There's no one to talk about it with.

"Do you miss him?"

I chuckle, though it's not with humor. "I miss what I thought we had."

He sighs. "Then maybe it's time you move on." He reaches across the seat to give my knee a friendly squeeze before pulling back.

And, after all this time, it dawns on me. I can't believe I haven't seen it before. Not in all these weeks, in the countless mundane, pointless conversations. "What did she do to you?"

Ronan's Adam's apple bobs with a swallow. He doesn't answer right away, but I already know there is a she. "She decided she needed time and space."

"How long were you together for?"

"Four years. We broke up about three months before I came here." A little softer, he adds, "Her name is Tasha."

I reach over to squeeze his knee, just as he did to me moments ago, because it feels like the right thing to do. He's still hurting over her, that much is obvious. "So, now what?"

He sighs, then shrugs. "I give her what she asked for."

"But you're messing around with other girls."

"She wanted the space, not me."

"And what if she tells you she wants you back?"

"Then she gets this version of me." His smile is weak and unconvincing. "But I'm guessing we're done."

"But what if you're not?"

"What am I going to do, *not* have sex with anyone until I know for sure? Because I know she is."

I swallow my pain. Just like I know Henry is sleeping with other women. He basically promised as much.

"What do you want, Abbi?"

"I don't know." Some miraculous turn of events that makes Henry not an asshole? That gives me a reason to forgive him for how he's treated me?

If that's the case, then I haven't really learned anything at all from this experience.

I stare out the window, seeing the steep roof through the trees. "To figure out how to let go, I guess."

∽

"All good down here. How about up there?" Ronan hollers from the bottom of the steps.

"Just a sec!" A lightbulb in the back bedroom blew when I flipped the switch and, according to Darryl, we're supposed to make sure *everything* is in working order. I've had to take my boots off and climb onto the bed to reach it. At least the beds have long since been stripped of their sheets from the grand opening ceremony weekend.

I turn around to find Ronan leaning against the doorframe, watching me intently.

"Okay. I think I've got it in." I move to jump off the bed but Ronan's voice stops me. "Don't."

"What?"

He strolls in slowly, his gaze drifting over my body. "What do you want, Abbi?"

He's yanked us right back to the conversation in the car.

That's the second time he's asked me that. I wish I had a good answer. "I don't know. To feel good. To not hurt. To move on." Those are pretty basic things.

Strong hands grip my outer thighs as he stops just in front of me, his head at waist level. "I can help you with that."

"We need to get back to the hotel, Ronan. We can't." Suddenly, *this* is exactly what I want. Ronan, making me feel good. Making me experience life again.

"There was a squirrel."

I frown, a laugh threatening. "A squirrel?"

"Yes." His hands begin sliding up and over my hips, his fingers curling tight around my body, until they come to rest on the button at my waist. "It was loose in the house, and we had to catch it." His green eyes lift to lock on mine.

And he pops the button to my pants.

I say nothing to stop him.

With a single finger, he pushes the zipper down, the tip of it running along my panties, down, to stop just above my clit. "It took a while to catch that fucking squirrel."

Why am I not stopping him? This is about to go way too far.

He tugs on my pants until they're sliding all the way down to my ankles.

"We can't do this in here," I whisper. This is Henry's grandparents' cabin.

He leans forward, his mouth landing between my legs. I feel the heat, the slip of his tongue, even through the cotton of my panties. "Why not? Do you think he cares?"

Henry doesn't give a fuck about me.

Ronan looks up again and he must see the answer in my eyes. His fingers coil around the sides of my panties and he pulls them down. My t-shirt is long but it doesn't cover me completely, and his mouth is *so* close.

My body begins reacting to him, a heavy pulse growing between my legs, even though this is wrong and stupid on so many levels. "This is going to make things weird between us."

His rough, callused hands slide up the backs of my thighs to land on my ass, squeezing almost to the point of pain, but not quite. "It won't. I promise it won't. I won't let it."

"You can't promise that."

"I can. Take your shirt off."

"You haven't even kissed me yet."

His sigh skates across the very tip of my clit. "You want me to kiss you?"

"Isn't that how all this should start?"

He pauses to look up at me through his penetrating eyes. "Sure. I can kiss you."

I'm about to step down from the bed when he leans forward. I gasp as his tongue slides over my slit, wriggling in to touch my clit, swirling around it.

I stop letting myself think—and worry—and just close my eyes and feel as Ronan kisses me between my legs, his hands gripping my ass, squeezing my flesh, pulling me closer to his mouth.

I watch him, eyes closed, mouth open, his tongue working away at me, and I can tell he enjoys doing it without even having to ask.

When his eyes flash open, they're darker and his pupils have dilated. "Shirt off. Now," he demands.

I peel off my t-shirt and unfasten my bra. My breasts fall

with heaviness, my nipples hard and sensitive. Ronan looks up, his mouth still on me, and heat flares in his eyes. "Get your pants off and lie down." Stepping back to give me space, he yanks his t-shirt over his head and pulls out his wallet to fish out a condom. He tosses it on the bed and then simply stands there, watching me sit down to tug my pants and panties off around my ankles. The bare mattress isn't exactly comfortable, but I don't really much care at this point, because I'm now completely naked in front of Ronan.

And, oddly, not at all uncomfortable. Maybe it's because I know him so well. Maybe it's because I somehow know he's going to be satisfied no matter what. Maybe because I'm doing this for me and not for him.

He unfastens his belt and pants, and pulls his hard dick out to hold it in his hand as he stares without shame at my body. "Open up for me."

My nerves are going wild as spread my legs apart, letting him see all of me. And admire all of me, as he seems to be doing. "You're so fucking fresh and innocent."

Henry used to say things like that to me. I close my eyes and push that aside.

But Ronan sees it. He always sees it. "What's wrong?"

"That's how he said he liked me," I admit quietly. "But he didn't really want that after all."

Henry doesn't want me.

Ronan doesn't answer for a long moment, his hand running up and down his cock in long, languid strokes, his thumb skating over the tip with each pass. With our gazes locked, he reaches over with his free hand to slide a single finger along my slit. "So you don't want to be fresh and innocent?"

I gasp at the intimacy of this, of Ronan, of that soul-searing look, even when I know he's having emotionless sex because he's still in love with another girl. I saw that same look the night I walked in on him, only now its intensity is tenfold. "I want to be wanted."

"You're wanted. Look at me. Look at this." He strokes himself to make a point. "This happens every time I see you. That first day we picked you up, to bring you here, I wanted to touch you. On the way home, your legs straddled that gearshift and I had to fight not to slide my hand up your skirt to touch you. Believe me, I want you. Connor wants you, too. We both want you." His gaze drops to rake over my chest, landing between my legs. "I like you fresh and innocent."

"I don't want to be so innocent anymore."

His mouth twists in thought. "You want to gain some real experience?"

I bite my bottom lip. And nod. A tiny bit afraid of what Ronan's idea of "experience" means, because I've already gathered that he's *very* experienced.

A soft smile curls his lip. "Turn around."

I remember how deep it felt from behind with Henry. I also remember how exposed I was. But I do as asked, tensing slightly as Ronan comes up behind me. I hear the soft slide of his pants, down past his knees. "Relax. I'm not going to do anything to you that you won't like." His lips skate along my neckline to place a kiss on my shoulder, making me shiver and drop my head back against him. I gasp as his hands come around the sides to cup my breasts. He pulls my entire body backward, closer to him, until I feel his erection lined up as the top of my crack, a bead of moisture leaking from the tip.

I instinctively grind my ass against him.

"Do you know how perfect these are? Most women need to pay for tits like these." He alternates between gripping my entire breast, or as much as his hands can manage, and rubbing my nipples between his thumbs and forefingers, squeezing them until almost just painful. Over and over again, a repetitive stroking that I feel through my stomach and down between my legs.

Until I'm squeezing my thighs together against the ache.

"I can't.... I need you to...." I don't have to finish my thoughts. He drops a hand down between my legs. I step farther apart to spread myself, giving him access as he slides his index finger through my slit and into me.

"That's it." Still, he clutches a breast with one hand while his finger pumps in and out of me. I close my eyes and revel in how wet he's making me.

At some point I've reached up absently, gripping the back of his head to give myself leverage as I grind my hips against him, working the end of his cock into my wet spot.

"Wait." He guides my knees onto the mattress with his, and pushes on the space between my shoulders until, leaning forward, I'm on my elbows, my face pressed against the mattress. I listen to him tear open the condom wrapper. Moments later he's pushing a finger inside me again, then two fingers.

"I think you may have the tightest pussy I've ever felt," he murmurs, thrusting his fingers in and out, hitting that spot deep inside that drives me wild and makes me drip with need.

Finally, he settles his cock at my entrance.

Is this really happening? Am I going to—

Ronan pushes himself into me with a moan. I close my eyes and clear my mind, breathing through the delicious pain as his cock pushes deeper into me with each thrust, only mildly aware of him dragging his wet fingers along my crack, smoothing over my tight, puckered skin.

"Oh, fuck. Abbi. I'm almost... I'm all the way in."

I revel in the feeling of being completely full of Ronan, of having him inside me.

Until he rubs that spot with a wet finger.

"Relax."

I clench instinctively but he keeps rubbing his thumb over and over and over, applying just a touch of pressure with each pass, all the while still pushing into me, again and again, helping to distract me.

Then a gob of something wet lands on my backside. "What is that?"

"My spit. I need you really wet."

People actually do that?

He rubs his saliva all over me, until everything feels slick and strange.

"Take a deep breath."

I do, and he begins pushing his thumb inside me, so slowly. There's a burn that's not entirely painful but not at all comfortable. "Relax, Abbi. And trust me. You'll be begging me to fuck this soon enough."

I don't know about that, but I take another deep breath and concentrate on Ronan's swollen cock pumping in and out of me at a slow and steady rhythm, his hips circling with each thrust. Soon enough, my body is loosening enough that I barely notice the burn as he continues to inch his thumb deeper into me.

First time having sex and Ronan is already sticking things into my ass. Even Henry didn't attempt that. Suddenly I can't help but giggle. "You *are* depraved."

"You love it. Don't worry, I'm almost there," he whispers with a groan, thrusting his hips at just the right angle to help build that delicious heaviness in my belly, even as I feel an almost unbearable feeling of fullness everywhere else. I can't help but spread my legs farther apart and stick my ass up higher, desperate for this orgasm that's hiding in the recesses.

"Did you touch yourself last night, like I asked you to?"

There's no room for shame with him, not right now. "Yes."

"I knew you would." He begins thrusting harder. "I need you to do it again now because I won't last. You feel too good, and I want you to come with me."

I reach back with one hand and begin rubbing my swollen, wet clit, my fingers catching the side of his cock every once in a while as it plunges into me.

"Faster, Abbi. Rub harder."

I obey, rubbing myself with quick strokes, my fingertips gliding over myself. Knowing that he's struggling not to come spurs me on, bringing my orgasm closer.

"Fuck. I'm about to explode." His fingers dig into my hip as he hammers against me, hitting my back wall over and over again hard and fast. I'm vaguely aware of my knees sliding against the abrasive mattress but I don't care, so focused on how Ronan both fills me and violates me but in the sexiest way. It doesn't even hurt anymore. It just feels strange.

I curl my head under and watch upside down as his thick, rigid cock disappears inside me over and over again, coated in my slickness. So much of it. I didn't think I'd ever get that wet for another guy again. But I have, for Ronan.

My orgasm comes on in a rush, and I cry out as I'm flooded with heat, my muscles not only pulsing around his cock but around his thumb as well, in what feels like a double orgasm. I ride the intense wave and then another intense wave, my body going wild with the conflicting sensations, until the spasms still and I'm left wanting to sprawl out on the bed.

Dropping a single soft kiss on my spine, Ronan pulls out, grabs the condom wrapper, and heads for the bathroom.

Leaving me to get dressed in bewilderment.

I can't believe I just had sex with Ronan.

I quickly pull my clothes on. How do I really feel about that? I honestly have no idea.

I'm lacing my boots up when he strolls in with his pants buckled but shirtless, his chest still gleaming with the slightest coating of sweat.

"We should probably take our trash."

"In my pocket." He yanks his t-shirt over him. "Ready?"

"Yeah."

He turns to leave. And stops. "You good?"

"I don't know. What's going to happen now?"

"Well, now there's going to be a wedding."

My eyes pop wide with his words. "What?"

He frowns. "Back at the hotel, remember?"

A wave of relief hits me. "Right. The planters."

He must finally clue in because he starts chuckling. "You're adorable."

"You're sure nothing is going to turn weird between us?"

"By weird, do you mean, am I going to think about fucking you constantly? Because I was already doing that in my head."

I blush.

His boots fall heavily on the floor as he walks toward me. "Yeah, things are a little bit different. We'd be idiots to think otherwise. I mean, we're closer friends now, right?"

"Yes." He's seen me naked and done things to me no one else has.

"But this thing you feel for me, it's not anything like you felt for him, right?"

I frown. What I felt for Henry. That all-consuming burn in my chest, the way my heart still stutters when someone mentions him even though I should despise him, the way my stomach twists when I see pictures of him.

No, I don't feel that with Ronan. What I feel for Ronan is a strange, close friendship, nothing more. I'd care if he were hurt, or sad, and I'll miss seeing him every day when we've parted ways. But I don't see a romantic future between us. I don't even hope for one.

As if reading my mind, he says, "See? Just good friends. Who sometimes fuck." He pushes a stray hair off my forehead. "Did it feel good?"

I hesitate for only a moment. "Yes."

He leans in to place a kiss on my forehead. "Good, because I'd love to do it again, sometime."

I think I'd love that, too. God, what am I getting myself into here? "Please don't tell anyone."

A somber cloud flickers across his face. "You should know me well enough by now."

"You're right. I do. I'm sorry."

"But just to warn you, Connor will probably figure it out."

I groan. "What's he going to say?"

"Seriously?" Ronan chuckles. "He's going to ask to join in next time." Ronan sees my expression and starts to laugh. He throws an arm around my neck like we're buddies and weren't just naked together ten minutes ago. "We better go. Remember, if anyone asks... it was a squirrel that made us late. A red one."

I snort and trail him out of the house, locking up behind me.

twenty-two

"I've gotta pull over for a minute," Connor announces. It's just a phrase though, because there's no "pulling over" around here. He simply stops the truck in the middle of the lone road.

"Fuck. We made it just in time." Ronan leans forward to look up toward the sky through the windshield. The rain is coming down in sheets. I can't see two feet in front of us.

"What about all the wood? Will the tarp hold up?" The back of the truck is full of freshly split wood, a half-assed attempt at covering it with a yellow tarp as we quickly cleaned up, the clouds rolling in faster than anyone anticipated.

"I hope so or Darryl will have our asses." Connor starts fussing with the dials, cranking the heat and turning up the music. "Might as well get comfortable. They used the word 'torrential' in the forecast."

"Well, in that case...." I reach behind the seat to pull out the tiny white box that I'd hidden this morning before we left. "Autumn went to Homer yesterday, so I had her stop at a bakery for me." I hand it to Connor. "Happy birthday!"

"It's not his fucking birthday!" Ronan argues.

"Yeah, it is, you asshole." His eyes light up as he opens the box to pull out the vanilla cupcake.

"Sorry, there weren't a lot of options."

"Where's mine?"

I turn to glare at Ronan. "Your birthday's not until November."

He looks bewildered. "How do you even know that?"

"Because I looked through your wallet when you weren't paying attention, Ronan *Clarence* Lyle."

Connor's head falls back with his deep bellow of laughter. "Dude, I think she's making fun of you."

I giggle as Ronan fakes a glower, but a devious smirk follows closely behind.

"Thanks, Abbi. You're a *real* friend." Roping an arm around my neck, Connor pulls me into a hug. Only he kisses me. Right on the mouth. And not a quick kiss either.

I pull away with flushed cheeks, and glance over my shoulder at Ronan, slightly panicked. He's watching us intently, his chin propped up by an elbow on the doorframe, his gaze flaring with heat. Only, not with anger. "Where's mine?"

"You'll get yours in November." I'll have to mail it to their place in Miami.

"What if I want mine right now?" He reaches out to wrap his arm around my waist and he slides my body backwards to him. "Come here."

He's not talking about cupcakes anymore. I'm not entirely sure what he's thinking is going to happen in this truck. It's been four days since that day at the cabin. True to his word, Ronan hasn't treated me any differently. Well, I feel him watching me more, and we're sharing a lot of secretive smiles. I haven't noticed him giving any of the girls who normally hit on him a second look.

He reaches up to slide the elastic from my hair, releasing my ponytail. Weaving his fingers through my long, thick hair, he guides my head back to rest against the seat.

And then he settles his mouth on mine in a kiss. A much deeper and more intimate kiss than the one Connor just gave me, his tongue slipping against the seam of my lips.

I push against his chest, forcing him away, so I can glare at him with warning. "What are you doing?"

"I know, Abbi." Connor licks icing off his fingers as he devours the cupcake, already half done. "Said you were the best fuck he's ever had."

My mouth drops open. I'm a mix between embarrassed that Connor knows and oddly proud that Ronan said that, especially since I really don't know what I'm doing yet, compared to someone like Rachel or Katie.

Still.... "What do you think you're doing?"

"I'm kissing you." Ronan takes a firm grasp of my hair again, tighter this time, and forces me backward until my head is resting against his lap and he's leaning over me, running the back of his knuckles against my jaw softly, affectionately. "I told you, he doesn't mind." And Ronan's mouth is on mine again, his tongue prodding my mouth open to slide in.

It's hard not to get lost in him, his lips so full and soft and skilled. I can't believe that I've had sex with this guy and yet I'm only kissing him now.

Music fills the truck cab as Connor turns the volume up. Ronan unweaves his hand from my hair, catching his fingers in the tangles. I startle against his mouth when his hand cups my left breast.

Is this wrong? Letting Connor watch him do this?

"Does it feel good?" Ronan whispers, somehow honing in on exactly where my nipple is, rubbing over it until it begins to harden.

"Yes, but—"

"No buts." He smiles against my mouth. "Just close your eyes and kiss me."

"But Connor—"

"Connor is crazy about you." He pulls back just long enough to show me his eyes. "I'll stop when you don't enjoy it anymore. I promise. Just say the word."

I hear myself whisper, "Okay."

His lips fall to mine again. And then his hand is sliding down and under, and back up my work shirt. Within seconds he's figured out that the clasp is in the front and, with a push of the button, my breasts spring free of my bra. He takes turns rubbing each one with his large, callused hands, in that almost too-rough way of his.

I whimper, reaching up to pull his lips closer to mine, not daring to look at Connor right now.

Ronan works my shirt up, and cool air touches my skin. I hear a soft, "holy fuck," come from the other side of the truck. Ronan's bared my breasts to Connor now.

Oh my God. This is really happening.

"You still good?" Ronan whispers against my mouth.

In some sick, depraved way, my heart swells for his concern for my comfort in all this. "Yeah." In some other sick, depraved way, having him expose me like this stirs my blood.

"Good." He smiles against my lips, continuing to kiss me deeply and touch my breasts so possessively, until I find soft pants escaping me against his mouth.

And then his hand begins sliding downward.

I suck in a gasp as his fingers skate along my abdomen to

my workpants. They rest on the button, his thumb toying with it. He breaks free from my mouth—my lips now swollen from all the attention—just enough to look into my eyes, to show me the lust he has for me.

And then he flicks the button open and unfastens the zipper. I hold my breath as his fingers slide down and under my panties. He hooks a finger and pushes into me.

I can't believe I'm letting Ronan finger me in front of Connor.

And I'm not telling him to stop.

Am I going to hell for this?

In and out, in a slow, repetitive flow, Ronan pushes his finger, his breathing growing more rapid against my mouth. I grow more and more wet, until the sound of it fills the truck's interior. I'll have to change my panties when I get back.

"Do you want to come?" Ronan asks against my mouth.

"Yes," I whisper, because I'm already almost there. A few more minutes of this and my moans will fill this truck. I've all but forgotten that we have a spectator at this point. Connor hasn't uttered a single word since he first saw my breasts.

"Okay. But we need to make it easier."

We?

A second set of hands settles on the top of my pants to grip and slowly pull them down over my hips, down my hips, to my knees. Past my knees.

Connor pulls my legs up onto the truck bench, bending them until my boots tuck against his thigh.

Ronan's hand slides out of me to guide my thighs part.

I try to swallow my nerves.

"Look at him. He wants this. Badly."

Steeling myself, I finally shift my gaze to where Connor

sits, taking my body in with hooded eyes, his chest heaving up and down with rapid breaths.

Ronan holds his finger—the one he had inside me—to my lips. "Suck."

I comply, opening my mouth and tasting myself on him as he pushes his finger in deep. I can't help the moan that escapes me as he pulls it out and begins lazily stroking my nipple.

"You're so fucking beautiful, Abbi," Connor murmurs, shifting in his seat to face me, his hands slowly running up the insides of my thighs, rubbing them as he goes, and pushing them even farther apart. His eyes are locked on mine, as if weighing my reaction.

Part of me wants to tell him to stop, to pull my pants up and end this madness. That's just my conscience, my "what would people say if they knew?" angel on my shoulder.

But body is humming with anticipation.

When Connor's hands have reached the apex of my thighs, his thumbs resting on either side of my swollen lips, and I haven't told him to stop, a strange look comes over his face. I can't explain it. It's a mix of shock, and happiness, and adoration.

Connor slides two fingers into me.

"She's nice and wet," Ronan murmurs, watching his friend finger me without a hint of jealousy or possessiveness, his focus on my breasts.

Connor's thumb lands on my clit and he begins rubbing that too. The feel of that, along with Ronan's fingers on my nipple, is almost too much. My muscles spasm.

Connor chuckles. "Don't you dare. Not yet." Leaning forward, he covers my mound with his mouth.

I gasp and then moan, looking up at Ronan as Connor sucks on my clit and blood floods toward my pelvis.

Ronan smiles—an "I told you" smile—and then leans forward to kiss me again.

This is too much. Ronan's mouth on mine, his hands on my breasts, Connor's tongue between my legs. It's enough to drive someone insane.

Thirty seconds later, I'm bucking against Connor's face, moaning and crying out as I ride a wave like I've never ridden before, all my inhibitions dissolved.

Connor sits up, letting his head fall back with a groan, his lips glossy from me coming on them. He unzips his pants. I don't even have to look to know he's hard. I'm sure Ronan is, too.

"He'd love it if you could help him out," Ronan murmurs, adding a soft, "but only if you want to."

I sit up and take Connor in for a long moment, stroking himself, his gaze still locked on me, still half-undressed, though my shirt has fallen down. I like Connor, I'm attracted to him just as I am Ronan, and after what he just did for me, I definitely feel like I owe him one.

Plus, I'm just curious about what it would be like to be with him.

So I reach forward to wrap my hand around his erection, reveling in the warm, smooth skin and hardness of it against my palm.

He lets go and allows me take over, lifting his hips off his seat to push his pants down, just enough to uncover himself fully and give me a good look. He's about the same size as Ronan, only thicker.

"Abbi...." He groans.

"Yeah?" I tease softly.

He reaches up first to graze my cheek with this knuckles affectionately, and then to hook his hand around the back of my head. He gently begins pulling my head down toward his lap.

I haven't done this since Henry.

Pushing that thought aside, I adjust myself onto my knees and lean forward, wrapping my lips around his tip first, before pushing down, filling my mouth with Connor. He gently thrusts his hips upward.

While I'm busy sucking off Connor, Ronan starts fussing with my boots, untying them and yanking them off my feet. My pants and panties come off next, until I'm in nothing but a t-shirt. Connor quickly slides that over my head, forcing me to break for a moment so he can pull it off.

And now I'm completely naked in the maintenance truck with Ronan and Connor. The rain is still coming down in sheets, but we've fogged up the glass with our hot breath anyway.

"So fucking perfect. She's unreal," Connor murmurs with adoration. Behind me, I hear the rustle of clothes—Ronan unfastening his belt and then his pants—followed by the crinkle of a wrapper.

And then I feel him shifting at my back, adjusting my hips, tugging my left leg off the bench so I'm on one knee and my hips are apart. Thank God for the wide benches in this truck or there's no way we'd be able to do this in here.

He lines his cock up against my opening and I pull away from Connor just in time to cry out as Ronan thrusts into me. How am I supposed to do this for Connor while Ronan's behind me doing that?

"You can do it, Abbi," Connor says as if reading my mind, pulling my head back down. This time I take all of him in, trying to focus on him and not on the swollen cock that's deep inside the other end of me. "Drag your teeth a little. I like that."

I do as asked and he groans.

We fall into a rhythm, of Ronan pushing into me and me taking Connor into my mouth, moving in the same direction to avoid bumps. Connor's hands are gripping my head and Ronan's hands are gripping my hips and I don't really know where to focus because if I think too much about what I'm doing—with two guys—it's all overwhelming, and I'm terrified that I'll be riddled with guilt once the physical high is over.

So I don't let myself think. I let myself feel.

Connor begins thrusting his hips into my mouth. "Yeah, that's it. Take it all in. Damn." He chuckles through his moans. "You don't gag, do you?"

As if to prove a point, I take him in even deeper, all of him, spurring him on, his hips thrusting harder and faster, his fingers weaving tight through my hair, all while Ronan keeps thrusting from behind.

A cry tears out of Connor's lips as hot, salty liquid spurts into my mouth, hitting the back of my throat in streams.

No sooner have I swallowed the last drop than Ronan pulls out and sits back, yanking on my hips to force me back onto him. "Straddle me," he demands, helping me get my knee over his thighs. Sliding his hand in between us, he lines himself up against my opening. Grabbing my hips on either side, he pulls me down hard onto his cock.

I've never done it like this before, but he guides me with his hips and his hands until I'm moving in sync with him. Connor sits with his pants still pushed down, his eyes glued to my breasts as they bounce up and down. Watching me fuck his friend.

Ronan's eyes are affixed to mine though, searing into me as I ride him, feeling heaviness grow in my belly once again. With a hand between my breasts, he pushes me back until

I'm leaning against the dashboard, my thigh muscles straining as they stretch.

"Can you touch yourself for me?" Connor asks. I look over to see that he's stroking his fully erect cock, ready to go again.

These two will be the death of me.

I'm far beyond feeling an ounce of self-consciousness by this point. I reach down and run my finger over myself, slick and sore but ready to feel ecstasy again.

"Fuck. If we weren't in this truck...." Connor murmurs, his hand gliding over himself faster, his grip firmer.

"The things we're going to do to you," Ronan whispers between pants, his chest heaving as much as mine. He's not far from coming now.

Like what? What could they possibly do that they haven't *already* done?

Ronan pulls me back up and tight to him, his strong arms curling around my body, burrowing his face in my neck, as we grind against each other. "You can't figure it out, can you?"

I'm embarrassed to admit it but, "No."

I think he's going to explain but his arms tighten and his hips speed up and suddenly Ronan's cock is pulsing as he explodes.

Next to me, Connor comes again too, this time into his palm.

And then, so suddenly, all is silent. The rain has stopped, and all I can hear is the three of us panting heavily in the car, my chest heaving against Ronan's. I didn't come but I'm strangely okay with it.

"Look at the three of us," Ronan murmurs.

I do. I take a good look at all of us. Me, naked and coated with a slick sheen of sweat, straddling Ronan's lap as he lies back with his eyes closed, and Connor with his dick in his cum-filled hand.

I start to laugh. "What just happened?"

Connor's deep bellow follows, and even Ronan's chuckling. "We're both yours, Abbi. That's what happened."

A tiny thrill jumps inside my chest. "What does that even mean?"

"It means we're *yours*." Ronan leans in to graze my nipple. "Did you enjoy that?"

Is there something wrong with me if I say yes?

I hesitate, then nod.

"Good."

I reach for my t-shirt, feeling very exposed now that the moment is over, but Connor manages to grab it and pull it out of my reach. He smiles sluggishly. "Do you think I could get in there tonight? It is my birthday, and all."

There's that little voice screaming in the back of my head. It's saying this is too much, I've gone too far. That I'm sinning.

I shove it aside, because that little voice is tainted with Mama's close-mindedness and Reverend Enderbey's constant preaching, and I'm not so sure we share the same beliefs anymore.

"Hey? What do you think?" Ronan's hands slide over my back, his fingers trailing all the way down along my crack until he's prodding my tight hole again. "How about both of us at once."

When I realize what he's suggesting, my mouth drops open in shock.

They both start laughing.

Even though I know they're not kidding.

∼

"Damn, look at that storm rolling in! We should probably pull over again." Connor slows the truck, peering up at the blue skies above.

"Keep driving!" I giggle, smacking his arm.

He grins and gives the truck some gas to get it going again. On the other side of me, Ronan rests his head against the headrest, eyes closed, smiling.

Things have been oddly normal—but better—between us since Connor's birthday a few days ago. We haven't so much as kissed since. They've been more than willing but they also haven't pushed it, somehow seeing that I need time to digest this new "relationship" between us.

A relationship that I'm finding myself craving more and more with each day that passes. The way they make me feel.... I can't describe it. It feels somehow right. I like being this close to them. I like the deep physical connection the three of us share.

But the last thing I want to happen is for anyone to figure it out. It's one thing for people to call them my "fuck boys," it's entirely different for them to know it's true. They might try to make me feel bad for what I want.

And right now, I want both Connor and Ronan. I want to see where they might want to go with this.

"Is there anywhere private for us? Maybe tonight?" I ask tentatively, staring ahead at the road, feeling both sets of eyes land on me.

No one says anything for a long moment, and then Ronan offers, "We might be able to catch the last ferry into Homer. We could rent a room."

I meet his gaze. "That'd be good."

His eyes flicker over my features, excitement dancing in them. "It'd be *really* good."

Connor throws an arm around my shoulder, pulling me

into his body to lay a kiss on my forehead. "You realize I'm going to be working with a raging hard-on all afternoon, now?"

"When aren't you?" I mumble, earning both their laughs.

We pull through the gates and park the truck along the service laneway. "Darryl said to check in with him before we head for lunch break." Connor hops out.

I slide out behind him. Ronan follows closely from his side, and the three of us stroll onto the main grounds.

"I didn't think it'd ever get this hot here." Despite my red hair and tendency to burn, I've somehow developed a rather unsightly golden farmers' tan. I don't know how to get rid of it, short of lying at the staff beach. "It's almost warm enough for a bikini."

"That's a visual I need right now, red." Ronan reaches up to cup the back of my neck, rubbing it affectionately for just a few seconds before pulling away.

I love it when they do that.

I look up to absorb the sunlight against my face. "I just mean that it's so nice. I'm so happy I get to work outside all day and enjoy this instead of being stuck inside."

When I drop my gaze, I find myself staring into familiar steely blue eyes.

twenty-three

My feet falter at the sight of Henry, looking larger than life as he leans against a service truck, powerful arms folded over his chest. He holds my gaze for three long seconds before shifting back to focus on Darryl. They're talking, and laughing. It's all very casual.

Meanwhile I may be moments away from passing out. My chest actually hurts, it's tightened so fast.

I hear a soft "Fuck" from Ronan beside me.

The only one who's clueless is Connor, who slows and looks back at us when he realizes we're not beside him anymore. "You guys coming?"

"Yeah." I finally croak, forcing myself forward, my work boots suddenly ten times heavier. My heart is racing by the time we're in front of Darryl.

And Henry.

"Hey, we've got another load in. We'll stack it after break, if that works for you?" Connor has absolutely no idea that my world is falling apart.

I was doing so well, too. I'd compartmentalized all of my

feelings—good and bad, mostly bad—into a little box and stuffed it into the recesses of my mind. I'd started to move on, letting myself enjoy life. Enjoy other guys.

And none of that matters anymore.

"Yeah, go on," Darryl mutters, just as clueless.

Connor nods, then shifts his focus to Henry, turning on a more respectful persona. "Good to see you around again, Mr. Wolf."

Henry eases off the truck and offers a hand. "Connor, right?"

A slight frown flickers across Connor's face. "Yeah, right." I know what he's thinking: how does Mr. Wolf know my name? But I'm not surprised. Henry knew every one of my roommates' names.

"And Ronan." Henry's jaw tenses as he offers Ronan his hand.

Finally, his eyes settle on me again.

And I feel the weight of my pain as surely as if it just happened. All this time... everything that's happened between Ronan, Connor, and me... none of it matters. My heart hasn't been able to dismiss and move on.

My heart is stupid.

He's evil, I remind myself. I can wish that he's different, but he never will be.

"Miss Mitchell."

I clear my voice. "Mr. Wolf."

"How is the Outdoor crew treating you? Is it everything you wanted?"

"It's been great. Everyone treats me well."

"I'm sure they do." There's a sharp edge to his tone, compounded by a lightning quick gaze to either side of me. To Darryl, he promises, "I'll have the truck back by four."

Darryl snorts. "It's your truck. Keep it as long as you want. You need help out there? I can send these guys out."

Henry lifts an ax that I didn't notice resting against the tire into the back of the truck. "Maybe. I'll see how I feel."

"Right. Well, radio in if you do."

I can't help but stare at his form—clad in a simple black long-sleeved shirt and cargo pants—as he climbs into the truck. He somehow looks better than he did before.

Henry's back. Who knows for how long. And it doesn't change anything. It doesn't change what he did.

But Henry's back.

"Abbi!" Connor's voice snaps my attention back. "Where'd you go to?"

I feel Ronan's gaze on me. When I meet his eyes, he simply nods to himself, sad realization filling his features. "We've lost her."

~

VOICES BUZZ around me but I easily tune them out.

Because Henry is here and everything has changed. For better or worse, I can't stop thinking about him, as much as I want to.

A corn kernel to the forehead pulls my attention back. I look up to find Connor watching me intently through a sip of beer.

I sigh. "Yeah?"

"You good?"

I nod.

He leans in slightly. "It's not because of... *you know what.*" He quirks a brow. "No regrets, right?"

For all that Connor may be, he's decent enough to be concerned that my boundaries were pushed too far. I feel bad that he has no clue what this is really about. If I could tell him, I would. But instead, I offer him a weak smile. "No regrets. I swear." Not about what I did with him and Ronan.

Regrets about Henry? That's an entirely different question, and one I can't answer. Had I not met him, not fallen for him, not given him me, would I still be that idiot pining over Jed?

Chalk it up to a life lesson. A brutally painful one.

Ronan smooths a hand over my back. "She'll be fine. Right, red?"

"You shut up. I'm still pissed at you. It's your fault we missed the last ferry," Connor grumbles, shoving a mouthful of meatloaf into his mouth.

I nod at Ronan with appreciation. He took the blame, disappearing mysteriously, only to reappear as John was leaving the docks. He knew a night in a hotel in Homer was not happening between us.

He also knows that nothing is going to happen between us again.

I just can't.

"Hey, buddy." Mark drops a hand on Connor's shoulder before settling in beside him, Corbin on the other side. The lodge is busy tonight, with people continuously joining our table.

"A grizzly can weigh up to fifteen hundred pounds," Corbin says. They're obviously mid-conversation. Or mid-argument.

"That's not just any grizzly. That's a Kodiak." Mark shakes his head at his friend. "Dude, have you not learned anything while in Alaska?"

"When the hell am I going to learn something? I'm always working!"

"Yeah, 'working,'" Mark jokes, making a jerking off hand gesture.

I get the feeling that Corbin and Mark are the type to argue about the sky being blue and the grass being green, just for the sake of arguing.

"So, what's new in the world of voyeurism anyway?" Ronan asks between mouthfuls of his burger.

"It's been pretty fucking dull lately," Corbin mutters. "Too many respectable guests. But, Wolf is back so maybe that'll change."

"He's too smart to let us catch him on camera, dumb ass." Mark shakes his head at his friend, but Corbin's already ready with a counterargument.

"Need I remind you about the smokin'-hot magazine writer?"

I'm ready to toss my fork at them. I really don't need to hear about this again right now.

Mark smacks the table with this palm. "I already told you, Wolf didn't hit that!"

"I *watched* him go into the cabin with her and that hot blonde with my own eyes!" Corbin emphasizes "hot" with two hands cupped and held out in front of his chest. "A guy like Wolf walks into a cabin with two women like that and the hell they aren't bangin.' He probably said 'get naked' and they were all 'yes, Mr. Wolf!' Dude's my hero."

Mark shakes his head. "That's not what happened."

"Basically, it was."

"No, it wasn't."

"Fuck! Shut up!" Ronan shouts, annoyance filling his face. "You two need to get laid."

Mark rolls his eyes at Ronan. "Fine, Corbin. How long was he in there?"

Corbin shrugs. "I don't know. I went on break."

"Well, I can tell you for a fact that that's not what happened."

"You weren't there!"

"No, but Andy was. Right, Andy?" Mark points his fork to the end of the table where Andy has just slid into a seat.

Heads turn toward him, waiting.

"I was where?"

"That journalist. The night Wolf shot her down."

I can't keep the frown from showing. *What?*

"Damn, just throw me under the bus, why don't you, Mark." Andy's shaking his head, but he's struggling to hide his smile.

"Wait. *You* were there with Wolf and those two hot chicks?" There's no small hint of envy in Corbin's voice.

"Oh, he was *there* all right." Mark waggles his brows.

Andy tosses a corn kernel at his roommate's head, pinning him in the nose.

But it doesn't distract Corbin from his need for the decadent details. "Bullshit. Like *there* there? What happened?"

Andy takes a sip of his Coke—I assume, because he's working tonight; he drinks as much as the crew, otherwise. "Fuck, Mark. If I get canned for this...." Andy shakes his head but then heaves a sigh. "I heard them come in so I went to see if they needed anything. The two chicks had stripped and were standing in the living room in *nothing*, waiting for Wolf. But he turned them down."

"What? No. He never turns ass down."

"How the fuck do you know?" Mark mutters.

"Because he has a Wolf shrine that he jerks off to, nightly," Connor jokes, earning a round of laughter from everyone but me.

Because I desperately need to hear the rest of this story.

Andy shrugs. "I don't know. He gave her some excuse

about being involved with a woman and not wanting to fuck things up."

"That guy doesn't commit. Not when he can have as much ass as he wants."

"Don't shit where you eat." Connor licks mayo off his finger. "She's from a big magazine. Smart guy. I guess that's why he's the boss."

"Yeah, well, I wasn't sure how smart he was. She was *pissed*. Tried to save face by blowing him off, saying she didn't care because she had the better fuck the night before with his brother, and she was going to destroy his hotel. And Wolf... damn." Andy's eyes widen. "Did he let her have it. Told her that if her article even suggested to him that she was acting unfairly, he'd make sure her boss knew what she'd been up to while here."

"Fuck. The guy's got some huge fucking brass balls on him." Corbin is officially in love with Henry. "Shut that bitch down. Crushed her."

Mark chuckles. "I wouldn't say that." His sideways glance at Andy tells me there's more to the story.

Andy shakes his head. "She called me in there and made me watch her and her friend do lines of coke off each other."

"And then?"

There's a long pause. And then Andy grins wide. "Then they broke my cock. I couldn't get it up for two days. Best night of my life."

They're all laughing and jeering. I feel Ronan's eyes on me, but I keep my gaze on my plate as blood rushes through my ears like a freight train. If what Andy's saying is true—and I get the feeling that it is—then that means....

Henry lied to me. He led me to believe that he slept with Roshana and that other woman.

I thought I felt ill before but this churning in my stomach, this guilt whirling around inside me, is going to make me lose my dinner.

My eyes begin to burn and I furiously blink away the tears, not wanting anyone to find out.

I need to know. I need to look Henry in the eye and get the truth from him.

Ronan, so in tune with me and having figured out the other piece to the story, leans in and whispers, "Go. I'll clean up for you."

Barely managing a nod of thanks, I slide out of my chair.

It takes everything in me not to run all the way to Cabin One.

twenty-four

My hands tremble as I hit the doorbell on Cabin One.

I have no idea if he's home. If he's alone.

Please be alone.

The door opens up and a freshly showered Henry stands there.

"You lied to me." It's barely a whisper.

He says nothing, stepping back to allow me in. I walk through, inhaling his cologne with a shaky breath. I haven't been in here since the day I discovered him gone. It looks the exact same.

The desk he laid me out on is still there, with his laptop set up on it.

The dining table he tied my wrists up on now holds dishes from room service.

Henry strolls past me, seemingly unconcerned. "Miles!"

A young, brown-haired guy who I've seen around pokes his head through the service entrance door. "Yes, Mr. Wolf?"

"You can call it a day. Please be back tomorrow at 8:00 a.m."

"Yes, sir." He disappears. Moment later I hear the door shut. I peer out the small window by the front door to see him trudging along the covered path.

"He's not the type to eavesdrop, if that's what you're worried about." A tiny smirk curls Henry's lip, but otherwise he shows me nothing.

I can't even begin to know how to approach this the right way, so I don't bother. I just blurt out, "You lied to me. You told me that you slept with her, but you didn't." My voice breaks at the end.

His eyes graze over me. "Isn't that what you wanted to hear?"

"What? Why on earth would I want to think that you slept with someone else? You should have told me the truth!"

He pauses, his fingers on a glass. Of water, it seems. The decanter of scotch remains untouched. "All I've ever told you is the truth, Abbi. I told you things would be different for a few days. I told you that I didn't have time for jealousy. I told you that I didn't fuck anyone on Friday night. I told you that my brother is a liar and manipulator. I told you that I wouldn't beg you to believe me." He fires the list off without pause, as if he's got them itemized on a sheet of paper, the anger seeping through his words. But then he falters. "I told you that I trusted you. All of these things were the truth. Truth that you chose to either ignore or interpret differently."

I squeeze my eyes shut. He *did* tell me all those things. "You should have told me the truth about what happened that night."

"Why?"

"Because then I wouldn't have hated you so much."

He steps closer to me. "I figured it would hurt you less

than telling you the truth. That, while you were lying under Michael, letting him fuck you, I was sitting in my cabin alone, considering whether I should be selfish and fire you as a Wolf employee so I could keep you for myself and avoid all this hassle."

His words are a kick to my stomach.

It finally clicks.

Henry didn't cheat on me.

Technically, I cheated on *him*.

Tears fall freely now. I don't bother holding them back. This is *all* my fault. I fucked up. I messed everything up between us.

"Did I *want* to hurt you?" Henry watches a tear slide down my cheek, but he doesn't reach up to catch it, to wipe it away. "Yeah, I did. Because I was angry. At you. At myself. Had I known you'd run off and fuck the first guy who put his arm around you, maybe I would have handled things differently." His jaw tenses. "Never in a million years did I think you'd go and do something like that. You surprised me, Abbi, and not in a good way. I didn't think you had it in you."

Tears spill from my eyes. "I saw you leave with them. I thought—"

"I *told* you I wouldn't, Abbi. But that wasn't enough for you." A brief wave of emotion flares in his eyes before he's able to get it under control, to ice me out. "And then you tried to threaten me, something else I never thought you'd do. So I did and said some things that I can't ever take back." He sighs. "And now there's no going back. There's no fixing it."

I try to stifle my cries with a hand over my mouth, his words stripping away the anger and blame I've used as a shield, leaving me unprotected and raw.

I wanted a miracle, a reason to believe Henry wasn't all bad. He's just given it to me, and it doesn't matter. I screwed up with Henry. Oh God, I screwed up *so* badly.

"I'm so sorry," I manage to get out through my sobs before I bolt out the door.

∽

Whispers surround my privacy curtain. I hear their questions, their concern, but I stay curled up in a ball, facing the wall, and no one bothers me. Not after I screamed at Tillie, telling her to mind her own damn business and stop looking for gossip.

This hurts a million times more than thinking that Henry cheated on me.

I cheated on him.

I mean, we weren't technically "officially" an exclusive item.

But he trusted me to believe him and *not* go and sleep with another guy, and I did exactly that. I fucked everything up. I caused this pain. Me, who was crushed by Jed only months earlier for sleeping with another girl.

My head tells me that it's nothing like what Jed did to me, because Jed and I were getting married. Jed and I shared a childhood of memories and promises, of plans. We already had a life. There was no doubt that we *were* exclusive and committed to each other.

And yet, down to my core—and every fiber of my body—I know that Henry owned me from the first time I gazed into his eyes, my head spinning from alcohol, my heart spinning from betrayal.

What have I done?

A knock sounds on the door and a moment later, angry voices.

"Is this because of you?" Katie hisses.

A guy sighs. "Yeah."

I immediately recognize Ronan's voice.

"You are *such* a dick!" The sound of skin slapping against skin ricochets through the cabin. "Make it better."

The curtain shifts and, a moment later, weight hits my mattress as Ronan crawls toward me to stretch out next to me. I can see the red mark where Katie's hand made contact with his cheek. It must have hurt, but he doesn't show it, wedging his arm under my head and pulling me against him. He leans in to place a soft kiss on my mouth.

I pull away. "Don't, Ronan. I'm not in the—"

"Shut up." He brushes the hair off my face. "I'm not here for that. I'm not Aspen."

I squeeze my eyes shut. I don't think I've ever regretted anything so much as that night.

Ronan's arms tighten around me, pulling my face into his chest, the smell of his soap comforting.

"You took the blame with them," I whisper, my fingertips sliding over his cheek.

He shrugs. "I'm sure I've already earned it somewhere. Now cry all you want, red. I'm not going anywhere tonight."

And I do, muffling my sobs against his t-shirt, soaking the cotton material.

I cry over Henry and what can never be fixed.

twenty-five

Someone is shaking me awake.

"Yeah. I'm trying.... Abbi?" Ronan's sleepy voice fills my ear. I'm still burrowed against his chest, exactly as I was when I fell asleep. I don't want to move, or even open my eyes, which I'm sure are swollen and red.

"Abbi, you need to take this."

Finally, the urgency in his voice clicks. I peel my face off him to find him holding my phone in his hand.

"It kept vibrating, so I finally answered it. Seemed important."

Oh crap. "Who is it?" If that's Mama, I will never hear the end of this.

"Some guy named Jed."

Jed? I frown. I haven't talked to him since the night I told him that we were done. I take the phone, a tiny bite of satisfaction lifting my spirits that Jed called here in the morning and a guy answered. "Hello?"

"Abigail, I've been trying to get hold of you all morning. Your dad had an accident."

I bolt up. "What do you mean *an accident*?"

"He rolled his tractor."

"What?" I heard him, but I don't believe it. My dad's been driving tractors in the fields since he was ten years old.

"On that slope near the back of the property. Your mom called our house on the way to the hospital, and she asked me to get hold of you."

"Well, how bad is it?"

There's a long pause. "It's bad, Abbi. You know him, not bothering to buckle up. He was tossed, and then it rolled onto him. Definitely broken bones, probably internal bleeding. I.... It doesn't look good. Look, you need to come home. We don't know if he's going to make it."

A strange wave of shock washes over me, throwing me into an odd state of calm. "Yeah. Of course. I just.... I don't know how long it will take. Just, tell Mama I'm coming. And call me as soon as you hear something."

"For sure."

"Thanks, Jed."

"Of course. He's like a dad to me."

I hang up the phone, my blood rushing in my ears. "My dad rolled his tractor. He's hurt really bad. They don't think he's going to make it." Is that even me speaking? It doesn't sound right. "I need to get home." I frown at Ronan. "How do I get home?" I'm in Alaska!

He checks his watch. "John leaves with the supply ferry in half an hour. Hop on that."

"Right." I look around at my little bunk cubby, at the shelf that holds a picture of my parents when they were young. I guess I should pack. I don't know how long I'll be gone. "Do I call Darryl?" Or Belinda? I haven't talked to her since the day I moved to the crew.

"Don't worry about Darryl. I'll tell him."

"Okay, then. I guess... I'm packing."

And leaving Alaska.

~

"Tell the airline that it's an emergency and they might be able to work something out for you," John says, spinning the wheel with ease. The small ferry that I arrived on oh so long ago churns water as it heads toward Homer. "It likely won't be cheap but emergencies never are, are they?"

"No. I guess not." I stare back at the hotel, at the guests out for early morning walks or preparing for a peaceful kayak tour of the cove, their days full of promise.

I haven't even had a chance to grasp my current reality. I stuffed my duffel bag in a mad dash and said a quick good-bye to Rachel and Lorraine, who were the only ones around. Ronan walked me to the dock and left me with a fierce hug. He promised to say bye to Connor for me.

But now I can't do anything but stand idly and wait for whatever's going to happen to happen, good or bad.

Penthouse Cabin One is now visible as we gain distance from the beach, perched atop the cliff and overlooking the waters. I can't help but watch it as we drift, wondering if I should have said good-bye to Henry. Should have apologized again. If that would have made today any less horrible.

Movement on the front porch catches my attention. I squint against the blue sky and morning sun to focus on the tall form leaning against the rail, coffee in hand.

My heart stutters.

It's him.

Does he see me? The red in my hair isn't as vibrant as it once was.

Does he even care?

Should I wave?

If I do, and he doesn't respond....

I grip the railing tightly to avoid the temptation and potential letdown, the hollow ache in my chest growing.

~

"Miss Mitchell?"

I hear my name called. An older gentleman stands by, watching as John docks the ferry. He's dressed in slacks and a golf shirt, and though I have to guess that he's local, he looks completely out of place next to the fishermen busy loading crates and supplies onto their boats, their beard unshaven, their clothes thrown on haphazardly.

"Yes?" I'm instantly wary. But John's here, I remind myself. He wouldn't let something happen to me.

"My name is Sam. Belinda from Wolf Cove asked that I bring you to the airport." He pops open the ferry door and holds out a hand, palm raised. "Here. Let me take your bag."

"Thanks." I hand it to him. The airport can't be more than a ten-minute drive from the port, but... okay. That was nice of her.

"You gonna be okay, Abbi?" John frowns at me. "You look a little green."

"I took my motion sickness medication on an empty stomach."

"Oh. Well, alright. Best of luck that you get that flight home as soon as possible. I'll say a prayer for your father."

I smile at the old man. It strikes me that I'll probably never see him again. "Thank you, John. Enjoy Alaska."

"Oh, don't you worry." He chuckles, his gray-blue eyes drifting over the mountain range in the distance. "I always do. Every morning, and every night."

With that, I trail Sam along the dock.

~

"Isn't that the turnoff?" I point at the simple driveway and the rustic rectangular sign that reads Homer Airport.

"Oh, yeah. But we're not going there. They asked me to take you up to the airstrip, about twenty miles north-east of Homer."

I catch Sam's eyes on me in the rearview mirror. He must see my confusion. "You have a family emergency or somethin', it sounds like?"

"Yeah." I don't really want to explain it, so I check my phone, even though I know there are no new calls or texts. My phone has sat clutched within my grasp since I left the hotel, as I anxiously wait for any news.

"Well, you probably weren't gonna have much luck gettin' a commercial flight out this morning. Maybe to Anchorage, but then you'd be waiting a while there. And God only knows where you'd end up next. This guy, he'll help get you where you need to go quick."

I'm picturing a small six-seater plane and a puke bag in my future, but if it gets me home, then I'll take it.

I just hope it's quick enough.

~

"Here we go." Sam pulls past the chain-link fence, past the helicopter pad to our left, and towards a white hangar. My mouth drops open when I read the large black lettering across it.

Wolf Private Airstrip.

"The family built this airport when Walter Wolf started

his hotel chain. He liked to come up to the cabin whenever he could get away. Would fly his jet up. That's why the long runway." Sam's hand waves toward the stretch of pavement to our right, where a sleek-looking plane sits on the tarmac, waiting. "It's a good thing Mr. Wolf was in Homer, or you'd be taking that helicopter to Anchorage and looking for a connection."

It finally dawns on me. This wasn't Belinda's doing.

This is all Henry.

He must have heard. I guess this means he doesn't hate me for what I did, at least.

That prickly ball already sitting within my throat swells.

"You staff?"

I nod, not trusting my voice.

He shakes his head, more to himself. "Then they must treat their staff well, because I can't imagine what this flight will run them."

Neither can I.

He throws the sedan into park. I don't bother waiting for him to come around to open the door.

A man waits by the plane to collect my duffel bag and quickly moves for the open cargo door, as if he knows we're in a rush. Despite the dire situation, I pause for a moment to take in this surreal scene.

Is this actually happening?

"Miss Mitchell. It was a pleasure meeting you. I wish you all the best," Sam offers.

With a nod of thanks, I make my way up the narrow set of stairs that leads into the private jet.

A man in uniform waits at the top of the stairs. "Good morning, Miss Mitchell. I'm co-captain Jack Rodan. We should be taking off within fifteen minutes." He gestures toward the back of the plane. "Any seat you want."

"Thank you."

He leaves me to study the cream leather interior. There are six seats to choose from, the two closest to me facing the back of the plane, and four more facing this way, each one wide and comfortable-looking.

I move toward the back, to allow me some privacy as I find Henry's number on my phone. With only a moment's hesitation, I hit dial.

Disappointment fills me when Henry's recorded voice fills my ear.

"Hi. I'm at your airstrip. I guess you heard about what happened." Did Belinda call him? Or did he see me on the ferry and ask? Not that it really matters. "Thank you. I don't know how bad it is but... this is a lot, and I just wanted to say, thank you. You didn't have to. But thank you." I hang up before I say too much, settling into chair to focus on the mountain range in the distance.

This may be the last time I ever see it again.

Will I ever be back? Seeing as I don't have to pay for a flight home, I could probably afford it. If Dad was somehow miraculously okay, which he very likely won't be, seeing as a tractor rolled over on him.

Please God. Please let him survive this.

A loud roar fills my ear as the engines kick in, and a flutter of nerves stirs me. This is only my second time in a plane, ever, and this one is a lot smaller than the last. How safe are these private things, anyway?

I sit patiently, because I can't be anything but, while Jack Rodan hits buttons near the stairway again. I guess on a small flight like this, there's no need for a flight attendant.

Five minutes pass.

Ten.

Fifteen.

Then twenty, and I begin to get antsy.

"Took you long enough!" Jack yells at someone. A moment later he's backing up.

And Henry steps on board.

twenty-six

Henry smooths the back of his windswept hair down. "Had to wake my chopper pilot up. He wasn't planning on flying me in again so soon."

"Neither were we." Jack chuckles and clasps hands with Henry. "Grab a seat. We're ready to go."

My heart is pounding like a jackhammer in my chest. Henry's here? He's going to fly to Pittsburgh with me?

Crystal-blue eyes land on me, weighing me down with a hundred emotions. "Where are we refueling?"

"Just outside Seattle."

"Perfect." Instead of taking a seat, Henry ducks into the cockpit, and I hear him exchanging greetings with someone else. The captain, I presume.

I watch quietly, brimming with excitement and trepidation, as Jack seals the door. Henry reappears. "Cooler's stocked?"

"Yes, sir." Adjusting his hat, Jack disappears into the cockpit, pulling that door closed.

Henry sets a brown paper bag on the table in front of

me. "Figured you didn't eat, so I had the kitchen make something for you."

"Thank you." I'm starving, actually.

He peels his jacket off and tosses it onto the seat. I admire the soft charcoal-gray t-shirt beneath, and the simple way it hangs over his jeans, in just that perfect way: not too tight, but enough to show his muscles.

How I miss the feel of him beneath my fingertips.

To think I was allowed to touch that—that he was mine—for even just a short period of time.

Until I got jealous, and possessive, and mistrusting.

And there's nothing I can do to change that, or make it better. If I regret anything for the rest of my life, it'll be that.

Folding into the seat across from me, he fastens his seatbelt and begins fiddling with the media system, until soft music fills the cabin. "You should eat, Abbi."

The world outside us begins to move as the plane rolls into position for takeoff. To distract myself, I dig out the contents of the bag and set them in front of me. Granola, yogurt, fruit, an omelet, bagels with various cream cheeses, lox, bacon, and danishes. Basically, most of the breakfast menu.

"I didn't know what you would want. I figured I'd give you options." Henry opens the fruit container and pops a grape into his mouth. "It's going to be a long flight."

"How long?"

"Nine to ten hours. We won't get to Pittsburgh until late tonight."

I take a deep, shaky breath. Nine to ten hours. Way better than fifteen to twenty, but will my father still be alive when we land?

"I almost forgot." He reaches into his jeans pocket and

pulls out two sticks of turkey jerky, tossing them onto the table alongside everything else. "Just in case."

I can't help it, I burst out laughing, thinking of that first day with Henry. All the hope and excitement and nervousness. The wonder. The impossible what-if.

Before I screwed everything up.

It's not long before my laughter morphs into tears. I'm not even sure what I'm crying about anymore. Henry, my dad. Leaving Alaska. Nothing seems to be going well right now. "I'm sorry." I wipe the tears with the back of my hand, but more replace them instantly, until I can't even see through the blur.

I hear his seat belt unfastening and then, a moment later, so is mine, and strong arms are lifting me out of my seat. Together we sit on the other side where there's no table, with me on his lap, wrapped within his arms, my face burrowed against his neck.

"Don't we have to be in our seats for takeoff?" I whisper, inhaling Henry's scent, hoping it will help calm my nerves.

"This is my plane. We can do whatever the fuck we want."

"Okay." I don't want to move. Ever. I curl my fingers around his t-shirt and stay put as the engine roars with the sudden increase of speed, and then we're off the ground and climbing high into the sky.

I don't want to say anything to scare him off, so I bite my bottom lip and keep quiet, letting the moments pass, memorizing the feeling of being in Henry's arms again—how lucky I was to ever experience it in the first place.

"I wish I could go back in time," I whisper against him.

His chest swells with a deep sigh. "Not now, Abbi."

He's shutting me down.

I close my eyes and let myself dream about his mouth, and his hands, of his bare skin against mine.

Wishing it was mine again.

And that's how I drift off.

～

I AWAKE in Henry's arms to the captain's voice over the intercom, telling us that we've begun our descent into Seattle.

The awful reality of the situation hits me like a brick to the chest. My dad. The accident. I instantly reach for my phone.

"He's still in surgery as of half an hour ago. I've been keeping an eye out," Henry says.

"I guess that's good?"

He pushes my matted hair off my forehead and then, as if catching himself, pulls his hand away. "Yeah, that's good."

"You could have moved me."

"I didn't want to wake you. You looked comfortable."

"Yeah, I didn't sleep much last night, and the anti-nausea meds sometimes knock me out." I let my eyes wander over his handsome face. "And I was comfortable."

He offers me a tight smile in return. Suddenly I feel awkward, like I should either climb off him or kiss him. He hasn't given any indication that he'd be okay with me kissing him, so I climb off his lap.

He must have been waiting for that because he stands and, stretching his arms over his shoulders, he makes his way to the tiny restroom in the back.

The food he brought is still all laid out on the table. I shift over to that seat and pick at the cold bacon and chewy omelet, too hungry to be grossed out.

"Don't worry. We'll have something hot delivered in Seattle." Henry slides into the seat across from me, checking his phone.

"I'm fine. I like fruit." I shift over to the yogurt and granola, accidently knocking a lid off the table in the process. When I reach down to collect it, I get a good look at Henry's shoes and socks.

I press my lips together to hide my smile but it doesn't work.

"What?"

"I take it you don't ask Miles to dress you?"

His eyes narrow. "Why?"

I purposely stall answering by dipping a strawberry into the yogurt and then sucking it off the end. I feel his eyes on my mouth and I revel in the moment of attention, remembering when those heated eyes would be looking down on me, when I was allowed to suck him like this. "Because you're wearing two different shades of blue socks."

He groans, but then he's chuckling at himself. "Dammit. It was nice, not to have to worry about doing that for a while."

Until I fucked it all up.

"I'm sorry."

"Don't, Abbi." His jaw tightens as he pulls his phone from his pocket and begins scrolling.

I do my best to keep my tears at bay. "Do you have a lot of work to do?"

"Always," he murmurs absently.

I sense he doesn't want to speak, so I focus on the view out the window as we approach Seattle.

"What's taking so long?" Henry doesn't hide his irritation well.

"There was a delay with the fuel truck. We'll be back in the air shortly," Jack promises on his way out the door.

Henry looks to me.

"Jed says he's still in surgery." That means he's still alive.

With a slight nod, Henry dials someone on his phone. "Yeah.... Where are we with the specs?" I stare unabashed at him as he watches the refueling truck outside the window and listens to someone on the other end of the phone.

Have those full, soft lips touched anyone? What about those hands. My eyes drop farther, to his jeans, and his belt.

What about the rest of him?

Not that I'd have any right to ever say a word, given what I've been doing. Both Connor and Ronan texted me to see if I was okay. I haven't answered. That world, them, me *with* them... it's already so far from my mind.

"Okay, here we go." Jack is back and carrying two food trays toward the table.

"Here." I scramble to help clear what's left of breakfast.

"Thanks. I don't have this flight attendant thing down pat yet," Jack mumbles.

"They don't teach that in flight school?"

He chuckles. "I guess I missed that day. All right. We'll be taking off in a few minutes, in case you want to stick your head out for some fresh air before you're trapped in this tin can again."

I giggle. "I think I can handle this tin can."

"Not a bad way to travel, hey?" He winks. "Come up and check out the cockpit later, if you want."

"I will. Thanks."

"...I don't care if it takes another year, we need to open with at least two runs!" Henry's impatient "do as I say" voice is creeping in. "The bottom's been clear-cut for three years already. Yeah. We used the wood to build the lodge."

He's talking about Wolf Cove. What is he planning now?

"No.... Shit, I can't remember. Hold on." Henry starts fumbling with the dossier on his lap, unzipping it with one hand. A piece of paper slips out and floats to the ground.

I don't think twice, crouching to retrieve it for him. My hand freezes when I realize that it's a picture of me.

The one that Hachiro took that day, on the deck at his grandfather's cabin, when I was staring off into the water, my thoughts drifting into a life with Henry.

Henry actually printed it off. He's kept it all this time.

"The permits are as good as signed. That's a nonissue." Henry is still staring out the window and talking. He doesn't seem to have noticed the picture. Would he be angry that I know? I never know with him.

I quickly tuck it into the back of my jeans.

"See if you can get a revised plan by end of week. I want to start the work before winter, which isn't that far off up there." He hangs up with a sigh. "What did they bring in to eat?"

Trying my best to sound normal, I lift the metal cover. "Looks like chicken parm."

He moves in across from me, unraveling the cloth napkin for his lap. "Good. I'm starving."

I alternate my focus between my food, Henry, and the view outside, as the engines roar and we're speeding down the runway, into the sky once again.

Deciding what to say. If I should say anything, or if I should just ignore it.

I can't ignore it. Why does he still have this picture of me in his dossier, nearly two months after our disastrous downfall?

I'd love to think it's because he still cares about me.

Finally, I decide to not say a word. I simply reach behind my back and pull out the picture, sliding it across the table to sit next to his plate.

He pauses with fork midair, his steady gaze on it.

And then he continues eating. Not saying a single word about it. Not until he's cleaned his plate and is wiping his mouth.

"It was my fault."

"What was?"

He tosses the napkin onto his dishes and then brings the can of Coke to his lips. I count four throat bobs before he relents, setting it down in front of him. "When you told me what Scott had done, I should have worried about you. Not about me, not about what he was up to."

"He was trying to have you framed for rape, Henry."

Henry's eyes drift out the window. "He scared the shit out of you. He introduced doubt into your mind that I didn't do anything to get rid of. Here you are, this twenty-one-year-old who's only ever been in one relationship, with that fuckhead who crushed you. Of course you're going to have a hard time trusting anyone so easily again. I expected you to take what I said at face value." His eyes flicker to me. "That wasn't fair to you."

"What happened with Michael—"

"The asshole took advantage of a distraught woman. I saw the video."

My mouth falls open. Oh my God. "There's a video?"

"Security footage. Of you running into him, and him leading you back to his cabin with his arm around you. And of you leaving the next morning. I wasn't sure you actually fucked him until I saw your face. Then I knew, right away." He shakes his head to himself. "I have to say, it's the first time I've ever had a woman I was with do that to me."

His words are soft and without accusation, and yet I flinch as if they're a slap. "I wish I could go back in time and change it all. Really, I do."

His jaw tenses. "Did you enjoy it?"

"No. I mean...." I close my eyes. "I did, for what it was, at the time. But I didn't want to be there. I wanted to be with you."

"I should have made you come home with me that night, instead of walking that...." His words drift off with a snort and an eye roll. "That piece of work back to her cabin." He sighs, chuckling to himself. "But I didn't. And then, to top it all off, I threatened you with a video. Knowing that would terrorize you. Not one of my finer moments, Abbi. But..." He hesitates. "I didn't like how you made me feel."

"Do you have a video of me? Of *us*?"

He pauses to peer at the bottom of his glass. "I would never do that to you."

"You did it to your last assistant," I remind him.

"No, I didn't."

"You didn't videotape the two of you together?" Was that a lie, too?

"No. To be fair, I *asked* if she'd be willing but...." When he looks up to see my mouth hanging open, he chuckles softly. "There's this table in the foyer of my penthouse. One night, Kiera decided to surprise me by stripping down and lying on it. She figured I'd enjoy stepping out of my elevator to that sight. She didn't realize that there's a security camera there, with a perfect angle."

"So you got a video of everythi—"

"Right down to the happy look on her face as I fucked her."

I cringe with mortification, putting myself in that unwitting position. "But you knew the camera was there."

"I did," he admits with a sheepish smile. "I pulled the security footage immediately after so no one could exploit it. The benefit of owning the building."

I frown. "But you kept it."

"I did." Heat flares in his eyes. "And I watched it. I enjoyed watching it; I'm not going to lie to you. But I also tossed it into my safe and had no plans of ever letting anyone else see it. I consider myself lucky for that choice. And stupid, for all my other ones. Had I listened to my father, the last eight months of my life would have been a lot easier. But it's all over and done with now, and everyone can move on." He reaches for my tray. "You done with that?"

I nod. I'm not sure if I feel better or worse about him taking some of the blame off my shoulders. The way he's speaking, it's like he's resigned to the fact that it's really and truly over.

"I guess we both made a lot of mistakes that we can't take back."

He carries the trays over to a small bar. "There should be some decent movies to watch on the TV. I'm going to grab some sleep." Reclining the seat back all the way, he stretches his arms back behind his head, the move lifting his shirt up to reveal that delicious thin line of hair that starts below his belly button. "Wake me up if you hear anything."

twenty-seven

I'm far ahead of Henry, rushing through the emergency room, my stomach in knots.

Jed hasn't updated me.

He hasn't responded to my messages.

I know my phone's working because Ronan and Connor have been texting me, but Jed has not.

I fear the worst. That my father has died and Jed doesn't want to tell me over the phone.

A nurse kindly points me in the direction of the emergency room waiting area.

The first person I see is Reverend Enderbey. His back is to me, but I'd recognize that short-sleeved button-down and summer vest ensemble anywhere. Jed's mom, a tiny blonde woman, stands next to him. They're talking with a man in doctors' garb. Jed and Mama are on the other side of him.

Jed's eyes widen when he sees me. "Abigail!"

"Oh, thank God!" Mama exclaims, her short brown curls matted, her eyes red rimmed.

My stomach sinks. Bernadette Mitchell doesn't cry. Ever.

They must see the panic on my face because Jed rushes

for me, arms up. "No! It's okay! He's out of surgery. They think he's going to be okay!"

What? I process this as Jed scoops me into his arms. I offer no resistance. "But.... Why didn't you call?"

"My phone died and nobody in this hospital has a freaking cord!"

That's a fair excuse, given he's been here all day. I hadn't even thought of that. "So, he's going to be okay?"

"Yeah, we think so. It's still early but it's mainly a lot of broken bones. One of his lungs collapsed and he ruptured his spleen, but they said it's a miracle that it wasn't worse."

I crumple against Jed's chest as tears of relief overwhelm me.

"Come here, baby girl." Mama waits with her arms open wide. She's still in one of her floral nightgowns, which looks a lot like most of the dresses she wears anyway—long and flowing and covering her girth. I dive into her arms, happy to be consumed by her overbearing presence as we listen to the doctor answer our questions.

Surprisingly enough, it feels good to be home.

"We didn't expect you until tomorrow, Abigail," Reverend Enderbey says.

"I know. I lucked out."

Henry!

I pull away from Mama long enough to search for him with my eyes. I find him near the registration desk, talking to an older woman in a suit. She looks like she works here, and perhaps knows him, because she's smiling and nodding in a friendly way. They part ways with a handshake and Henry's thanks.

"I'll be back in a second." I feel everyone's eyes on me as I make my way over to Henry.

He offers me a smile. "Good news, I take it?"

"Yeah. It looks like he was really lucky."

"I'm glad." His gaze drifts over to where Mama and the Enderbeys wait, his eyes narrowing slightly. At Jed, I assume. "There's a suite booked at the Wolf downtown, if any of you need to grab some sleep or a shower. They just need to give your name at the front desk."

"That's.... Thank you."

"No problem. I'll be heading back first thing in the morning. Call Room 4001 if anything changes. Otherwise...." He sighs. "Take care of yourself, Abbi." He turns to leave.

"Wait!" I'm not ready to say good-bye to him again, even if what we had is done.

I don't care who's watching. I don't care if he's not okay with this. I throw myself at him, wrapping my arms around his neck in a tight hug, reveling in the feel of his strong, hard body against mine.

With a slow exhale, his arms wrap around me, returning the embrace, his nose grazing the top of my ear. I'd like to think it's an intentional sign of affection from him. "I've gotta go, Abbi," he whispers into my ear.

Reluctantly, I peel myself off him, and watch his back all the way down the hall.

~

"You should go and get some sleep, Mama. May said there are two bedrooms and a couch there."

"I'm not goin' nowhere until he wakes up." Mama holds Dad's still hand. They let us into his room an hour ago, and I burst into tears at the sight of all the machines and tubes. Outside, the beginnings of daylight creep into the sky, warning of the coming sunrise.

A nurse strolls in. "How are we doing in here?"

"We're doin' just fine. Got my man alive and my baby girl home, where she belongs. I'm counting our blessings." Tough Mama is back in full force.

The nurse smiles at me as she checks the machines and drips. "It certainly was a blessing. I hear they pulled Dr. Eisenhower out of surgery and threw him right into a helicopter."

I frown. "You mean he doesn't work here?"

"Dr. Eisenhower?" She chuckles. "No. He's out of New York. And he's considered to be the best trauma surgeon in America. Your father must be someone pretty special to the Wolf family."

My heart starts racing.

That's why Henry was talking to that lady in the suit. She was probably the Chief of Staff or something. He must have made that phone call the second he heard about my father's accident, before he met me on the plane.

Without Dr. Eisenhower, would my father have survived?

"Where you goin'?" Mama glares at me as I grab my sweater and purse.

"I'll be back as soon as I can."

"You are not goin' anywhere, young lady. Your father is going to wake up any minute. He'll want to see you here when he does."

"I'll be back as soon as I can. But I have to go."

"This doesn't have anythin' to do with that *man*, does it?"

I snort. "That *man* is Henry Wolf, and he's the reason I got home so fast, and the reason Daddy had the best trauma surgeon in America."

"So we can all call him and thank him together, later. Now it's time to focus on your family."

I head for the door.

"Just so you know, Jed broke up with Cammie. He's still in love with you. He's determined to win you back."

She obviously thinks that's going to matter to me, that the news will stop me from wanting to run to Henry.

"Sorry, Mama. Gotta go." I charge out the door.

twenty-eight

"Come on.... Pick up, pick up, pick up." I've had the hotel dispatch put me through three times already, but no one's answering. No one can tell me if he's checked out yet.

Please still be there.

I rush down the quiet hall, nodding at the room service guy on my way past, to the very end, to hammer on the door with my fist.

Henry opens the door, holding a towel around his waist, beads of water still dripping from his body, a confused look on his face. "What happened? Did something happen?"

I step forward, forcing him back inside. The door shuts with a noisy bang. "Dr. Eisenhower. Did you fly him in?"

He frowns. "I called in a favor, yeah. Why? Is your father okay?"

"Yeah. He's fine. He's...." My eyes drag over this man as my chest swells with an overwhelming amount of emotion.

Of love.

I no longer care what he put me through, or how badly he hurt me, or how badly I hurt him.

I dive for him, for his mouth.

He pulls away, his jaw cording with tension. "Abbi—"

"No. Don't. It is *not* too late for us. We can't go back, but we can go forward, and we can do it better. I know we can. It is *not* too late for us so don't you dare say that. I know you still feel something for me."

He tips his head back as if to find an answer in the ceiling. I so badly want to drag my tongue over his throat, but I restrain myself, and instead let my fingers settle on his chest, reveling in the beads of water and his nipples, pebbled from the cold, the gooseflesh covering his hard muscles, even as his breaths become ragged.

Beneath my fingers, I feel his heart beating hard and fast.

"Abbi, I can't. I'm—"

"Then end it!" The thought that Henry may be—probably is—involved with another woman crossed my mind in the cab on the way here, and I quickly decided I wouldn't accept that excuse. "Tell her you're sorry, but you never should have started anything because your heart has always been with me. End it now because I *need* you *right* now." My hands slide down to grip the top of his towel. It would be nothing to uncover him, a quick tug.

"Oh, fuck me." He closes his eyes and heaves a sigh. "I'm not seeing anyone, Abbi. I just…. I can't do this again. Not with you."

I step in to him, pressing myself against him. "Give me one good reason why not."

He finally drops his gaze, and it's a pensive one. "Because it hurt. It hurt you." He squeezes his eyes shut. "And that nearly killed me. I can't…." He's shaking his head, some internal dilemma going on inside his mind. He's struggling though, I can see that much. Because I can feel him hard under the towel.

"Look at me."

It's a moment before he does, the fire burning within his cold blue eyes enough to make my knees wobble. "Don't make me beg, Henry." I lift up onto my tiptoes, letting my lips float over his. I drag the tip of my tongue over the seam of his lips, so slowly. I give his towel a yank, releasing it to drop to the floor. "I will, but please don't make me." Without shame, I reach between us to wrap my fist around his length and stroke it, a loud moan escaping my lips. I don't know what it is about Henry's cock, but no one else's compares.

He's like a bull released from his gate.

Strong hands seize my head, his fingers weaving through my hair to get a good hold as his mouth attacks mine, his tongue plunging into my mouth, claiming it with aggressive, almost angry swirls. He leads me backward toward the bedroom, stumbling and bumping into tables and a wall on the way, not breaking free of me even once.

The backs of my legs hit the bed and I'm suddenly being pushed backward, with Henry's naked form crawling on top of me, overwhelming me with his size, his hands on my shirt, tugging it over my head, and then on my jeans, unfastening the buckle and yanking them and my panties off in one fell swoop.

He's pulling down the front of my bra, making my breasts spring free even before he has the back unfastened.

In a matter of seconds, I'm naked and straddling Henry's lap, my arms cradling his head as I savor the sight and feel of his mouth clamped over my nipple, his tongue teasing me mercilessly.

Unable to wait, I reach down between us and guide his

cock into me. I'm so wet, I offer him little resistance as he slides into me, dragging out a deep moan from my lips.

His hands seize my hips, holding me still. "You've been smart? Safe?" He doesn't look at me when he asks that, but his jaw tenses, like he knows exactly what I've been doing since he left Alaska.

And maybe he does.

"Yes." I hesitate. "You?"

"Yes." Now he finally peers up at me, letting me see the plain truth.

Oh my God. "You haven't been with anyone else."

A pause, and then he shakes his head.

I drop my forehead against his and beg, "Kiss me, please. I need you to kiss me right now." Because I need him to tell me it's okay, that what I did wasn't wrong. That he won't hold it against me now, or ever.

He flips us over to put me on my back. Dominating me with his body, he pins my hands above my head by my wrists with one strong hand.

And simply stares down at me.

"Please don't be mad. I kept seeing pictures of you with these women, and it made me feel horrible. Ronan and Connor helped—" I cry out as Henry thrusts into me, spearing me with how hard and long he is.

"I *am* fucking mad." He seethes, pulling out and then thrusting once again, earning another cry from me. "This is mine and no one gets to fuck you unless I say they can." Stilling his hips, he leans down and kisses me deeply. "But I'm not mad at you. I let you go. You had every right to want someone else."

I break free of his grip, working one hand out to grasp his jaw, to force his eyes to me. "I don't want anyone else but you. Ever." I grind my pelvis into his and he groans.

Hooking one leg up over his arm, his hips start moving in that languid, slow, but forceful way he has, pumping in and out of me, each stroke pure ecstasy.

No one can fill me the way Henry does.

No one can make me feel this all-consuming level of lust as Henry does.

And I can say that based on a modicum of experience now.

I don't wait for him to tell me to; I reach between us and begin working my clit with my finger, stroking it hard and fast, not wanting to miss the opportunity to come with him.

"Fuck," he curses, finally climbing to his knees and hoisting my hips up. He drives into me at a ruthless rate, his eyes locked on my fingers stroking myself.

Henry's mine, again.

This man.... The sight of him alone, straining and glistening with sweat as he fucks me mercilessly, it's enough to set me off, tearing an orgasm from me as I buck wildly against him. He follows closely after, his face contorting with pleasure as he grunts. I open myself up completely to him, reveling in the feel of him pulsing inside me, filling me with him.

~

"Your mother?"

I set my phone on the side table. "No, Ronan. They wanted an update."

Henry's hard swallow carries through the room.

"Don't fire them."

He pauses, and then chuckles. "Or what? Are you going to try and blackmail me again?"

I curl into his chest, draping my naked body over his,

hoping I can keep him here forever. "No, I'm asking you. Please don't fire them. They're just friends, and they mean a lot to me. They—"

"I won't fire them, even though I want to. And I didn't fire Michael, either. Even though he deserved it."

I frown. "What do you mean?"

"I gave the asshole a promotion. And a raise. He's a manager in Aspen now. The deal was he packed his shit, got on a ferry, and didn't say a word to you or anyone about it."

"But you let me think—"

"Because *I'm* an asshole." He hesitates. "I wasn't going to let you come back here, where your mother would make your life hell and you'd end up miserable and back with your ex, but there was no way I was letting anything serious start between you and Michael."

I prop myself up on my elbow to peer down at Henry's handsome face. "Truce?"

A wry smirk touches his lips, pink and puffy from kissing me so much. It falls off with a groan as he glances at the clock. "I need to get going. The crew has been waiting for two hours." He plants a quick kiss on my lips and then rolls me off him and climbs out of bed.

I admire his muscular naked body as he strolls toward his dresser to pull on his boxers and jeans. "I wish I could go back with you."

"Yeah. You're not going anywhere for a while, from the sounds of it."

"I know. I don't know what I'm going to do about school in the fall." Defer a year, maybe? Mama's going to need me.

A thought crosses my mind and I smile. "I'm no longer a Wolf Hotel employee."

"Well, you haven't handed in your resignation. Or been fired."

"Yeah, but either way, there's no more workplace conflict."

His hands pause on his zipper, his gaze drifting out the window to the cityscape. "We lead very different lives, Abbi."

My heart sinks with his words. Stupid me. What did I think was going to happen? Just because we reconciled between the sheets doesn't mean we're all of a sudden "together." I'm going back to Greenbank, Pennsylvania—population five thousand—to farm my family's land and take care of my parents, while Henry jets around the world, opening hotels and ski hills. Our worlds are even farther apart now than when I was bringing his coffee to him in Alaska.

That's what the old Abbi would have accepted, anyway.

Henry just dropped everything, flew me across the continent, and basically saved my father. He cares for me, even now. And he was telling me the truth before. We *do* have something special.

"Yeah, I guess we do lead very different lives. I fight for what I want, while you just roll over and give up."

His head snaps back from the window to lock on me, his eyes flashing with surprise. "What did you just say?"

I climb to my knees and let him take my naked form in for a long moment. "You heard me."

Leaving the window, he wanders over to stop in front of me. "That sounded like a challenge."

"Maybe it was."

His gaze drops down to my chest, and I feel my nipples pebbling just with the touch of his eyes. "I'm difficult, and quick-tempered, and demanding. I've already caused you a lot of pain."

"And I wouldn't trade any of that for anything."

He heaves a frustrated sigh. "What's going on with fuckhead?"

"He broke up with Cammie and is apparently going to try to win me back." I roll my eyes.

"And you're not at all interested in reconciling with him?"

"No. Absolutely not."

"And is that because you were with"—his jaw clenches—"the other two?"

The idea of Ronan and Connor is really bothering him. But, like Ronan said when I asked him what would happen if his ex ever took him back, Henry's got to want me for who I am now, not who I was before he left me. "No. It's because Jed is in the past and I'm not the same girl I was."

He chuckles, reaching up to run the pad of his thumb over my bottom lip. "No, you definitely aren't."

I take the opportunity to pull his thumb all the way into my mouth, sucking it hard before I release it with a pop.

He steps in closer, forcing my head to tilt back to keep his gaze. "What happens when I fly in to see you?"

"I'll be waiting for you."

"And what about when I can't make the time but I need you. What if I'm in New York and I want you there with me? What if I send for you?"

"Then I'll come running."

His brow spikes. "Your mother will never approve."

"No. She won't." Bernadette Mitchell is going to fight this every step of the way. "But I can live with that, if you can."

His fingertips skate over my bare skin, over my breasts and down my stomach, reaching down to plunge deep into me, where his cum is still spilling out. I lean back on my haunches and spread my thighs to give him better access.

"I can live with it. Actually, this could be fun." He kneels in front of me, trapping my nipples with his teeth, earning my hiss. "You sure this is what you want?"

I lean down to catch his mouth with mine, trying to convey exactly how much this is what I want with my tongue.

Henry's eyes are hooded when I pull away, and my body buzzes with adrenaline because poor Jack is going to be waiting another hour, at least. "Okay then. It's official." A wicked smirk touches his lips. "You're fired."

Did you enjoy Break Me?
If so, please leave a review!

Abbi and Henry's story continues in Teach Me, The Wolf Hotel #3, available now.

teach me: the wolf hotel #3

Enjoy this excerpt...

The hospital doors slide open to welcome in a nurse, her purse slung over her shoulder. Coming in for her shift, I'm guessing.

I really should get out of the car and go in there. Jed texted about an hour ago to tell me that my dad was awake. I *do* really want to see him.

But going in there means leaving Henry, something I'm just not ready to do.

"I'm already hours late, Abbi. I have to get to my plane." Henry delivers that softly, his hand squeezing my thigh.

"I know. I'm sorry, it's just.... How long before you're back in New York, do you think?"

We've just reconciled in his hotel room and now he's flying back to Alaska and I'm staying in Pennsylvania, and I have no idea when I'm going to see him again.

I fight the tears that are threatening.

And fail.

He reaches up to brush them away from my cheek. I'm

so thankful that Henry's driver stepped out of the car as soon as he pulled up to the curb, giving us privacy.

"It's hard to say. I need to bring these engineers to the site to assess it for the ski hill I want to put in. Then I'm flying to Colorado to meet with the builders who put in the runs at our Aspen location."

I fight the cringe. I can't hear "Aspen" without thinking about the disastrous night back on the grand opening weekend, when I believed Henry was sleeping with another woman and I let my broken heart be distracted by Henry's masseuse, Michael.

The weekend that, technically, I cheated on Henry.

I regretted it when it happened because I'd used Michael. But now that I know Henry lied to me, that he never slept with Roshana Mafi....

I force that stomach-churning guilt aside for now. "Can't someone else do these things? I mean, you're the CEO. You own Wolf Hotels now." Or a controlling 61 percent of it, anyway.

He smirks. "This isn't just some other hotel. You know that. I don't trust anyone with it."

I nod, trying to contain my emotions. I know how important Wolf Cove—and Alaska—is to him. He spent his childhood summers there. He considers it home. "So, I guess...."

"We'll keep in touch."

I can't help the frown. Keep in touch? That sounds like something casual friends say.

"Hey." He grips my chin between his thumb and index finger. "This isn't going to be easy, Abbi. I warned you. We lead very different lives, and right now, you're stuck here. You could be stuck here for a long time." He softens that reality by drawing the pad of his thumb across the bottom of my lip.

He's right. That tractor that rolled over Daddy did a real number on him, breaking multiple bones and puncturing his lung. It could have been much worse but, still, it's going to be months before he's back on his feet and running the farm. "I know, it's just...." I settle my gaze on his steely blue eyes, still amazed at how they can sometimes look so cold and hard, and yet other times melt my heart with their softness and warmth. "What *is this*? What are we?"

Henry officially fired me this morning, more a joke than anything. I left so abruptly that I hadn't had the opportunity to hand in my resignation, but it was pretty clear I was quitting anyway. Either way, I'm no longer a Wolf employee, which means that dating me isn't against company policy. Even though Henry would say he can do whatever the hell he wants now that he has controlling share, I think it would still bother him to be so blatantly and openly disregarding his own corporate rules. He has a lot of pride in the Wolf name.

He sighs. "We'll figure things out as we go. You need to get in there and spend time with your family. And I need to get back to doing what I need to do. Okay?"

"Okay." I know Henry enough to know that's as far as this conversation is going. I nod. Do I need an official label for what we are? Or is it just enough to know Henry's in my life? That he cares about me. Because I know he does. He dropped everything to fly across the country with me because he didn't want me sitting in a plane for ten hours alone, given the tragedy. He's gone out of his way to make sure my dad has the best trauma surgeon in the country and that my family is set up in his hotel while we're here. He's been carrying around a picture of me—the one the Japanese photographer Hachiro took that day so long ago—in his portfolio.

I *know* he cares.

The question is, will it be enough?

"So... I guess I'll see you when I see you?" I reach up to graze his handsome hard jawline, admiring the feel of his soft, freshly shaven skin.

"Something like that." Henry turns his face to kiss my fingertips, and then he leans in to capture my lips with his, his tongue finding its way in to brush against mine in a slow, erotic dance that's not outright scandalous but is probably inappropriate right in front of the hospital. "I love this mouth of yours," he murmurs, taking the back of my head in his hand to deepen the kiss.

And I love you.

I've felt those words sitting on the tip of my tongue, threatening to tumble out, since he stepped onto the plane yesterday morning. I've somehow managed to hold on to them though. It's too soon for me to tell him. We've only just reconciled.

Henry breaks away with a groan. "Okay, you really need to go or I'll be unzipping my pants right here."

My blood rushes with the thought, my fingers digging into his forearm. I didn't get nearly enough of him this morning. "Maybe I want you to," I tease, catching his earlobe between my teeth.

"I don't think fuckface and his parents would enjoy the show so much though."

"What?" I spin around to find Jed with Reverend and Celeste Enderbey standing on the sidewalk.

Staring.

The Reverend and Celeste have the decency to look away when we make eye contact, but Jed continues staring at me, a mixture of shock and hurt filling his face.

They saw me come in with Henry yesterday. Sure, I told

them he was my boss when they asked. If they were wondering what was going on... I guess they have their answer. "I guess I'm going."

I reach for the door.

Henry's hand seizes my thigh, holding me in place. "Just so we're crystal clear..."

I turn to find a hard gaze on me. "When I say 'let's see where things go' that means make sure he keeps his fucking hands off you. And that goes for every other asshole out there, too."

Maybe it's odd that my heart swells with his words, but I smile anyway. It's his way of telling me he cares. "I only want you, Henry. Always."

He opens his mouth, and I hold my breath, wanting him to tell me that he only wants me, too. That he misses me already.

That he loves me.

"I'll call you later."

My cue to leave. "Bye, Henry." I force myself out of the backseat. Thank God Jed and his parents have already gone inside. It allows me the chance to watch his car pull away in private, my throat thick with emotion for that man.

With a sigh, I turn to face the hospital doors.

And prepare for what my life back in Greenbank, Pennsylvania, is going to be like.

∼

Continue on with Henry Wolf!

also by k.a. tucker

The Wolf Hotel Series:

Tempt Me (#1)

Break Me (#2)

Teach Me (#3)

Surrender To Me (#4)

Empire Nightclub Series:

Sweet Mercy (#1)

Gabriel Fallen (#2)

Dirty Empire (#3)

Fallen Empire (#4)

For K.A. Tucker's entire backlist, visit katuckerbooks.com

about the author

K.A. Tucker writes captivating stories with an edge.

She is the internationally bestselling author of the Ten Tiny Breaths and Burying Water series, He Will Be My Ruin, Until It Fades, Keep Her Safe, The Simple Wild, Be the Girl, and Say You Still Love Me. Her books have been featured in national publications including USA Today, Globe & Mail, Suspense Magazine, Publisher's Weekly, Oprah Mag, and First for Women.

K.A. Tucker currently resides outside of Toronto. Learn more about K.A. Tucker and her books at katucker-books.com